INDUSTRY LEADERS
SPEAK THEIR MINDS

The

# CONFERENCE BOARD CHALLENGE TO BUSINESS

Edited by Peter Krass

With an Introduction by
Richard E. Cavanagh
President and CEO, The Conference Board, Inc.

John Wiley & Sons, Inc.

New York • Chichester • Weinheim • Brisbane • Singapore • Toronto

ISBN 0-471-38471-2

Printed in the United States of America.

10 9 8 7 6 5 4 3 2 1

# Contents

Contents

# Introduction

This important new book from Peter Krass reminds us that knowledge is not just power but destiny.

This highly readable book gives us rare access to the insights and wisdom of some of the world's most influential business leaders and thinkers. The two score of leaders featured in these pages represent a wide range of business philosophies and management styles. Some are brilliant innovators, some superb strategists, and some bold visionaries. But because all of them have led or advised world-class organizations, they can add value to our enterprises and our careers.

The rich blend of ideas in this book reflects uncommon management wisdom. From Andy Grove to Warren Buffett. From Peter Drucker to Tom Peters. From Lord Marshall of Knightsbridge to Robert Townsend. From Anita Roddick to Katherine Graham, Larry Bossidy to Akio Morita, Simon Ramo to Charles Wang, Raymond Gilmartin to Robert Haas. And from Joseph Juran to Michael Bonsignore. And so many more.

Krass, the editor of a series of compelling books on business wisdom, again shows his keen eye for assembling ideas that truly matter. Although the published and spoken words of these leaders span 50 years, the prescriptions in this book are aimed at the most formidable challenges facing business executives today. Most significant, the views presented here are not based on speculation and theory but on real-life insight and practice.

I'm delighted that all of the wisdom presented in this book was first shared with members of The Conference Board at our conferences and in our reports and publications. The Conference Board has been engaged in knowledge sharing since we were founded nearly 85 years ago: a pioneer in convening the best in business to exchange experiences and in creating economic and management intelligence. Mr. Krass adroitly weaves recent research findings throughout this book to underscore today's critical issues. Like The Conference Board itself, this book celebrates the power of shared knowledge.

If you're looking for authoritative tips on leadership and strategic management, you'll find them here. You'll also learn about the dangers of unethical business behavior and how to link quality to profitable growth. If you're searching for ways to strengthen your brands or gain more control over fast-paced technology, you've also come to the right place. And you'll also find new ways to stimulate greater productivity by breaking down the walls of bureaucracy.

The concepts and ideas are portable. They can be used by all of us to strengthen our decision making. Two cases in point are Warren Buffett's highly successful recipe for selecting corporate winners and Andy Grove's practical checklist on how to tell whether your organization is suffering from that often fatal disease—organizational inertia.

Are you seeking ways to gain a competitive edge over your rivals? Read Peter Drucker's prophetic insights about the power of knowledge workers and midsize companies and Robert Townsend's iconoclastic views on how to lift productivity by ridding companies of their us-and-them mentalities.

Some legendary marketing and brand builders also share their expertise. Here's Akio Morita on why investments in marketing are important, Howard Morgens on what advertising can and cannot do to open new markets, and Melvin Goodes on the lasting value of internal branding.

Perhaps the most winning feature of this book is that it is completely reader friendly. Ideas are expressed clearly and concisely. A valuable case in point are the prescriptions for meshing quality and profitability: Joseph Juran, a founder of the quality movement, on how to make quality part of your everyday business; Paul Allaire on why management cannot delegate quality responsibilities; and Michael Bonsignore on how to overcome hurdles in building a company-wide quality ethos.

The book also strongly warns us about the dangers of operating our businesses without an ethical compass. Read Robert Haas and Raymond Gilmartin on the many ways ethical behavior assures corporate success, and Anita Roddick's call for "fair trade, not free trade."

Employees at all levels of enterprise may want to take notes when reading the final section of this book. It contains some market-tested tips on the dangers of corporate bureaucracies and how to level them. There's Larry Bossidy telling us how to eliminate irrelevant work, Edgar Woolard on the urgent need of large organizations to move faster, and Lord Marshall of Knightsbridge on the profitable art of self-management.

The collected wisdom in this book makes it clear that there are no singular solutions to business problems, only multiple options. But what a rich menu of options.

Richard E. Cavanagh
President and Chief Executive Officer
The Conference Board

# PART I

# Leadership Dynamics

One of The Conference Board's primary research studies in 1999 was the *CEO Challenge*,* a survey in which chief executive officers (CEOs) were asked to select the top three marketplace and the top three management challenges in the next year from a list of about 15 issues in each category. According to 29 percent of the 656 responding CEOs, "Engaging employees in the company's visions/values" is one of their top three management challenges. To engage employees, leaders must have an inclusive philosophy that, for example, destroys any divisive walls between headquarters and other groups in the organization. Toward that end, Robert Townsend, retired chairman of Avis, Inc. and author of the best-selling book *Up the Organization*, states in the opening essay of Part I that one of his top leadership principles "is to fight the them-and-us lines that separate people in a company." One of Townsend's tricks was to have headquarters staff work the car rental counter to better appreciate the frontline troops. Another concern gleaned from the survey: 24 percent of the respondents said that "developing and retaining potential leaders" is one of their top three challenges. To retain potential leaders, business guru Warren G. Bennis declares that the CEO must create a vision with clear direction that is "compelling, plausible and attractive." The vision must include real and tangible elements so that it is truly inviting, according to Bennis. Today, a clear vision is more important than ever to navigate a sometimes murky future; just consider that 43 percent of the CEOs participating in the survey said that "changes in type/level of competition" is one of their top three marketplace challenges and 41 percent placed "industry consolidation" in their top three. All of the authors in Part I offer leadership advice to meet today's and tomorrow's challenges in a rapidly evolving business environment.

*See the Appendix B for further research information and findings referenced in this and the other part introductions.

# ROBERT TOWNSEND

Robert Townsend, author of the best-selling book *Up the Organization* and a hugely popular business speaker, has always promoted independence and creative thinking. While working for American Express, he wore pink shirts to express his individuality and was soundly criticized by senior executives. Townsend was imbued with the rebellious spirit; one American ancestor was a revolutionary spy working against the British. After earning an English literature degree at Princeton University, Townsend served in the military as a gunnery officer during World War II.

Townsend then made his way to Wall Street, joining a brokerage firm. In 1948 he took a job with Hertz American Express International, a car rental company jointly owned by Hertz and American Express. He later became senior vice president of the investment and international banking operations for American Express. The company was not the most tightly run, according to Townsend, who later reflected, "During those years, the company was rich enough to do—and did—almost everything wrong," and he learned from that. In 1962 he left to become president and chairman of Avis, Inc., and turned around the then ailing company with the "We're Only No. 2. We Try Harder" advertising campaign.

To create a team environment, Townsend forced all managers at headquarters to go to rental agency school. At first they protested, but they soon realized how hard it was to work the counter and how important it was to support the frontline troops. During his tenure, which lasted until 1965 (when ITT bought the company), Townsend increased their market share by 28 percent and tripled revenues. He felt executives should do their own share of grunt work and delegate some of the meaty stuff. "Many give lip service, but few delegate authority in important matters," he wrote. In *Townsend's Third Degree in Leadership,* he elaborates on his leadership philosophy and boldly declares, "The first lesson is: To hell with centralized strategic planning. If you don't have a good leader, it's all nothing; it's just a bunch of papers flying around."

# Townsend's Third Degree in Leadership
### *Robert Townsend*

I'm going to try to give all of you a Ph.D. in leadership. The first lesson is: To hell with centralized strategic planning. If you don't have a good leader, it's all nothing; it's just a bunch of papers flying around.

Let me tell you what leadership is not. In some companies the chief executive has retired on the payroll, and there aren't any leaders. The companies are run by strong planning departments, strong purchasing departments, strong human-resources departments, and strong management-information services. What generally happens in those strong staff organizations is that you get very mediocre performance from otherwise able people down the line.

Some companies have gotten out of that trap. I'll give you one: Kollmorgen, 5,000 people, 16 divisions, had a marvelous management-information system with a 360 computer to tell everybody in the company wherever a sparrow fell. The whole company was so mesmerized with information that nobody did anything. And, bless his heart, Bob Swiggett [the CEO], practically over the dead body of the Harvard Business School, which was telling him to centralize management-information services, shot the 360 computer between the eyes. He called up his 16 division

3

presidents and said, "I am instituting a return-on-net-assets incentive compensation system for all of you; I want you to think of your divisions as your own, run them as if you owned them, and telephone in 10 numbers every month so that I can consolidate a P&L and a balance sheet."

Well, the organization came to life. It became much more profitable, a good, fun place to work. It turned around fast, without any consultants. They didn't have a strategic-planning department to think about it for three years; they just did it.

---

Profits are made in the divisions, not at corporate headquarters.

---

Brunswick, a little company, sold its crown jewels to avoid a takeover and was left with three businesses that Wall Street thought were very dull—outboard motors, fishing tackle, and bowling. Fortunately, they put in charge of the company a guy who thought those were exciting businesses, and he also had a strange philosophy:

Profits are made in the divisions, not at corporate head-quarters. So when he became CEO, he eliminated the group vice-presidents concept—and there went 400 people—and he reduced corporate staff by two thirds—there's another 400 people. He took the division managements and sent them back to the fields, where they would be near the companies they were running. Then he leased out two thirds of the crystal-palace space so that nobody would ever get back in there, and then he gave nine shares of stock to every employee. And he never wrote a memo, never made a speech, and the company turned around on a dime, and it's a lean, happy organization. And much to Wall Street's amazement, the stock went from 5 to 35. They didn't have a strategic-planning department.

The second point about leadership I learned while working for American Express many years ago. I was a security analyst, and I worked for a boss who was very typical of bosses then and maybe now. He was tall, he was handsome, he was ambitious, intelligent, articulate, and he was never there when we needed him. He took credit for everything we did that was any good and blamed us for everything that went wrong. We spent all our time coming in late and leaving early and bitching about the conditions. We were all underpaid; we didn't have the right mix of people.

All of a sudden he died, and the company in its infinite wisdom named me head of the investment department. I called everybody in and said, "I don't know anything about management; I'm very uncomfortable. But one thing's for sure: We don't have to talk about what's wrong; we haven't been doing anything else since I've been here. Why don't you people form a partnership and be the best investment department you can," I said, "and I'll try to get us the proper pay, the proper titles, the proper machinery, and the proper mix of people." And they said, "That's a pretty good idea, because you're a lousy analyst anyway, and we won't miss you."

So I did. I started to go around. And these people started coming in early and doing good work and making good decisions. And I remember once that Bobby Clarkson, who was chairman of the board, stopped me in the hall and said, "Townsend, that was a good bond swap you made last week." And I said, "Bond swap? I don't know anything about a bond swap. I don't even get to read *The Wall Street Journal.*" I said, "I'm working full time to get bowls of rice for my peons, so they don't starve on your front steps and embarrass you."

Well, gradually we started getting what we should be paid, and the titles we should have, so we could go in to interview top management. And I got more and more power from their performance, and one day Charlie Cuccinello, who invested our traveler's-check float, which was billions of dollars in short-term securities, came to me. "If I had one of those new Japanese calculators," he said, "instead of the hand-crank machine I've been using" (his predecessor used an abacus—this was an old company), "I could make us a ton of money." I said, "Charlie, you're right, you're absolutely right. Why didn't I think of that? I'll go get you one." Listen, that's what a leader does. He doesn't say, "I'll call in one of my three secretaries and dictate a purchase requisition, which will sit in some out-box for three days and when it gets back to me for my signature I'll be in Europe, so it will wait until I get back and will just miss the monthly purchasing meeting, and it will be two months later when it is returned to me, rejected." I said, "I'll go get you one."

So I get in the elevator and go down to the fifth floor to the purchasing department, and say, "Hi, my name's Townsend. I work up on the 14th floor and I need an electronic calculator, and here's the make and model number." And the man on duty says, "Is it in your budget?" And I say, "No, it isn't—because I made my budget out last October, and I only found out I needed it today. So I've come to my purchasing department for help." The purchasing man says: "If it's not in your budget, you can't have it."

I was carrying my resignation around, so I pulled it out—it was battered. I said, "Would you please sign this," and he looked at it and he read it and said, "Why should I sign that? That's your resignation, and you don't work for me." I said, "Because when I leave here I'm going up to the president's office, to whom I report, and I'm going to resign. He may ask me why I'm resigning, and if he does, I'm going to tell him it's because some stupid son of a bitch in the purchasing department won't give me a machine that would pay for itself the first two and a half minutes that we owned it. And if he asks me which stupid son of a bitch in the purchasing department, I want to show him your name."

Well, we got the machine. But that's not the point. The real point is that I was using the power that those people in the investment department were giving me not to get goodies for myself, but to get things for them, to enable them to do the job even better. If you ever break that circle and start stealing the goodies that come from their performance, they'll find out about it before you will, and they'll stop cooking and they'll stop trying, and you won't know what turned the organization off.

---

Another principle of leadership . . . is to fight the them-and-us lines that separate people in a company.

---

What I was really doing, though I didn't know it at the time—and this is the lesson that belongs in your leadership kit—was eliminating their excuses for doing lousy work. An excuse may be just "I'm underpaid," or "I'm undertitled," or "We don't have the right machinery," or "We really don't have the right kind of people here," or "We don't have an economist." I was eliminating their excuses.

At Avis I discovered another principle of leadership, which is to fight the them-and-us lines that separate people in a company. These lines are easy to see. There are the people you trust and the people you don't trust. The people you don't trust park outside the gate, have to punch a time clock, and have to get coffee out of a coffee machine. The people you trust park inside, don't punch the time clock, and get free coffee. You want to fight those lines.

One of the interesting lines in America is that the difference in salary between the CEO and the highest-paid blue-collar worker is 36 to 1; in Japan it's 7 to 1. Now that's a them-us line that I find hard to swallow, knowing what chief executives don't do for their companies.

The way we got around it at Avis was that we had a rental-agent school taught by our finest rental agents, ladies in red uniforms. It was a tough school, at O'Hare airport, with an exam every night. I made the whole management go through it, as an absolute condition of employment. We had to study, and we had to spend two or three hours renting cars at the airport.

---

Fire all your management consultants, all of them.

---

I went through it, too. One night, I had my trainee button on and was renting a car and trying to get the right keys with the right agreement—this was before the computer did this. I was trying to get the figures in the right boxes when my customer said, "Can't you hurry up? I'm on a real bummer of a trip." I said, "Give me a break, I'm a trainee." I kept on doing it, and I dropped the keys, and he said, "You're certainly the worst trainee I ever saw. Where did they dig you up from?" And I said, "You want to know something really sick? I'm the president of the company."

I tell you, when we got back to headquarters we were so proud of those ladies out there on that firing line and the difficulty of the job that they were doing that we started wearing red jackets around the executive office as a sign that we were part of their team. When we went into a city, we'd look at them with different eyes; they were our heroines now, instead of being the dopes who were renting cars. Them and us. Get rid of those lines; it's not an act, it's a career. You have to fight it like the weeds in your garden—continuously.

As you know, I've recommended that you fire all your management consultants, all of them. Promise them a bonus if they'll get off the premises by 5 P.M., and another bonus if they won't submit a report. Let me explain this to you.

Let's say we've got three divisions in a mythical company, and you are the chief executive. You've already gone to four board meetings a year, so you're already in that mode.

You have three divisions and one of them is sick. It's old Joe's division. He keeps reorganizing, missing his targets, reorganizing, missing his targets. It's time to face up to the fact that old Joe is no longer the guy to run that division.

So you say to your board: "I'm going to go over and run old Joe's division for three months, and I'll see what's going on." You tell old Joe to go skiing in Vail or go to Palm Springs and play golf with Gerry Ford or something. You say that when he comes back there will be a job with equal pay and benefits, but it sure as hell will not be running this division.

And then—and this is very important—you actually go over and sit at Joe's desk. You don't bring anybody with you, like your secretary, to make your life comfortable; you go sit at old Joe's desk. You call everybody in who reported to old Joe, and you say: "Now, you people know a lot about this problem. I'm your new division president, by the way. You know a lot about it, and you all have different views about what it will take to make this thing cook. I'm going to call you in one at a time and ask you for your help. But I don't want your goddamn private grievance committee; I don't want to hear about any goddamn coffeepots. I want you to tell me how to save this division and make it a credit to the company, because if we can't do this in a relatively short period of time, I'm going to shut the mother down."

---

Charisma is not generally associated with a true leader, in my opinion. It is more associated with the opposite: the corporate politician, who is what is the matter with our country.

---

Now that's motivation. Contrast that with the normal approach of the big company, in which the chief executive is too lazy to get out of his office and give up all those comfortable surroundings. He calls McKinsey & Company and drops six Harvard Business School graduates on these poor beleaguered people. Then they *know* they're in trouble. They might love to solve the problem themselves. But now you have to educate six people who don't know anything about the business.

---

A good leader is decisive. This is why you shouldn't have lawyers or accountants or MBAs in a corner office.

---

Now let's go back to the alternative. You are sitting in old Joe's chair and you may have to call in your people one at a time, three times each, but at some point you'll wake up and they will have given you the plan of how to turn that thing around. Then you call everybody in and say, "This is the plan you've given me, this is what you want to do, and, Bill, you are the obvious one to be division president. So you sit up here and run the division and carry out this plan; if you want to change it tomorrow because you run into something, change it. I just want you to save this division and make it a credit."

In six months those people will be 10 feet tall, and they will have forgotten that you were ever there. And it's all very proper that they do so, because they really did save the division themselves, and you'll be back in your own office with your cockamamy outside directors.

For the final part of your Ph.D., I'm going to tell you from my experience the characteristics of a leader. This is something that's very important and very difficult and misunderstood. They come in all shapes and sizes and colors and sexes; some are bright, some are dull, some are articulate, some can't speak a whole sentence, some are Type A's, some are lazy and laid-back. You cannot recognize them physically. Charisma is not generally associated with a true leader, in my opinion. It is more associated with the opposite: the corporate politician, who is what is the matter with our country. There are too many of this type in our corner offices.

Now here are the characteristics of a real leader to help you identify them and become one, if that is your desire. They have their personal ambition under control; they seem to get their kicks out of seeing their own people succeed and their own organization succeed. They are visible or available to their people, and they are good listeners. Listening is a very painful thing because, depending on how much pain they're in, you may have to listen to your people say something four or five times until they get that look in their eyes that says, "By golly, he really understands." When they get that look, you can say, "Fred, I understand what you're saying. Now get the hell back to work and do it my way." Then they'll go back home and sleep like babies and tell their spouses, "At least the son of a bitch listened."

That takes the anger out, but it's very painful to the listener. That's why you need a new CEO every five or six years, because after five or six years he or she can't listen anymore.

A good leader is decisive. This is why you shouldn't have lawyers or accountants or MBAs in a corner office. They want to get the last shred and scrap of information; they're happy with numbers and words, and they don't trust people. They need more information, and by the time they've collected all the information for the decision, the timing is off and they might as well forget the whole project.

At some point a good leader with inadequate data will say, "Ready, fire, aim—and if it doesn't work we'll correct it, but at least the timing is right to start with what we have." A good leader sees the best in his people, not the worst; he's not a scapegoat hunter. He sees winners, and he uses "the rule of 50 percent," which makes him high on promoting from within. The rule is that if you have anybody in your organization who looks like 50 percent of what you need for a job and who has the support of the people around her and wants the job, give that person the job and she'll grow the other 50 percent.

The corporate politician with no faith in his people hires a search firm, and they wind up bringing in an electric blue suit. He raises salaries all around, and a year later you're still teaching him the business. A good leader is simplistic, not complex. He makes things seem simple. He's persistent. If he can't convince his people and he really thinks it ought to be done, he'll find a different way to come at them until either they convince him, or he them.

He's fair and has a sense of humor, and he has humility. If you ever become chief executive, remember: You are still the same lovable, stupid, lazy slob you were the day before you got the job, and don't try to rush out and buy a whole lot of three-piece suits to fool people.

You're not going to fool anybody. You got there on your program, so stay on your program. But just remember to work a lot harder, and work for your people.

---

A good leader is simplistic, not complex. He makes things seem simple. He's persistent.

---

About the time of my first meeting with the board at Avis, General Sarnoff did what all outside directors do: They try to impress the other outside directors with how smart they are. He said, "I would like a run of all the cars we have in Avis, by the location and model number." I thought of the weeks that that would take our accounting department to run down, and I said to him, "General, if I don't need that statement to run the company, you sure as hell don't need it to be an outside director of the company." Bless his heart, the general turned purple; it was a joy for me to behold it.

But what I was doing was protecting my people, so they could get on with what the company was really trying to do. It was also in the first 100 days I was hired; I wouldn't have dared to do that six months later. You're bullet-proof in your first 100 days; the man who hired you can't fire you without looking stupid.

I suppose the best way to tell a leader is if you find a place where people are coming to work enthusiastically and they're excited to come to work and would rather work there than anywhere else, you can bet they've got a leader.

Well, there's your Ph.D. in leadership. Good luck and God bless.

# WILLIAM T. ESREY

Sprint came out of nowhere to take on AT&T and MCI in the long-distance phone market, and the credit goes to William Esrey, who has guided the company like a telecommunications guerilla leader since 1985. After earning an economics degree from Denison University in 1961 and an M.B.A. from Harvard University in 1964, Esrey actually joined his future enemy, AT&T, that same year and remained there until 1969. He left to become a managing director at the investment banking firm Dillon, Read & Company. In 1980 he resurfaced in the telecommunications world as vice president of planning for United Telecommunications (UT), a rural telephone company. Esrey became president and CEO in 1985, adding the title of chairman in 1990.

In 1984 the tiny upstart UT forged the way into an all-digital, all-fiberoptic long-distance system. Soon they were buying 80 percent of all the fiber in the free world. Upon reflection, Esrey said, "The risk was very, very high. But if management did not pursue that opportunity, our shareholders should have lined us up against the wall and shot us." One of its partners in the venture was Sprint, with which UT merged, assuming the Sprint name in 1991. Few gave them a chance of successfully competing against AT&T, but the company was able to develop a niche in the business market because Sprint could handle high-speed data transmission.

To break out from their niche, Esrey built a global alliance with Deutsche Telekom and France Telecom. Most recent, in 1999 MCI WorldCom made a $115 billion takeover offer that Sprint agreed to take. Part of the deal is that Esrey remains as chairman; however, the merger requires regulatory approval at the time of this writing. Regardless of the outcome, Esrey looks forward to a future business environment in which the lines between telecommunications, cable, and the Internet become further blurred. In *Leadership in the Next Century*, he foresees information zipping through the global economy at light speed and believes that "the leaders of future-oriented companies will need to be innovative users of communications."

# Leadership in the Next Century

*William T. Esrey*

We have a divided government in Washington with one party controlling Congress and another controlling the White House. The president retains his popularity despite relentless attacks from the media and political foes. He has visited China, and the entire Asian continent is on our minds for other reasons as well. The news of the day focuses on antitrust activity at the Justice Department, progress toward true European union, and hopes for peace in Northern Ireland.

The year is 1972, and the president is Richard Nixon.

This scenario raises the question: Are we making any progress? The cynical answer is no, and some say things are getting worse. Yet, despite its ups and downs, the world is on the whole more competitive and prosperous. National and world leaders are better equipped than ever to cope with today's thorny and dangerous economic and political issues.

The recent track record of U.S. corporate leaders has been impressive. Over the past decade, they have:

- expanded into new markets at a speed and on a scale that has never before been possible;
- taken remarkable strides in creating efficiencies, reducing costs, and tapping new sources of talent;

- made more information readily available to their employees so they can work smarter and faster;
- flattened their organizations and driven decision-making closer to the front lines so that customers are being served better and quicker; and
- partnered and outsourced so they can take advantage of resources and subject matter experts in much more effective ways.

A primary enabler of these gains is advanced telecommunications. New technology has provided the speed and has broadened the capabilities to make employees more effective and our companies more profitable. For example, a newspaper ran a story about a group of IBM computer programmers employed at a Beijing university. At the end of the day, the Chinese programmers send their work over the Internet to other IBM facilities. Programmers in the United States and Europe work on it and then electronically send it to workers in India, who pass it back to Beijing by morning, and then the cycle repeats itself. This kind of ability has changed the economics of business.

---

The leaders of future-oriented companies will need to be innovative users of communications.

---

Use of modern communications can, of course, be much more comprehensive than this. For example, Cisco, the global leader in networking products, has developed a wide and intricate web of suppliers, contract manufacturers, and assemblers. Using the company's extranet—an extension of a corporate intranet—outside contractors directly monitor orders from Cisco customers and ship the assembled hardware to buyers, often without Cisco ever touching the product.

As one informed observer said, Cisco can be considered the quintessential outside-in company. It has mastered how to source talent, products, and momentum from outside its own walls. A recent article in *Business Week* identified Cisco as a model of the corporation of the future. Business leaders would do well to study this model, not necessarily as a precise formula for success and not because Cisco is in the telecommunications industry, but because of how it uses communications to manage in an innovative way, tying diverse groups of people into one very flexible organization.

The leaders of future-oriented companies will need to be innovative users of communications. The power of communications is going to grow phenomenally, and it will yield potential opportunities to redefine business. For example, every day the Sprint network electronically transmits data equivalent to all 17 million books in the Library of Congress. In just two years, the telecommunications networks in the United States will carry more electronic data traffic than voice. By 2003, voice traffic could be less than 2 percent of the total traffic that is carried. Additionally, the World Wide Web is the fastest-growing communications technology in history. To reach an audience of 50 million people, it took the Internet just 4 years, compared with 13 years for television and 38 years for radio.

With these facts in mind, one might be tempted to think that technological change is just a straight, upward trajectory—a rocket that you simply jump onto and you will be okay. To the extent that technology shapes leadership imperatives, a very simple message would be to be prepared to lead as we have in the 1990s, but at a much faster pace. That would be very bad advice, indeed.

## THE NEW NATURE OF LEADERSHIP

The shift in our leadership challenge is much more profound than it appears on the surface. Leaders need to prepare for a change in emphasis that our experiences and education have not fully prepared us to consider.

The heart of this shift lies in the fact that technological changes are making the modern organization more far-flung, complex, decentralized, and diverse. At the same time, information is exchanged and communicated in enormous volumes and at breathtaking speeds. These trends are likely to continue and thus raise a number of questions:

- What happens to leaders when the group they are leading is spread out over ever increasing physical distances?
- Does there come a point when the tried and true leadership approaches of the 1990s are stretched too far, to a point where these methods simply will not work anymore?
- Can you flatten your corporate hierarchies so far that traditional systems of controls will break down?
- Can you spread your talent across such a wide swath of the globe where people can communicate and operate very efficiently, but where language and cultural barriers stifle ideas and creativity?
- Can you parcel out your work to so many independent sources that you lose the cohesiveness, the vision, and the emotional commitment needed to make any team function well?
- Can you as a leader create the culture and teamwork that act as the glue to hold together an organization that, even if very fluid, will still function as one?

Knowing the answers to these questions could define the difference between those who survive and thrive, and those who do not. The best answers can come from the people within our organizations, but they may emerge only over time. How well we answer these questions may determine how well we respond to the profound challenge of how to direct and manage a profusion of relationships between hundreds or thousands of people involved in running our business without impeding them.

That challenge may not be as overwhelming as it first appears. The answer comes down to giving people clear objectives, and then providing them with the right tools and incentives to break down the barriers of time, distance, and culture. In doing so, they can get the job done in a way that is right for the business.

## A GLOBAL ALLIANCE WITH A POSSIBLE SOLUTION

How can leaders open the gates of communication and collaboration between diverse organizations, including suppliers, distributors, and customers, so that creative solutions will emerge naturally and continuously and by applying as little force as possible to elicit these solutions? Global One, Sprint's global alliance with two of the world's leading telecommunications companies — Deutsche Telekom and France Telecom — may provide an instructive example.

Sprint and these two companies agree that you should never underestimate the challenge of operating a multicultural business enterprise in a very dynamic industry. In the end, working through our organizational differences is going to make us better and a more effective global competitor, but it takes an unbelievable amount of energy, devotion, and patience. All of us have had to change our perception of what it takes to be strong leaders. We have learned to put relationships among ourselves as executives as well as among employees at a much higher level of priority. We have to arm employees with timely access to accurate information if they are to effectively communicate and learn from one another and grow together. These are very top priorities of our global partnerships and increasingly for Sprint itself. Our experience is not unique; it is just one manifestation of an aspect that can be found in corporations across the gamut of business enterprises.

As businesses are being intimately linked in the global economy, and as they partner with competitors (and compete with partners), we become more and more reliant on each other. But within this crush of activity is a great potential for an organization to learn. To learn quickly and to respond effectively to the marketplace, people within organizations must break out of their traditional, rather comfortable confines—confines that, in fact, have become somewhat limited in geographic or cultural breadth. Rather, they need to communicate with one another clearly and frequently.

For example, the ultimate success of Global One will come as people throughout Sprint, Deutsche Telekom, and France Telecom communicate often and on a much larger scale. The answer to managing a far-flung, diverse business effectively is found in the people who are already within your company and within the companies of your partners, vendors, and distributors.

## LIGHT-SPEED COMMUNICATIONS: INCREASING THE LEADERSHIP CHALLENGE

Leaders in this environment will have to work differently if they are to succeed. Leaders of the future must:

- be able to assimilate facts and ideas much more rapidly because of the shear volume of data that is at our disposal;
- develop the skills to work in an increasingly interconnected and often convoluted web of business relationships, which will require understanding and encouraging diversity;
- master the art of projecting goals, values, and strategies to many different people with many different viewpoints, all of whom are listening practically all the time both to you and to each other; and
- learn how to utilize the tools of advanced communications, not just to expand their organizations but to make their businesses more flexible and more agile.

Today's advances in telecommunications are not just more of the same. We are now introducing technologies that offer more than just increased speed and capacity. They offer capabilities that are also different in what they can do for you.

For instance, in the summer of 1998, Sprint introduced ION, the integrated, on-demand network. With ION, a home or business will be able to conduct multiple phone calls, receive faxes, run new advanced applications, and use the Internet at up to 100 times faster than a 56-kilobit modem—all through a single connection. Even the distance between local and long-distance will disappear because distance becomes irrelevant when communications travel at the speed of light. In short, you will be on the network all the time, and you will have blazingly fast communications speeds in your arsenal.

ION technology means that people are going to have a remarkable new tool for communicating. It will enable us as never before to develop very close, more productive, personal relationships that will collapse both space and time because it will allow people to share so much more all at once. Capabilities like this are going to change what we can do at our businesses. Thus, the leadership challenge increases.

As telecommunications instantaneously, intimately, and intricately interconnect us, it can take us well beyond what had been our limited horizons. It will allow us to communicate not just faster and more frequently, but more fully as human beings with special talents, perspectives, and ingenious ideas. The best, most effective, and most influential leaders of the future will be those who recognize and employ that power effectively. They will be the ones who will learn how to unleash and direct that power to the fingertips of a dispersed, diverse, and global workforce. They will be the ones who will welcome and promote a significant decrease in corporate viscosity, creating a highly fluid and very flexible organization while at the same time acting to develop teamwork and learning that ties the organization into one unit that moves in the same direction—your direction.

Crawford Greenewalt oversaw DuPont's participation in the top-secret Manhattan Project (the building of the atomic bomb) and went on to become DuPont's president three years later. During World War II, DuPont constructed the necessary testing labs and production plants, produced the raw materials, and then built the A-bomb under the supervision of government scientists. At the University of Chicago, Greenewalt witnessed the first controlled atomic reaction, convinced neither he nor the city would survive the experiment. While the Manhattan Project certainly was high-profile work, Greenewalt's real break came in the late 1930s when the Massachusetts Institute of Technology (MIT) chemist brought nylon from the test tube to mass production. This synthetic material became a huge moneymaker for DuPont.

Greenewalt was a unique and dichotomous leader, whom a colleague described as having "energy, charm, a chain-reacting mind, and some seeming contradictions. He has the cold precision of a trained scientist. . . . Just as quickly, he can become as gregarious as a travelling salesman." The cold precision was a necessity in order to focus on problems and make decisions in an extremely complex business. When it came to problem solving, Greenewalt was fond of saying, "Don't scatter your fire." He was also the type of leader who could leave problems at the office. Greenewalt's favorite hobby (for which he was also famous) was the study and photography of hummingbirds; he also enjoyed playing the clarinet. Amazingly, he could witness and comprehend a nuclear reaction one minute and write an article on ornithology for *Audubon* nature magazine the next.

A humanistic approach to life and business contributed to Greenewalt's capacity as a leader. He understood that all people are not created equal in terms of both their skill sets and the degree to which they use them. "Suppose one were an artist and asked to portray a business leader in his proper posture, how would one go about it?" he asks in *A Philosophy of Business Leadership.* His answer: a conductor faced with bringing together a variety of players with different talents, of course.

# A Philosophy of
# Business Leadership
*Crawford H. Greenewalt*

Suppose one were an artist and asked to portray a business leader in his proper posture, how would one go about it? I believe I would do it by showing him standing on a podium, a baton in his hand, confronting a hypothetical orchestra comprising all of the various talents that he must effectively bring together if his presumably large and complex business were to pursue a harmonious and successful course.

A good conductor need not be able to play the bassoon or the trumpet or the bass viol, but he must recognize the potentialities of the instrument and the character of the performer and deal with them in such a way that he produces an ensemble which is harmonious and effective. In the same sense, a business leader need not have expertise in science or in law or in marketing, but he must understand their significance. He must know and be able to measure the capacities of the individuals who will carry on in these various fields. And he must acquire the spiritual qualities which will induce the people under his direction to put forth their best efforts in the interests of the enterprise as a whole.

I have come to the conclusion that differences in managerial competence are due not to one person, nor to the few geniuses that cross the stage from time to time, but arise out of the creation of an atmosphere that induces every person connected with the enterprise, no matter what his position, to perform his task with a degree of competence and enthusiasm measurably greater than what could be called his normal expectations.

Business success then can be measured by summing up the small increments of extra effort on the part of all the people who are joined together in a given enterprise. If one looks at the question quantitatively, it would seem inescapable that five percent or so extra performance on the part of, let us say, 90,000 people will far surpass extraordinary competence in a small executive group.

---

A business leader . . . must acquire the spiritual qualities which will induce the people under his direction to put forth their best efforts in the interests of the enterprise as a whole.

---

The important qualifications that make for high competence in business leadership are intangible rather than tangible. They involve such things as the ability to deal with people sympathetically and understandingly, the ability to recognize competence in others, and the courage to weed out incompetence when necessary. They involve the ability to stimulate high performance at all organizational levels and to insure unity of purpose among individuals differing widely in temperament and experience. It is simply not possible to define these characteristics in any quantitative way.

Because business equates success or failure with profitability, the superficial conclusion is that profit is the sole objective. If this were true, the role of business leadership would be vastly simplified. All of us know, however, that profit is only one of many factors influencing corporate decisions. Business leadership must, of course, be concerned with profit, but the difficult decisions, and those calling for the highest level of insight and judgment are those involving the conditions under which profit may be realized.

---

Business success then can be measured by summing up the small increments of extra effort on the part of all the people who are joined together in a given enterprise.

---

Profit under what conditions? The grab for a quick killing is the mark of the worst kind of leadership, for it places immediate profit above the long-term interest of the organization and can lead ultimately only to disaster. The successful leader will define objectives within limits that his organization will find consistent with professional pride, personal satisfaction, and public esteem. He will take into account all parties at interest—employees, customers, shareholders, and his country, finding the way to an equitable distribution of the fruits of progress. The leader who establishes viable guide lines compatible with human values and public policy will insure to himself and his organization the essential backing and support of his associates, his subordinates, and his nation.

Business leadership has a far more important role than has been the case in past generations, since business leadership holds in effect the key to the stature of a nation in the world's political arena. The implication seems clear that industrial leaders can no longer insulate themselves from public affairs; they can no longer consider their responsibilities as dealing solely with the profit and loss position of their enterprises.

They must accept responsibility at highest levels of national policy and must form an association with leaders in government that is at the same time harmonious and purposeful. For government leadership would be weak indeed if it did not have strong industrial sinews behind it. In short, the problems of a nation's government are in a very real sense the problems of its business establishment. Neither can proceed in a given direction without the sympathetic support of the other.

---

The grab for a quick killing is the mark of the worst kind of leadership, for it places immediate profit above the long-term interest of the organization and can lead ultimately only to disaster.

---

By this I do not mean that business leaders should seek political office, nor should they necessarily attempt to insert themselves at the council table of their governments. There must, on the other hand, be complete understanding and harmony between leaders in both fields if there is to be national unity and continued national strength.

---

Business leadership has a far more important role than has been the case in past generations, since business leadership holds in effect the key to the stature of a nation in the world's political arena.

---

To sum up, it seems to me that any philosophy of business leadership must take into account not only the size and complexity of modern enterprise, but the influence it has come to exercise in determining national well-being and national stature. Management competence can no longer be equated to distinction in particular technical or nontechnical disciplines, but must embrace those larger and more spiritual qualities that make for inspired leadership of diverse groups of individuals dedicated to a common cause. No longer can business leaders concern themselves solely with their own enterprises—they have a larger role to play in national and even in international affairs.

# RICHARD G. LEFAUVE

It takes more than a natural disaster to incite the powers that be in the automotive industry to radically depart from their set ways; it takes a Japanese invasion. By the early 1980s Japanese car manufacturers had a lock on the small car market in the United States, prompting General Motors (GM) to create their vaunted Saturn division. The plan was to set up a new factory in a new place, but transplant GM people. Richard LeFauve, who was at the helm for ten years, knew not all would be open to change due to past corporate oppressiveness. He reflected, "The classic corporate statement was, 'We're going to make all these improvements and eliminate all these jobs. So we'd like you to help us. . . .' And you wonder why employees don't want to change. The change has to make their jobs more exciting." So when Saturn set up its Tennessee operation with 6,000 transplanted GM people, it asked for their input in designing the best operation.

Although Saturn was founded in 1984, LeFauve wasn't made president until 1986. With the sudden change in the executive suite, the fledgling company's employees immediately questioned GM's commitment to Saturn, because part of the plan was to build a tightly knit team-based culture. LeFauve was up front with them, "I believe you will find that I am a team player, for I have believed for a long time that cooperation is the way we will beat our competitors—not confrontation." The early years were not easy; besides keeping the team together, his GM counterparts were jealous of all the attention Saturn received. Finally, the first car rolled out of the factory in 1990.

After ten years with Saturn, LeFauve moved on to other responsibilities in GM, and in 1997 he was charged with developing standard management and engineering practices across GM; in other words, the unconventional, team-oriented management style at Saturn was recognized as a success. LeFauve discusses how "each individual is an agent of change" in the aptly named *Leaving the Comfort Zone.* One of his conclusions is that leaders "must show some humility and accept that you do not know all the answers."

# Leaving the Comfort Zone
## *Richard G. LeFauve*

Saturn was less a new product than an entirely new way of doing things: our novel relationship with the United Auto Workers (UAW) union, the notion of suppliers as partners, and our emphasis on making the experience of buying a new car enjoyable. Each of these initiatives had a learning curve and the common denominator of an organizational learning effort that management, the union, and rank-and-file employees went through together. One result: Rather than having new procedures and standards imposed on employees from the outside, each individual is an agent of change, and union leaders educate union members. That gives us credibility in convincing our people to leave the comfort zone. It is credibility that will help sustain and drive the process of change in the future.

## MANAGING THE MESSAGE

The key to change is a shared vision of the future. And at Saturn, the key word is "shared." You can ask anybody in our organization, "Where are we going?" The response would be the same. But it is also important for us to convince our managers that simply telling employees what to do — even repeatedly — does not necessarily get the message across. In some cases, in fact, telling evokes confrontation.

The answer is to begin an education process together. It is similar to voting in a presidential election. Someone who voted is able to say, "I may not have selected that candidate to win, but at least I participated in the process." Participation creates a sense of identification and support.

Certainly, training also plays a big part. At Saturn—at the insistence of the UAW, no less—we commit 92 hours a year to training. That means 5 percent of the time we are participating in a learning process.

One of the first things the union wanted to teach was the history of the UAW. As a manager, I thought that would be a complete waste of time. But sitting across the table from people you had learned to distrust over the years, learning about their background and discovering that you have the same problems, helps to generate respect and support—for them and for the learning experience.

Along the way, other difficulties arose. Management felt we could not spare 92 hours to sit in a classroom. So someone came up with the idea that teachers should receive double credit. Not only did that improve management support for training, it also enhanced the educational experience, because you really learn when you teach.

Some of this training is technical, but a lot of it is social. It focuses, for example, on how to make decisions as a team. If Saturn is going to have self-managed teams—a key to employee empowerment and increased productivity—we have to spend time teaching our people how to identify and solve problems, and how to come to a consensus. You have to develop a common vocabulary.

The critical point is that you may have doubts about whether and how much learning needs to occur. But ultimately, companies need to make time for the process or face the loss of a significant competitive advantage.

## PLANNING TO WIN

Properly conceived, a learning organization creates the opportunity for employees to have some fun. From a business perspective, it has been exciting for us to watch many of the things we have learned at Saturn circulate back into the broader General Motors environment. Based partly on the Saturn experience, GM is developing a corporate-wide vision called the "Plan to Win." We are going to teach that plan to more than 1,800 top GM managers, then help them teach it to others.

Learning enables you to identify the need for ongoing change, and an awareness of what to do about it. In the small car group, for example, we determined we had people in Germany, Detroit, and in Saturn itself engineering cars simultaneously. These were essentially the same cars; they might have looked slightly different in size and shape, and maybe they had different brake lines. Does the consumer really care what the car's brake lines look like? Obviously not. The consumer just cares that the brakes stop the car. So why were we engineering it three times? Why didn't we engineer it once and use it across the organization?

In order to rectify this situation, we had to bring people together and create a vision. One of the first things we did was to break down the cultural barriers between different areas. It was interesting to watch the disciplined Germans interact with the more relaxed Americans. We may not see the project's results until after the year 2000, but the end product may be something really special in small cars.

Many business people look at learning as a "soft" skill, or "goody-goody" stuff that you might do if you really had the time and money, but that is short-sighted. Learning is an immensely important business decision, and the results are superior.

What are the lessons for leaders who must generate a common experience and drive the learning process? You must show some humility and accept that you do not know all the answers. But take heart; the people around you probably do. You need to bring them together, get to work, and enjoy the journey.

# WARREN G. BENNIS

As founding chairman of The Leadership Institute at the University of Southern California's Marshall School of Business, where he has taught since 1979, Warren G. Bennis is recognized the world over as an expert on leadership. Bennis, who has written more than 25 books and 1,500 articles on management and leadership, earned his undergraduate degree from Antioch College in 1951 and a Ph.D. from MIT in 1955. He stayed at MIT for several years as a faculty member of the Sloan School of Management and as chairman of the Organizational Studies Department, and then taught at Harvard and Boston Universities. Bennis himself took a management job as provost and executive vice president of the State University of New York at Buffalo and then as president of the University of Cincinnati.

In researching leadership, he determined that there were five key characteristics of leaders: "(1) They have passion and purpose . . . (2) They generate and sustain trust . . . (3) They are purveyors of hope and optimism . . . (4) They manifest a bias for action . . . (5) They keep learning and growing." He has also found that Americans, more so than others, tend to enshrine charismatic leaders such as Jack Welch and Bill Gates, when it's a team effort that builds a company. Bennis argues that leaders who think they can do it by themselves à la John Wayne are nuts. In particular, he dislikes CEOs who consider themselves heroes for downsizing, such as Al Dunlop (late of Sunbeam) and Bob Allen (late of AT&T).

As for the future, Bennis believes that "the key to competitive advantage in the nineties and beyond will be the capacity of top leadership to generate intellectual capital know-how, imagination . . . knowing how to orchestrate, knowing how to bring about general intellectual capital in small groups is going to be key." Also, he believes that in the near future leaders must "embrace ambiguity" and not be frightened by surprises. In *Leaders and Visions* Bennis focuses on the significance of a leader's vision and how one creates new realities for those around oneself.

# Leaders and Visions: Orchestrating the Corporate Culture
## *Warren G. Bennis*

### THE ROLE OF THE CEO IN CORPORATE CULTURE

I believe that the single most important determinant of corporate culture is the behavior of the chief executive officer. He or she is the one clearly responsible for shaping the beliefs, motives, commitments, and predispositions of all executives—from senior management to the operators of the organization.

What is this corporate culture that the CEO shapes and sustains? First and foremost, a corporate culture presents a shared interpretation of organizational events so that members know how they are expected to behave. And it generates a commitment to the primary organizational values and philosophy—the vision that employees feel they are working for and can believe in.

"Shared vision" is the significant element in that system. The idea of corporate culture, or any culture, has to do with significance, with a web of meaning that allows people to make sense of their organization. Successful companies have a very deep set of symbols and beliefs that create meaning, a shared vision, for its employees. And leaders create and transmit that meaning, that vision, so that people identify with it, or "enroll" in it.

33

## THE LEADER AS PRAGMATIC DREAMER

Perhaps a brief definition of leadership will highlight its role in corporate culture.* In studying leaders, I made a very rough distinction: I defined leaders as people who do the right thing, and managers as people who do things right. Management has to do with efficiency, with making things run properly. Leadership, in contrast, is concerned with identity—why we are here; what our business is; what our destination, goals, mission and values are. In an era of transition, that function of leadership—of vision—is very important.

Without exception, all of the leaders I had an opportunity to get to know were "pragmatic" dreamers, people with a realistic sense of destiny and identity. The late President John F. Kennedy presented an admirable illustration of what I mean by vision when he talked about having a man on the moon by the end of the 1960's, which actually came about. As that example implies, a vision is more than just another interesting idea. A lot of people have attractive but unrealizable dreams. But Kennedy's idea of a man on the moon by the end of the decade worked for several reasons. First, it recognized a barely discernible, but deeply felt, public aspiration. Second, the technological know-how to achieve it existed. Third, because he had correctly sensed public sentiment, he got the political support to fund the program. Leaders' visions are pragmatic.

The leaders I studied were very diverse in their personalities and styles. Even their managerial philosophies ranged widely from participative management philosophy to an autocratic attitude. But there are some common characteristics of leadership that bear directly on corporate culture.

*Warren Bennis and Burt Nanus, *Leaders: The Strategies for Taking Charge*, New York: Harper & Row, 1985.

# The Leader's Inviting Vision

I spoke to executives from both the profit and not-for-profit sectors, governmental agencies and corporations, and they all seemed to have a set of guiding concepts that enroll other people. When these leaders spoke about their organizational vision, they caught your attention. When they were involved with or talking about their organization's goals they were obsessive and passionate. But outside of that all-consuming interest, they could be as dull and boring as the next person.

---

In studying leaders, I made a very rough distinction: I defined leaders as people who do the right thing, and managers as people who do things right.

---

A leader's appeal, that is, has nothing to do with an innate or charismatic power of appeal. A leader creates a new social reality that is compelling, plausible and attractive. A leader's vision invites other people into that social reality; it takes people to a new place. Vision is really an interactive process between a leader and followers—the stakeholders and the work force.

---

All of the leaders I had an opportunity to get to know were "pragmatic" dreamers, people with a realistic sense of destiny and identity.

---

Vision is crucial for a company. Without a clear vision, the organization is either dreamless, with no direction, or it has so many different visions that people have no consistent understanding of their direction. In companies buffeted by changes, takeovers, and what not, it can be very difficult to know which vision is the real one or what the vision will be next month. In that situation, people can feel lost, even catatonic: They do nothing, hoping that the turmoil will all blow over.

## TRANSMITTING A SHARED VISION

Having a shared vision is absolutely essential if an organization is to be effective. It creates alignment among employees and motivates them. People would much rather have lives with a sense of purpose and direction than lives of aimless diversion.

---

A leader creates a new social reality that is compelling, plausible and attractive. A leader's vision invites other people into that social reality; it takes people to a new place.

---

Creating that kind of vision entails more than simply communicating it; it means turning the abstract into something real and tangible. Leaders have an almost obsessive drive not just to create but also to transmit that vision. They are able to do that because they can communicate meaning.

---

Leaders convey meaning by example. That is, the leader's style pulls rather than pushes people along.

---

(The distinction between information and meaning is important here, because all of us are inundated with information, ambushed by data and discrete facts. What we need is meaning.) Leaders have a knack for using analogies and other kinds of creative explanations to get the meaning across.

Furthermore, leaders convey meaning by example. That is, the leader's style pulls rather than pushes people along. A pulled style of influence works by attracting and energizing people to enroll in an exciting vision of the future. It motivates through identification, rather than through rewards and punishment. Leaders articulate and embody the ideals toward which the organization is striving.

# PART II

# Principles of Management

The primary task of management, Intel chairman Andrew Grove declares in the opening essay, is to energize people "in order to increase productivity." Considering that in The Conference Board's 1999 *CEO Challenge* survey, 48 percent of the responding CEOs said that downward pressure on prices was a top market-place challenge, increasing productivity is indeed crucial. Grove provides his own test to measure organizational effectiveness, giving readers the opportunity to rate their respective company's ability to communicate and to develop new products, among other topics. As for day-to-day management skills, he offers classic maxims such as never shoot the messenger and suggests new ideas such as organizing autonomous SWAT teams to solve problems or attack new markets. According to Peter Drucker, a manager must link specific strategic goals directly to the performance of individual employees to motivate them; each knowledge worker must understand how his or her job contributes to an end result. Taking it a step further, Richard Branson espouses tying compensation directly to performance. Another Branson management tip: Keep your organization broken down in small, autonomous groups not only to avoid inertia, but because internal and external customers identify better with small teams. The predominant themes in this section center around the need for organizational structures to become more fluid to encourage innovation, to increase productivity, and to better serve all customers.

# ANDREW S. GROVE

Consider that from 1985 to the fall of 1999, Intel's stock rose 6,300 percent versus S&P 500's 800 percent. Numbers, however, are not everything to Intel's chairman Andrew Grove, who is deeply introspective and lives by the motto, "Only the paranoid survive." The paranoia was bred in his youth: Life for Jewish families in Hungary, where he was born and raised, was not easy. During World War II, his father was taken to a labor camp on the eastern front, while young Andrew and his mother survived the Nazi occupation by obtaining false papers. When the Soviets invaded Hungary during the popular uprising in 1956, Grove and a friend escaped to the United States. After taking a train close to the Austrian border, they hired a smuggler to sneak them past the Soviet troops.

Upon earning a Ph.D. in chemical engineering from the University of California, Berkeley, Grove went to work for Fairchild Semiconductor, where he met the future founders of Intel, Gordon Moore and Robert Noyce. When they founded the company in 1968, Grove joined them and became president in 1979. *Fortune* magazine named him toughest boss in 1984. Being tough has been necessary in the rapidly changing technology sector and Grove encourages "constructive confrontation" to solve problems. This process involves gathering all the appropriate people involved with the problem and encouraging them to butt heads as issues are worked out. The idea is to accelerate the problem solving. "Dealing with conflict," he states, "lies at the heart of managing any business."

Grove is also concerned with inflection points—the critical points when a company must adapt to a changing environment. Most recently, for Intel that meant quickly reallocating resources to manufacture low-cost chips for personal computers that cost less than $1,000. Companies, even the largest, must be nimble, a topic he tackles in *Elephants Can So Dance*. He declares, "To be sure, elephants don't move as rapidly as rabbits. But if you have some substantial work to be done, you have to mobilize an elephant rather than harness 1,000 rabbits. The truly important jobs in our world are elephant-size jobs."

# Elephants Can So Dance
## *Andrew S. Grove*

W hen the day-to-day protocols and procedures of a company get in the way of employees trying to do their jobs, that company suffers from organizational inertia.

Organizational inertia is a terrible disease that saps the will and energy of individuals and, in the 1980s, [as well as in the twenty-first century] may be devastating to a company's ability to compete.

The older and bigger an organization, the more inertia it will tend to have. But the solution to the problem is not to fracture large, mature organizations into smaller, more agile parts. To be sure, elephants don't move as rapidly as rabbits. But if you have some substantial work to be done, you have to mobilize an elephant rather than harness 1,000 rabbits. The truly important jobs in our world are elephant-size jobs.

Before you read on, try to get an idea of how your organization stacks up by taking the mini-quiz on the following page.

Organizational inertia is not a new phenomenon. Even in the 1970s—which, in retrospect, seems like a benign time for everyone—it could hurt a company. But some companies with a high degree of inertia did all right; they were able to survive. Business conditions were favorable enough to hide the sins of organizational inertia.

## A Test of Organizational Inertia

For clues to whether your organization is an agile or a sleeping giant, try this mini-quiz devised by Dr. Grove. Circle one of the three alternatives for each question and add up your score at the end.

1. An employee from three levels down calls your secretary and urgently requests to talk with you about a recently made decision. In your organization, do you:
   A) Take the call?
   B) Ask the employee to send a memo through his manager?
   C) Contact the employee's boss and let him handle the problem?

2. One of your junior marketing managers, while reviewing some manufacturing procedures, discovers several steps that seem to accomplish nothing but cost money. In your organization, does he:
   A) Write a memo to the manufacturing manager responsible?
   B) Document the problem in a report to his own supervisor?
   C) Doggedly pursue the problem himself until it is solved?

3. Your archcompetitor launches a new product. It catches you off guard and rapidly takes market share. In your organization, do you:
   A) Request weekly reports from the marketing manager detailing what he or she is doing to solve the problem?
   B) Hire a consulting firm to verify your own understanding of the market?
   C) Create a multidisciplinary task force, make it responsible for resolution of the problem, and turn it loose?

4. The last three or four products that your company has introduced have done poorly in the marketplace. The products were released on time, according to the schedule set by engineering. The sales force says they are good products, but the competition is getting there first. In your organization do you:
   A) Give the marketing manager more control over the engineering schedules?
   B) Replace the engineering manager?
   C) Scrutinize your product-development procedures with the goal of eliminating half of them?

## SCORING

| If You Answered | Score Yourself | If You Answered | Score Yourself |
|---|---|---|---|
| 1. A | 2 | 3. A | 1 |
| B | 0 | B | 0 |
| C | 0 | C | 2 |
| 2. A | 1 | 4. A | 0 |
| B | 0 | B | 0 |
| C | 2 | C | 2 |

| | |
|---|---|
| 0-2 | Bad Case of Organizational Inertia |
| 3-5 | Signs of Creeping Organizational Inertia |
| 6-8 | Agile Organization |

The 1980s have brought both enormous technological developments and changes in the marketplace. Distributed computing, for example, is wreaking havoc with the mainframe computer industry right before our eyes. It is restructuring the entire industry, weakening old established companies and permitting upstarts to take their places.

Deregulation and internationalization have combined to change the rules under which many industries operate. The enormous impact of deregulation in the United States is evident to anyone who frequently travels by air. As for internationalization, Intel bears witness to the pain that it has brought to organizations that sailed through the 1970s without stumbling.

---

Organizational inertia is a terrible disease that saps the will and energy of individuals.

---

To be a significant force in the 1980s, a company has to be an *agile giant*. Both words need to be stressed equally. You need to be able to react quickly and you must be of significant size to make a difference.

Recently, many people have argued that the way to make organizations more agile is through intrapreneurialism. The notion is to form small groups within the larger organization—sort of little SWAT teams freed of normal regulations and constraints—and encourage them to solve problems aggressively and independently, respond to opportunities, create new products, and attack new markets.

---

The truly important jobs in our world are elephant-size jobs.

---

Intel has tried intrapreneurialism, quite successfully. We set up intrapreneurial units inside the company to pursue specific projects. One unit, for instance, pioneered the "Above Board," a new electronic board that can be inserted into a personal computer to make it much more powerful. This group built a substantial business in a very short time. A second intrapreneurial group made phenomenally powerful supercomputers out of our own microcomputers. It developed a family of products in just nine months.

But, I submit, such intrapreneurial units are not the answer to the problem of organizational inertia. These are two islands of success in the sea of a major company. Although they were successful, they operated independently and their activity did little to affect the company as a whole.

We have, however, developed a few principles that I think can reduce organizational inertia. Admittedly, we have not been uniformly successful in adopting them. (On the mini-quiz, I give my own company a grade of only 5.) Where we have not succeeded, I am convinced that it is because we have not been able to implement the principles in the entire company, not because they aren't right.

**1. Quick-Trouble Communication.** The first question in our mini-quiz concerns how the boss responds when an employee three levels down calls and asks urgently to speak with him. The principle here is the old admonition: "Never kill the messenger."

Now, very few of us have actually killed messengers. But do we in fact cultivate the kind of environment in which all messengers can feel confident that they will not be in trouble when they bring us some bad news? The expectation of how the bearer of bad tidings will be treated is every bit as critical as how he actually is treated.

**2. The Doctrine of Assumed Responsibility.** If an employee identifies a problem or an opportunity, he should assume responsibility for the solution without waiting for anybody to tap him on the shoulder and tell him to do it. We formally teach this "doctrine" to our employees in all orientation courses. We encourage champions to step forward, grab problems, and attempt to find solutions themselves.

This principle is closely tied to the previous one: Only if members of an organization feel free to report problems, and believe that their careers won't be tainted by doing so, will they take the next step and assume responsibility for finding a solution. Remember the second question in the quiz, which dealt with the junior marketing manager who discovered a problem in manufacturing. How he acts will depend on how comfortable he feels with the doctrine of assumed responsibility.

**3. The Corporate Crusade.** At various times every organization is going to encounter a problem that is bigger and more urgent than it can cope with using ordinary means. What one needs at such times is a corporate crusade. The situation described in the third question of the mini-quiz, where an archcompetitor launches a new product that catches you off guard, may be the type of problem that demands such a step.

---

Intrapreneurial units are not the answer to the problem of organizational inertia.

---

In a corporate crusade, you have to turn the organization loose to act more energetically than it normally does. First, you have to clearly target a corporate need. Second, you have to empower people to break barriers, remove blockages. Such a crusade brings enormous energy to solving a problem, and also energizes the entire organization. It rejuvenates people and evokes such comments as, "Hey, I haven't felt like this in many years."

An example of a successful marketing crusade occurred at Intel in the early 1980s. We were losing market share in the then new 16-bit microprocessor market. We were faced with becoming an also-ran in a product area that we had pioneered and in a market that we had developed. Our crusade involved mobilizing all the marketing, sales, and engineering people in the company and focusing them on winning every significant design for 16-bit microprocessors. The campaign was a success and as a result, Intel's architecture enjoys about two thirds of the 16-bit marketplace today.

But a crusade is extremely expensive in terms of the energy it takes and the emotion it mobilizes. You can't use it

46

Andrew S. Grove

too often or you will burn out your organization. Even worse, you will wear out your welcome, and your people won't respond when a real need arises. A corporate crusade should be mounted only to meet a key need in your organization.

**4. Reducing "Time To Market."** Nothing shows the presence or absence of organizational inertia as clearly as the time it takes for an organization to bring a product or service to its customers. Time to market, the subject of the fourth question in our mini-quiz, is a result as well as a measure of the vitality and responsiveness of any organization. It is also one that is close to our hearts at Intel, which has been consistently in the forefront of new products and technology.

The rate at which we brought products to market was fast enough for us in the '70s, but it's not fast enough for the '80s. To address this, we have mounted a major effort to cut down the time involved in our product- and market-development programs.

I have to say there is no single stroke of either a pen or a magic wand that can accelerate this process. It has to be done a step at a time, until the steps add up to a significant total.

---

We encourage champions to step forward, grab problems, and attempt to find solutions themselves.

---

We have one campaign called the "52-week chip" program. Our semiconductor product development has become more complex and it now takes more than two years to develop a new chip. We have dedicated ourselves to reducing the time to less than a year. We are already plotting the framework for a 26-week chip program, which will begin when the 52-week goal is achieved. How we work to cut down development time is very interesting. Of course, a great deal depends on pushing ahead in the use of computerized techniques. But the most important thing is to make

47

sure that we reuse the products of our previous engineering efforts in our new developments.

Anyone who has worked with engineers knows that this is easier said than done. Engineers like to develop everything from first principles themselves, and take delight in pointing out the weaknesses of previous engineering work. So what we have here is more than a procedural task. We have to change the attitudes of our most creative individuals. We have to encourage them to use capabilities developed by others.

**5. Internal Deregulation.** Government deregulation of industry causes our society to be more competitive, at the price of increased disorder. Deregulation within a company similarly enables a large organization to be more competitive, with the same penalty. What this means, basically, is pushing control down to lower levels in the organization.

Intel's normal practice was to require multiple levels of approval for every dollar we spent. If a person wanted to buy a piece of data-processing equipment, he had to get the consent of his own functional managers, the finance department, and the computer department. To cut through this cumbersome process, we came up with a program called "One dollar, one spender": Only one approval would be required for an expenditure under this rule.

---

To energize the middle manager, we have to find ways of mobilizing his heart and mind and energy in order to increase productivity.

---

We have also busted our planning process, delegated it to each of the divisions, and removed our corporate hand from overseeing how they do it. The divisions do their own planning, and they can do it in whatever form they want. If they want to do it on the back of an envelope, over a couple of beers, that's fine. If they want to do it in a big committee meeting, that's also fine. What we're concerned with is the result—the outcome of the planning process.

The common thread running through my five points is that they energize middle managers throughout the organization. We must achieve this in order to make a difference. Unfortunately, we face an agonizing dilemma. In the '70s, increased productivity plus growing and expanding markets meant increased employment. In the '80s, the markets that are available to us are more limited. Increased productivity in such a situation means decreased employment.

The 11-year history of prices for one of our most important products, an erasable programmable memory chip (EPROM), provides a good example. The graph on this page shows the price per bit for our EPROM products, declining more or less steadily, from $1 in 1975 to about a fiftieth of a cent at the end of 1981. In this period, we had become increasingly efficient in producing such devices, and we were

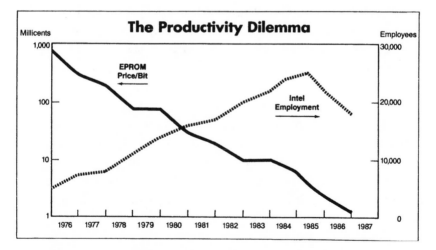

Employment rose steadily at Intel as increased efficiency helped bring down prices for its EPROM chips. But by 1985, the continued price declines required layoffs.

able to pass the result of our higher productivity on to our customers, who have found more and more applications for EPROMs. Our market grew, and so did our employment.

But the situation has become very different in the past five years. Prices for the chips have continued to decline, even more steeply than in the previous six years, reaching one one-thousandth of a cent per bit. That's a huge reduction in price over an 11-year period! Our growth in employment came to a sudden stop, and in the past two years we have had to substantially cut both our domestic and international work force.

Measured in terms of physical units per manufacturing employee, our productivity grew by 64 percent in 1985 and 1986. The result was a tragic 29 percent reduction in the head count at Intel. The process of increasing productivity that brought us prosperity for so many years has suddenly rewarded us with a round of layoffs.

Our manufacturing industries face a new problem today. In the trade wars, in which countries fight for a share of more slowly growing markets, our country has engaged in unilateral disarmament. Our markets are a free playing field for everybody, including countries whose markets are closed to us. The result is bad enough in each specific case, but when you add it up, has frightening implications for the future.

While the United States, person for person, is still the most productive nation in the world, unilateral trade disarmament is allowing our most productive industries to bleed to death. Those of us who have been fighting this battle in the trenches have been doing our share to combat organizational inertia. It is not an abstract task; it is a fight for survival. We are dedicated to continuing this fight as we finish up this decade and look to the '90s.

But we face a terrible dilemma. To energize the middle manager, we have to find ways of mobilizing his heart and mind and energy in order to increase productivity. But how long can we energize our middle managers to pursue their tasks with vigor and enthusiasm when the reward for innovative productivity increases turns out to be more layoffs? This is a problem for all American manufacturers, not just Intel and other electronics firms.

We need the help of a friend, our own Government. We don't want it to protect the stodgy giants that are, and should be, slated for extinction. But we do need the Government to provide rigorous enforcement of the international rules of trade, with unshakable insistence on the principle of reciprocity. For no matter how agile we are, we cannot remain giants unless we can play on as large — and as free — a field as our competitors do.

# PETER F. DRUCKER

**R**ecognized as the father of management, Peter Drucker has been a student and a teacher of business for 70 years. He was born in Vienna, Austria, where his father was a prominent lawyer and Viennese government official. After graduating from secondary school, Drucker studied law at the University of Hamburg and the University of Frankfurt in Germany. When Adolph Hitler came to power in 1933 Drucker knew it was time to leave Germany. At the outbreak of World War II, Drucker wrote a series of insightful articles on Germany's economy that caught the attention of United States's policy makers who sought his help. As a result, his consulting business was launched in 1940.

During the war years, Drucker focused on helping the government boost wartime production, but his interests soon included the American corporation and in 1946 he published his seminal book, *The Concept of the Corporation.* It was based on his consulting work with and analysis of General Motors, and in it he promotes decentralization and empowerment. Over the years he has advised top companies such as General Electric as well as governments around the world. Meanwhile, he also taught philosophy and politics at Bennington College (from 1942 to 1949) and then management at New York University (from 1950 to 1972.) Eventually he moved on to the Claremont Graduate School in California.

Drucker coined the term *knowledge worker* in his 1969 book, *The Age of Discontinuity,* in which he predicted the age of information, now being fully realized with the growth of the Internet. He wrote, "Though the knowledge worker is not a labourer, and certainly not a proletarian, he is not a subordinate in the sense that he can be told what to do; he is paid, on the contrary, for applying his knowledge, exercising his judgment, and taking responsible leadership." Thirty years after coining knowledge worker, Drucker refines his ideas in *The Rise of the Knowledge Worker.* One realization: "Historically, *keeping* knowledge a secret was the key to power and success. But in today's society, *sharing* knowledge is the key."

# The Rise of the Knowledge Worker
## *Peter F. Drucker*

The world economy is growing at a compound rate of 8 or 9 percent. If a company does not grow that much in its key markets where its core competencies should produce rewards, no matter what the chairman says in the annual report about it being another banner year for the company, it is not growing; it is looking at finance only. If the business has not grown, the year was dismal, dangerous, and catastrophic. Growth is hard work, but it is a survival necessity.

Every company needs a growth strategy. If it does not grow at least at the same pace as the market, it actually shrinks and becomes marginal. The fact that a company manages for shareholders and for increasing shareholder wealth becomes ludicrous once it becomes marginal. Such a company is put on the defensive and profit margins dwindle. The only way it can stay in the market is by leading on price, but that will only work for three years and no longer. By pursuing a no-growth policy, large companies around the world are simply condemning themselves to a slow death.

# BIG COMPANIES ECLIPSED?

The center of economic gravity in every developed country is no longer the big companies, but rather medium-sized companies. They have considerable advantages: as much access to information and money as the big organizations, and better access to "knowledge workers" who, in the United States and increasingly in Japan and Europe, prefer the medium-sized company precisely because it has a growth strategy. This is the market with growth in revenue, market share, and leadership.

---

In today's society, *sharing* knowledge is the key. That is very hard for people to do—withholding knowledge is how people have operated for thousands of years.

---

Large institutions are apparently resigned to decline. Leaders of these institutions receive enormous salaries and bonuses for downsizing—a total misunderstanding of what makes and keeps a company prosperous: growth, not cost control. Cost control is hygiene; growth is strength. Without growth, big companies will soon become also-rans, marginal, and defensive; they are putting their profits at risk no matter how much they downsize or reengineer.

# KNOWLEDGE IS EVERYTHING

Knowledge is between the ears; it is not the Internet. What to do with the data is the knowledge. Because we are starting out with superior knowledge, we need to pare it down and ask: "What knowledge do we *need* for our mission, our market, and our core competencies?" If you focus on knowledge, you do not have to worry much about the knowledge foundation. The knowledge foundation is simply people who are eager to see results stemming from what they know. Historically, *keeping* knowledge a secret was the key to power and success. But in today's society, *sharing* knowledge is the key. That is very hard for people to do—withholding knowledge is how people have operated for thousands of years. Now, we have to learn to share. Only then will we be able to attract and hold knowledge workers. Both Sony and Intel understand this very well and have built an incredible knowledge base. They focus the knowledge worker on unique performance and results. You do not hear much of people leaving Sony or Intel because their knowledge people are challenged, are focused on results, and see the results of their contribution.

---

Cost control is hygiene; growth is strength. Without growth, big companies . . . are putting their profits at risk no matter how much they downsize or reengineer.

---

They also have the right tools placed in their hands. About 150 years ago, when the large enterprise first arose, the only model was the military. So we built hierarchical, control-and-command structures under the assumption that only a few people at the top had any knowledge and that the rest were undistinguished and interchangeable people who were at best doing semi-skilled and repetitive work. That is no longer true. The model now is like a symphony orchestra. A good conductor knows that he cannot play the clarinet. But he challenges the clarinetist at every rehearsal. Maybe the clarinetist has only a small part in a particular score; in the next concert, he may have a huge solo. These people are motivated by the challenge to grow as specialists. The conductor has to meld dozens of individuals into one team. The difference between an orchestra and business is that an orchestra has a written score already. Business produces a score as it goes along, so the first step is for the people at the top to have clear and challenging goals and relate them to the performance of each of their knowledge workers. A few companies are working on this, but most of them are small and medium-sized companies. The big companies still believe they are in control of the knowledge worker, whereas in reality they can at best offer a promotion or threaten to fire him. They cannot command him.

## Setting Minimum Goals

Everybody today competes in a global market. To do so effectively and with a pool of knowledge workers, a company has to work on three tasks simultaneously. First, it has to *improve processes, products, and services* constantly without any additional investment. At the minimum, a quantitative goal of 3 percent compound per year, is a steady, albeit not a terribly fast, rate.

Second, a minimum investment must be made in *exploitation* —building on what already exists and then extending it. For example, Sony has grown by exploiting the tape recorder one step after the other. The Walkman is only a tape recorder with earphones—not a great technological breakthrough, but a great commercial breakthrough. The same is true of the cellular telephone. In emerging countries, that is the only way people can get telephone service. Companies are not going to wire all of China or India—it would take too long and cost too much. Exploitation has to be done by moving products and services to new markets, new uses, new geographies.

Third is *innovation.* The key to innovation is to abandon things that no longer produce; that were mistakes from the beginning and were not realized to be so until five years later; or that do not utilize an approach that systematically exploits changes in society, the economy, and technology as opportunities for the enterprise.

---

**Knowledge is between the ears; it is not the Internet.**

---

None of these three things cost a lot of money, but they do require an enormous amount of very hard work. As we are shifting toward knowledge organizations, companies without a growth plan will not be able to attract and hold knowledge workers — the linchpin of future success. The key is to constantly challenge them and make it worth their while so that they can say: "I have a purpose and a goal."

# WARREN E. BUFFETT

**W**arren Buffett knows what he wants in a management team, ideally, nothing: "I like a business that, when it's not managed at all, still makes lots of money. That's my kind of business." The oracle of Omaha knows how to pick them; today he is one of the world's richest people. Even as a boy, he is said to have discovered money like "Mozart discovered music." He worked hard for it too, operating two paper routes, retrieving golfballs for resale, and operating pinball machines in barber shops. Buffett attended the University of Nebraska and then Columbia University, where he earned an M.S. in economics in 1951.

In 1956 Buffett created his first fund with 100 partners, and from inception to 1969 he averaged a 32 percent annual return for his clients. He preferred buying companies that had monopolistic-like positions in their industries such as Coca-Cola and Disney. But then he did something radical; in 1969 he dissolved the partnership, declaring the market overpriced. He also admitted, "My idea quota used to be like Niagara Falls—I'd have many more than I could use. Now it's as though someone had damned up the water and was letting it flow with an eye-dropper." Ah, the investor's version of writer's block. It didn't last long and he had a new project to manage—Berkshire Hathaway, his publicly traded company.

Buffett had come to control Berkshire when it was a down-trodden textile company in the late 1960s and then transformed it into a holding company through which he bought stocks in other companies. The first 2,000 shares he bought cost $7.50 each; in the late 1990s Berkshire's shares hit a high of $84,000, but then fell back down to the mid $50,000 range as some of his investments such as Coca-Cola and Disney suffered set-backs (although the consensus is he'll fly high again soon). In *Track Record Is Everything,* Buffett provides the investor's eagle-eye view on management and what separates the good from the bad. "Watch that track record," he writes. "The best judgment we can make about managerial competence does not depend on what people say, but simply what the record shows."

# Track Record Is Everything
## *Warren E. Buffett*

I've often felt there might be more to be gained by studying business failures than business successes. In my business, we try to study where people go astray, and why things don't work. We try to avoid mistakes. If my job was to pick a group of 10 stocks in the Dow Jones average that would outperform the average itself, I would probably not start by trying to pick the 10 best. Instead, I would try to pick the 10 or 15 worst performers and take them out of the sample, and work with the residual. It's an inversion process. Albert Einstein said, "Invert, always invert, in mathematics and physics," and it's a very good idea in business, too. Start out with failure, and then engineer its removal.

In Berkshire Hathaway Inc.'s 1989 annual report, I wrote about something I called the "institutional imperative." I didn't learn about it in business school, but it tends to have an enormous impact on how businesses are actually run. One of its main tenets is a copycat mechanism that decrees that any craving of a leader, however foolish, will be quickly supported by detailed rate-of-return and strategic studies prepared by his troops.

For example, every time it becomes fashionable to expand into some new line of business, some companies will expand into it. Then they get out of it about five years later, licking their wounds. It's very human; people do the same thing with their stocks.

To illustrate, let me tell you the story of the oil prospector who met St. Peter at the Pearly Gates. When told his occupation, St. Peter said, "Oh, I'm really sorry. You seem to meet all the tests to get into heaven. But we've got a terrible problem. See that pen over there? That's where we keep the oil prospectors waiting to get into heaven. And it's filled—we haven't got room for even one more." The oil prospector thought for a minute and said, "Would you mind if I just said four words to those folks?" "I can't see any harm in that," said St. Pete. So the old-timer cupped his hands and yelled out, "Oil discovered in hell!" Immediately, the oil prospectors wrenched the lock off the door of the pen and out they flew, flapping their wings as hard as they could for the lower regions. "You know, that's a pretty good trick," St. Pete said. "Move in. The place is yours. You've got plenty of room." The old fellow scratched his head and said, "No. If you don't mind, I think I'll go along with the rest of 'em. There may be some truth to that rumor after all."

---

A group of lemmings looks like a pack of individualists compared with Wall Street when it gets a concept in its teeth.

---

That, unfortunately, is what happens in business and investments. People know better, but when they hear a rumor—particularly when they hear it from a high place—they just can't resist the temptation to go along.

It happens on Wall Street periodically, where you get what are, in effect, manias. Looking back no one can quite understand how everyone could have gotten so swept up in the moment. A group of lemmings looks like a pack of individualists compared with Wall Street when it gets a concept in its teeth.

When I was a graduate student at Columbia University, I got a piece of advice from Ben Graham, the founding father of security analysis, that I've never forgotten: You're neither right nor wrong because other people agree with you. You're right because your facts are right and your reasoning is right — and that's the only thing that makes you right.

---

What counts is how the company does over a five- or 10-year period. It has nothing to do with charts or numbers. It has to do with businesses and management.

---

And if your facts and reasoning are right, you don't have to worry about anybody else. Watch that track record. The best judgment we can make about managerial competence does not depend on what people say, but simply what the record shows. At Berkshire Hathaway, when we buy a business we usually keep whoever has been running it, so we already have a batting average. Take the case of Mrs. B, who ran our Furniture Mart. Over a 50-year period, we'd seen her take $500 and turn it into a business that made $18 million pretax. So we knew she was competent. She's also 97 years old. In fact, now she's competing with us; she started a new business two years ago. Who would think you'd have to get a noncompete agreement with a 95-year-old? Clearly, the lesson here is that the past record is the best single guide.

Then you run into the problem of the 14-year-old horse. Let's say you buy The Daily Racing Form and it shows that the horse won the Kentucky Derby as a four-year-old. Based on past performance, you know this was one hell of a horse. But now he's 14 and can barely move. So you have to ask yourself, "Is there anything about the past record that makes it a poor guidelines as a forecaster of the future?"

> You're neither right nor wrong because other people agree with you. You're right because your facts are right and your reasoning is right—and that's the only thing that makes you right.

The situation may also arise in which there is no clear past record. Let's say that when you left college they gave you a little bonus: You got to pick out anybody in your class and you'd get 10 percent of his or her future earnings. All of a sudden you look at the whole group in a different way. You've seen them in class; you know their grades and their leadership capabilities. Taking these factors into account, you ask yourself, "Who do I pick?" But how good a choice do you think you could make? It would be a lot easier if you could make that decision at your tenth class reunion, after you've seen their actual business performance, wouldn't it?

> Watch that track record. The best judgment we can make about managerial competence does not depend on what people say, but simply what the record shows.

These are the judgments that Berkshire Hathaway makes about management all the time. We try to find businesses that we really felt good about owning. What a company's stock sells for today, tomorrow, next week, or next year doesn't matter. What counts is how the company does over a five- or

10-year period. It has nothing to do with charts or numbers. It has to do with businesses and management.

Another thing I learned in business school was that it doesn't help to be smarter than even your dumbest competitor. The trick is to have no competitors. That means having a product that truly differentiates itself.

Say a customer goes into a drugstore and asks for a Hershey's bar. The clerk says, "We don't have any, but why don't you take this other chocolate bar instead; it's a nickel cheaper." And the customer says, "I'll go across the street." It's when the customer will go across the street that you've got a great business.

# I. MacAllister Booth

Edwin Land, founder of Polaroid, resigned as CEO in 1980 and sold all his stock in 1985, later declaring, "I had been such a dominant influence in the company for such a long time that I had to separate myself completely." He understood that his successors, including MacAllister Booth, "had to learn to be proud of what they were doing." No doubt, Booth had rather large shoes to fill. He joined Polaroid in 1962 as a supervisor in the film division. He worked his way up on the manufacturing side and in 1983 he was named president. The title of CEO was added in 1986 and chairman in 1991.

In a unique chapter of Booth's career, Polaroid won a major patent infringement suit against Eastman Kodak in 1986, but not until October 1990 were they awarded the $1 billion judgment. Unfortunately, in 1988 and early 1989 the company was forced to defend itself against a hostile takeover led by Roy Disney (Walt's nephew) and his company, Shamrock Holdings. So before he even had the $1 billion, Booth was forced to use it to protect the company and finance a stock buyback program. He reflected, "There was a multi-dimensional tic-tac-toe game going on. The borrowing of the money . . . and the attempted takeover were all influenced greatly by speculation on what the Kodak settlement would be."

There was a bright side—Booth realized Polaroid had to become more vigilant in protecting shareholder interests: "It was a cold shower. It made us recognize the importance of the shareholder." To become more competitive, the company cut the workforce by 15 percent, introduced an (overdue) employee stock ownership plan, and then went through a second restructuring in 1992; the purpose was not to cut but to focus on growth through new products, such as photographic imaging using laser technology. Through it all, the biggest lesson Booth, who retired in 1995, learned was the importance of involving the employees at every level. In *Much Ado About Worker Participation* he argues for team building; however, he warns that creating a collaboratory atmosphere does not mean a company will be one big, happy family.

# Much Ado About Worker Participation
## *I. MacAllister Booth*

Fact: Business and labor leaders nationwide agree that increased worker participation in corporate decision making improves decision quality, boosts productivity, and leads to greater customer satisfaction, shareholder return, and improved competitive position in the global marketplace. So why are we struggling so much to make greater worker involvement in decision making a workplace reality?

The answer varies from company to company. In some, the change to a participative workplace may be alien to the company's history and culture. There may be fears that greater worker participation threatens traditional management. And last, but by no means least, our legal environment greatly hinders worker participation in decision making outside the context of traditional collective bargaining. Companies must overcome these obstacles. Organizations must be allowed to be as innovative with worker participation as any good, learning organization must be in developing new processes or products. We must be able to experiment, evaluate the results, and experiment again without artificial constraints on subject matter or form. If we cannot do this, we will not be competitive.

## PERSONNEL POLICY 101

Polaroid's core values regarding worker participation date back to the employee philosophy of its founder, Dr. Edwin Land. In the 1940s, Dr. Land published "Personnel Policy 101"—a credo that describes two basic aims at Polaroid:

1. To manufacture products that present an attractive value to the public and an attractive profit to the company.
2. To provide a worthwhile working life for each member of the company in which he or she shares the responsibility and the rewards.

Sharing the responsibility and the reward has been a way of life at Polaroid from the beginning and remains so today. Each Polaroid employee is encouraged to share in decision making by participating in at least one problem-solving group activity in addition to his or her "line" job. In the 1960s and 1970s, we called our participative groups "vertical councils" because their membership was typically a vertical slice of any given work group. Today, through continuous experimentation and improvement, the groups have evolved into "critical process teams" or "corrective action teams" because membership comes from anywhere in the company where people have relevant knowledge. We are also experimenting with self-directed work teams that make hiring and pay decisions autonomously, and we have an internal grievance process where employees serve as decision makers.

In any kind of participatory arrangement at Polaroid, we try to be as clear as possible at the outset about who has what authority and responsibility. Participants must not be misled into thinking they will always have an equal say in every decision. Our self-directed work teams and employee grievance panels, for example, are empowered to make certain final decisions without further managerial review. But other groups operate in a "test and respond" mode. That is, a manager or team leader presents proposals to the group and

group members provide feedback upon which a final decision is ultimately made by the manager. The underlying
intent of each participation mode is that authority for decision making be commensurate with responsibility and
accountability for the outcome of the decision.

This entire process of participation helps blur the
"we/they" line at Polaroid. However, it does not mean that
people at every meeting are one big, happy family. Team
members often disagree on how to best solve a problem, but
when the problem is defined so that each participant sees it as
his or her own and understands that his or her best interest is
served by a good solution, disagreements take on a different
character. Almost invariably, ultimate decisions are more
credible, more sound and more effective as the result of having been forged by thoughtful people with divergent views.

Additionally, employees acquire knowledge, perspective,
and ultimately transferable skills that stand them in good
stead if and when they need to move to different assign-
ments, as job security becomes a thing of the past. The experience of interacting with other people from different parts
of the company and from different levels builds new learning
and self-confidence and provides great networking, all of
which become invaluable to the individuals and to the company as a whole.

## So What's the Problem?

In spite of all the benefits, our teams and committees have
come under attack. In 1949, an employees' committee,
elected by the entire work force, was founded to provide a
voice for all Polaroid people in matters of pay, benefits, personnel policy, and assistance in our dispute resolution
processes. For more than 40 years, the committee operated
openly and effectively. It was cited in numerous articles that
extolled its virtues, and Polaroid itself was listed in national
surveys as an outstanding place to work. In 1992, however,
the committee was dissolved—a painful decision that

stemmed from the Department of Labor's finding that the committee's officer election procedures were out of compliance with national labor laws.

However, we did not want to abandon our commitment to worker involvement in decision making, so we set out to find a new, legal arrangement through which employees could influence company decisions. We set up a critical process team of 30 people who reflected the diversity of our work force by age, race, gender, seniority and pay level. They were selected from a pool of volunteers by still another group of people who had originally volunteered to serve as grievance process panelists.

The critical process team studied what other companies were doing. They learned about unions and the legalities of worker participation. With some help from our lawyers, they designed a new forum, the Employee Owners Influence Council (EOIC). Yet this structure too has become the subject of a complaint, this time from the National Labor Relations Board, which alleges that we have created an illegal, company-dominated labor organization.

We do not agree that the EOIC is a labor organization at all. Rather, it is an informed focus group that provides decision makers with a range of reactions to possible modifications of our personnel policies and benefits. Each person on the EOIC speaks only for himself or herself. None of them represent any other employee in the company. It is simply a forum where management can talk to 30 employees and learn from their opinions about choices the company faces.

## SEARCHING FOR A SOLUTION

Whether in a union or nonunion setting, employers must be able to involve any and all of their workers in decisions that affect their lives and to hear and take advantage of their ideas. To be an effective CEO, I need the freedom to hear the direct voices of employees unfiltered by layers of executives or by any other employees. Polaroid's people are independent minded, articulate and perceptive. I need the best and broadest range of what they have to offer to make my decisions and manage my company.

If the law prohibits the practices that led to Polaroid's being named one of the 100 best places to work in the United States, then surely it is time to reexamine the law. If workers and management are not working cooperatively, the pie that we are trying to make bigger actually shrinks instead. Such situations are marked by greater distrust and disloyalty and by litigation that is costly to business and society at large.

I am not suggesting that there should be no legal regulations of the labor/management interface. On the contrary, our laws must continue to protect worker rights, including employees' rights to engage in collective bargaining without coercion or restraint by their employers. Perhaps the time has come to raise the ante on employer interference in worker rights with serious monetary penalties for employer misconduct. But such misconduct must be based on actual evidence of wrongdoing, not simply presumed on the basis of a particular model of dialogue between employer and employee. Our laws must not prevent organizations from having the latitude to innovate and experiment with different models of constructive engagement among all workers—managerial and nonmanagerial.

There is much talk about horizontal and borderless organizations. This reflects the need to enlist everyone in the mission of the company at all levels. We need more open, interactive, dynamic engagement, not stiltedness where there are just a few single leaders and everyone else is a follower. It is the "we" companies that will succeed in global competition.

Perhaps the solution is simply a matter of looking at our old laws in new ways and reinterpreting them for today's realities. We need to accept and promote learning through experimentation. Without these opportunities for learning, we will suffer all the problems evidenced in any situation where there is only one choice. Our country cannot afford that. Our labor laws are our social engineering that set the boundaries and framework of how we interact in the workplace. They must not be allowed to hamstring us as we move into the 21st century.

# RICHARD BRANSON

To some, Richard Branson is a serious businessman to be contended with; for example, Branson's Virgin Atlantic airlines, which he founded in 1984, has taken away market share from powerful British Airways with aggressive pricing and top service. To others, he is the British version of P. T. Barnum; in 1998 the self-promoting Branson drove a World War II tank into Times Square to promote his new Virgin Cola. The reason: "I want Virgin to be as well known around the world as Coca-Cola." He also flaunts his flamboyant personal life in his 1998 autobiography, *Losing My Virginity.* He opens his book with the following childhood memory: "My mother was determined to make us independent. When I was four, she stopped the car a few miles from our house and made me find my own way home across the fields. I got hopelessly lost."

Branson founded his first notable company, the record label Virgin Records in the early 1970s, which he put on the map when he signed the notorious Sex Pistols in 1977. Unfortunately, during the recession in the early 1990s he was forced to sell his gem to pay off bank loans needed for his other renowned start-up, Virgin Atlantic, which has proved a risky but successful uphill battle against British Airways and other established airlines. Branson appears to thrive on risk, both business and personal (in 1997 he crashed his hot air balloon in Algeria while trying to circumnavigate the world).

Having to sell his record company left a bad taste in his mouth and Branson now prefers joint ventures with wealthy partners over bank loans. In terms of which business opportunities to pursue, he relies on his gut instinct: "Perhaps my early problems with dyslexia made me more intuitive: when someone sends me a written proposal, rather than dwelling on detailed facts and figures I find that my imagination grasps and expands on what I read." In the following interview Branson does provide some concrete views on management, including "Small is beautiful." To keep that small feeling, Branson goes to great lengths to stay in touch; for example, every month he writes a personal letter to employees.

# The Virgin Iconoclast
## *An Interview with Richard Branson*

*When you look at your career, what do you see as the critical decision points?*

I suppose the first one was deciding to leave school at a young age, being only 15 years old. I started a magazine at school. The aim of it was to give young people a voice, to put the world right. At the time, the headmaster gave me a choice: Either you do your education or you do your magazine. You can't do both. I decided to leave school to run the magazine. Obviously, that was a critical decision point. The magazine turned out to be my form of management education. I spent four or five years running it, going out and doing interviews, meeting people, and perhaps most importantly, learning the art of survival. I had to sell enough advertising to pay the bills. I needed to have a table big enough to dive under when somebody came to collect the bills that hadn't been paid.

From then on, things just evolved. Never was there any sort of mapping things out five years ahead. Perhaps I should have done that, but I never did. One day, for instance, somebody turned up who loved popular music, a cousin of mine from South Africa. He led me to think maybe we should consider setting up a record company, and of course we did. Actually, a lot of companies evolved out of

71

that record company. If you had a record company, you needed shops to sell your products; you needed an export company to export your records; you needed foreign companies to distribute records abroad and market them well; you needed editing suites to edit film, video, and so on.

---

I find that I spend a lot of time trying to motivate people. For instance, once a week I go down to the airline to make sure I meet all new employees at least once.

---

We decided to create companies that would stand on their own, companies in themselves. Looking back, I suspect, the biggest difference between us and other independent record companies was that we decided to set up our own companies around the world ourselves rather than giving the rights for our products to other people. Suddenly, we had substantial companies in Germany and France. Japan and America were also signing on local bands as well. . . .

*Is there anything distinctive about your company that accounts for its success?*
I'm absolutely certain that it is a question of the kind of people we have and the way we motivate them. If you can motivate your people, you can get through bad times and you can enjoy the good times together. If you fail to motivate your people, your company is doomed not to perform well.

I find that I spend a lot of time trying to motivate people. For instance, once a week I go down to the airline to make sure I meet all new employees at least once. If the cabin crew joins a company like Virgin, they join for the romance, for the flying. Yet, with most airlines, they soon realize that there is no romance in flying. What we try to do is to make sure that there is. Thus, the kinds of hotels where they stay in are nice hotels, not airport hotels—hotels with swimming pools and pleasant environments. If your staff is happy and smiling and enjoying their work, they will perform well. Consequently, the customers will enjoy their experience with your company. If your staff is sad and miserable and not having a good time, the customers will be equally miserable.

I go to great lengths to be in touch with the staff. We have 3,000 or 4,000 people now. Every month I write them a letter with lots of chatty details about what's going on and what we are planning to do. At the end of the letter, I always give my home address and telephone number. I tell them, if you have any suggestions, any problems, any ideas, just call or write me. On average, I get maybe 15 or 16 letters a day from staff members, and I always make sure that these letters are the first to be answered. I've gotten some superb ideas from letters, and also learned about some bad decisions that have been made. Some staff members even write me about personal things. That's fine as well. I personally believe that if each chairman of every company were to communicate directly to every staff member and get them to write about their problems, the need for trade unions would be much less, and the company would also run that much better.

---

If your staff is sad and miserable and not having a good time, the customers will be equally miserable.

---

In some ways I place more importance on the junior people in my companies than I do on the senior people. I do get quite angry when senior people come in saying they want another 30,000 pounds, while at the same time they are asking their junior people to tighten their belts. Given the way we value our people at Virgin, we will very rarely ever fire anybody. To do that kind of thing is very demoralizing for everybody.

*Could you say something about the way you design your organization, its architecture?*

I suppose our record company [now divested] still provides the best example. My philosophy was always that if there were 50 people in a building I would go there and ask to see the deputy managing director, the deputy sales manager, and the deputy marketing manager, and I'd say: "You are now the managing director, the sales manager, and the marketing manager of a new company." I would put them into a new building. Then, again, when that company got to a certain size, I would do the same thing again. We actually set up about 25, 30 small record companies. Cumulatively, they became the biggest independent record company in the world. And they never lost major artists. Major artists stayed with them because they would identify with the small teams. Also, if you're given a card by somebody who says he is the managing director you might take him very well more seriously than if you were given a card saying that the person was the deputy to the deputy to the deputy to the deputy managing director.

---

Given the way we value our people at Virgin, we will very rarely ever fire anybody. To do that kind of thing is very demoralizing for everybody.

---

*What about your reward systems? You once said that you were in the business of making millionaires.*

Yes, I suppose that we have made maybe 15 or 20 multimillionaires through this structure. In the last two years we have also paid out over 150 million pounds to people whom we have given stakes in companies to. I think, however, as a private company it is more difficult to bring in schemes to involve everybody in the same way you can with a public company, where you have shares. But that is something which I think in the future we have got to try to address. We have to make sure that it is not just part of the wage package. There is a danger in doing so. At the moment we tend to reward our people more in a paternalistic way. If somebody has performed really well, we all sing from the mountain and thank them the best we can. But we need to formalize that a bit in the future.

*Do you have any characteristics or weaknesses that get in the way of your work?*

I suspect not being able to say no. Hopefully, I am getting better at it now. But there are so many wonderful ideas. And I do love new projects; I love new ideas. We are in a position where almost anybody and everybody who has got an idea loves to bring it to us. There aren't many companies like us, which have a certain amount of entrepreneurial flair; companies which seem accessible to the public. Therefore, in any one day we receive hundreds of proposals of all sorts. And some of them are very good ones.

My weaknesses really go back to the fact that I have spread myself too thin. In a purely business sense I suspect if I wanted just to maximize profits I should have stayed more focused on one area. That's the most conventional way that I'm sure most business schools teach. Perhaps that way is right. But having said so, I have to say it wouldn't have been half as much fun as doing it my way. I have no regrets at all in trying to break the mold and taking a different approach. That different approach has resulted in Virgin, as a brand name, being one of the best-known and well-respected brand names in the world.

And as a matter of fact, we actually have started companies just because of the name. For example, we started a skiing company called "Virgin Snow" just because the name was so delightful. We now have gone into launching "Virgin

Water" and "Virgin Cola" because these seemed like such great names. We're also driven to start something new when we feel that something hasn't been done very well by others; that we can do it better.

---

> In a purely business sense I suspect if I wanted just to maximize profits I should have stayed more focused on one area.

---

The importance of having a name like Virgin for the company cannot be overemphasized. Over the next 20 years, we can use that brand name to break into a number of different areas and hopefully create a number of other quite successful companies.

But in spite of all these new ideas flowing in, we do make an effort to be firmer, to say no, simply because we don't have the time to concentrate on what we have already taken on.

As an aside, my wife says my biggest weakness is sticky pudding and pretty women.

# PART III

# Marketing and Brand-Building

Without the customer there is no company, so it makes sense that in The Conference Board's 1999 *CEO Challenge* survey 40 percent of the responding CEOs said that "customer loyalty/retention" is one of their top three management challenges. In a separate 1999 research report entitled *Consumer Expectations on the Social Accountability of Business*, The Conference Board discovered that brand quality and image/reputation influenced consumers most, with more than 54 percent citing it as the most important factor in judging a company. The authors in this section tackle not only the importance of creating the right image for a company and its products, but what qualities are needed to be a superlative marketer. Akio Morita, cofounder of Sony and author of the first essay, declares "Good marketing, I believe, requires some degree of courage . . ." One of the first lessons he learned was that "no sale can be achieved unless the buyer appreciates the value of the merchandise." Howard Morgens, the legendary Procter & Gamble leader and pioneer in consumer research, adds, "Advertising can only create a new market for products which fill a genuine— though often unexpressed or latent—consumer want." In a 1998 research report, *Managing the Corporate Brand*, The Conference Board discovered that the top three success factors in promoting a brand are "(1) The strength of the brand logo, (2) The effective use of visuals and imagery, and (3) The ability to capture the brand in a slogan." No doubt advertising executive Jennifer Laing concurs. As CEO of Saatchi & Saatchi's North American operations, she has learned that the proliferation of media channels such as cable and the Internet can fragment brand messages. Laing concludes, "More than ever before, brands need advertising that will carve a special, distinctive place in consumers' hearts and resonate long after the spot is gone."

# AKIO MORITA

The cofounder of Sony had his work cut out for him when in war-devastated 1946 Japan, he and his friend, Masaru Ibuka, set about building "a clever company that would make new high-technology products in ingenious ways" and help rebuild Japan's economy. Morita had always been obsessed with electronics and credits his unwitting mother for his interest: "My mother was very fond of Western classical music, and she bought many phonograph records for our old Victrola. . . . and I believe my interest in electronics and sound reproduction began because of her." Morita's father was hoping his eldest son would follow him into the sake business, a family tradition for fourteen generations. Morita, however, went on to study physics at the Osaka Imperial University just as World War II was breaking out.

During the war, the lab in which he worked became a naval research facility and Morita himself became a lieutenant. After the war he went into business with his friend, and their first innovative product was the tape recorder—Morita finally conquered voice recording—only postwar Japan was not interested in toys. At the time, the courts were overwhelmed with cases and stenographers were scarce, so he marketed it as a replacement for them. He was always on the lookout to take advantage of technology. For example, while it was Bell Labs that invented the transistor, it was Sony that put it into a pocket radio.

Morita also realized that "having a unique technology and being able to make unique products are not enough to keep a business going. You have to sell the products, and to do that you have to show the potential buyer the real value of what you are selling." The technologist turned showman took a global view in building Sony and personally sought overseas opportunities. Morita moved his entire family to the United States in 1963. He discusses some of the lessons he learned from the United States and why and how they came up with the name Sony in *Moving Up in Marketing by Getting Down to Basics*. While the name Sony was created for marketing purposes, Morita eschews market research simply for the sake of it.

# Moving Up in Marketing by Getting Down to Basics
## *Akio Morita*

Good marketing, I believe, requires some degree of courage, and so I shall try to draw on mine in discussing frankly my marketing concepts. These come from my experience and not from theory. I was a physicist by education and have had no formal training in the field of marketing. I shall, therefore, lean on my past experience rather than try to theorize.

In 1946 our present chairman, Mr. Masaru Ibuka, and I established our company with a little over 20 persons and less than $600 of capital. We started making communication equipment for the reconstruction of Japan. We dealt with various government agencies.

It required a great deal of effort to get the purchasing officers in these large organizations to understand that we were a company that could be relied on for its unique technology and sincerity. We were finally able to gain their trust and get a continuous flow of orders from them. However, one day a horrible thing happened. The person in charge of purchase, whose trust I had won after long effort, was transferred to another position. An entirely new person now sat in the purchaser's seat. This meant that I had to start all over again to convince him of our capabilities.

79

After a few repetitions of this experience, I began to think about the problem. I realized that it is not good business if our efforts do not accumulate and continue to bring results. From the standpoint of efficiency, our efforts should accumulate and remain as an asset of the business. When we deal with a large organization it is true that a large, one-time sale may be achieved if the purchasing agent of the organization has been convinced of our company's ability. However, such large sales are influenced by a small handful of individuals in charge of the purchase. Once these individuals disappear, all the effort of the past is lost. I began to wonder whether this manner of doing business was a wise policy or not.

---

Good marketing, I believe, requires some degree of courage.

---

I discussed this matter with Mr. Ibuka, and we arrived at the conclusion to go into the consumer market. In other words, we decided to do business with unspecified millions of individuals instead of with a specific few. On this basis we started to produce the first tape recorder and tapes in Japan.

We had dreams of making a great fortune, and we devoted huge amounts of money and personnel, in comparison with the size of the company, to the development of the product. But this dream disappeared when we started to market this first tape recorder, for we visited many prospective customers, demonstrating the new tape recorder ourselves, and they would only say that the device was very interesting but too expensive for a toy. Facing this fact, we spent many days trying to find out how we could sell the product.

One weekend I took a stroll in my neighborhood and stopped in front of an antique shop. I am not interested in antiques, but I gazed at the various articles displayed in the show window. Out of curiosity I walked into the shop where a customer was asking the salesman various questions. And then the customer paid an amazingly high price for an antique that would not have attracted me in the least, and he walked out happily with it. I thought that our tape recorder was much more valuable, but he had gladly paid an even higher price for an antique.

I was surprised and intrigued by this behavior. It taught me a basic principle of sales. This principle is that no sale can be achieved unless the buyer appreciates the value of the merchandise. I would not have paid such a price to buy the antique piece, because I am not interested in such things. But the other person, who understood the value of antiques, was willing to pay the price.

The tape recorder was a tremendous technical achievement in the eyes of those of us who had struggled to create it. For us it had a very high value, and we thought that the price we had put on it was even less than its true value. But the general public looked on it only as an interesting toy. This meant that unless the customer understood that the tape recorder was a valuable device with a wide variety of uses, he would not pay the price. The principle was this simple, but we realized that we were ignorant of even this basic principle. We therefore embarked on the task of teaching people how useful the tape recorder was in practical life.

---

No sale can be achieved unless the buyer appreciates the value of the merchandise.

---

This experience taught us a basic lesson in the marketing of our product, which has guided our policy ever since. A company such as ours, which is constantly developing new products, must always have the capability of educating prospective customers. Otherwise, new markets for new products will never be created. However, it is impossible for us, who are limited in time and number, to educate large numbers of customers. We realize that marketing means increasing the number of persons who can communicate to customers the usefulness and value of our new products in the same way as we would ourselves.

Firstly, therefore, I had to educate our marketing group in this purpose, and then they would transfer my concepts to the next stage of marketing. In this process an accurate message had to be communicated fully from myself to our marketing group, and from them to distributor salesmen in each region, and then from the distributor salesmen to the dealer salesmen. This meant that our marketing task was a communication task.

## MARKETING AS COMMUNICATION

In the technology of electronic communication, the more relay stages there are in the channel, the greater is the possibility for distortion to accumulate. It is important, therefore, to keep the number of relay stages to a minimum. Yet in earlier days in our industry Japan had a very complex sales distribution system. So it took a very long time to build up our own sales organization to enable our sales personnel to deliver the message directly to the dealers.

---

In our type of society, where new technology is constantly being developed, I think it is risky to rely too heavily on market research.

---

Now the concept that marketing is communication has become very firmly established. Moreover, this concept is not limited to the sales network alone. It is very important inside our own company whenever we develop a new product. It involves transmitting the intent of top management in the development of a product through all stages, from the production department to the floor salesman of the dealer and to the customer. Moreover, the communication is not just one-way. Customers' views must be fed back accurately through the marketing network to the factory. Only when this two-way communication is adequate can it be said that the marketing mechanism works out well.

People nowadays pay great attention to market research. The belief has grown that by learning promptly what things the consumers want and by producing those things, good sales will be achieved. However, in our type of society, where new technology is constantly being developed, I think it is risky to rely too heavily on market research. The customer in general has some knowledge about the products he presently owns, but he is not usually an expert who knows the technology involved. Therefore, if we are too strongly influenced by his demands in our development efforts, we may end up working on a product which other manufacturers may already have introduced on the market by the time we are able to put ours on sale. This would mean that we could not be competitive.

Utilizing our technological capacity, we must create products having new features that customers have not expected nor have had any knowledge about. These products and features, when they are created, must then be communicated to the customer so that he can understand what benefits he can obtain. In this way a market is created. This is the concept that our company has about marketing.

## DEVELOPING AN INTERNATIONAL MARKET

In referring to the need to reduce the number of relay steps in order to improve communication, I also indicated that each relay step should be manned by those having the same concepts and interests as we have. When we began to produce the world's first small transistor radio, we decided that our products should be sold all around the world, and these ideas of relay steps in communication were also applied to the system of exporting our products.

At that time Japanese manufacturers found it very difficult to sell their products abroad. They felt that the only way to sell their products outside Japan was to rely on various trading companies. However, we felt that we could not communicate our new knowledge adequately through trading firms that had different interests from ours. We therefore decided to export our products ourselves.

I took the small radio myself to the United States to sell it. I spent a great deal of time learning how best to conduct sales in the United States. My knowledge of the country was nil. I was amazed at the huge market; I was amazed at the huge size of the country; and I was amazed at the strength of the competition. But I became confident that our marketing concept need not change and that the basic principles need not be different.

However, we ran into a very big obstacle. That was the name of our company, Tokyo Tsushin Kogyo. I found that no American could pronounce it. We realized that we needed a trademark that could be easily recognized by Americans. The establishment of a reputation for reliability among the public is of prime importance in consumer marketing, but this could not be achieved unless the name of the company could be easily remembered. It would be impossible to ask the public to trust a company whose name they could not even pronounce.

Realizing, therefore, that the company should be identified easily and clearly, we concluded that the name of our company was not appropriate for international business. We started a search for a name that would be the best. We set up three conditions to be met. One was that it must be an internationally acceptable name. Another was that it must be short, and thirdly, it would have to be pronounced in the same way wherever it was seen.

Thinking of various possibilities, we came across the Latin word *sonus*, meaning "sound." We also thought of the English word "sonny," or "sonny boy," and we combined it with the Latin word to form SONY. At that time we were a group of young people handling sound equipment, in other words, "sonny boys" dealing in "sonus." And so the name SONY was coined, and on that first tiny radio, therefore, we put the letters S-O-N-Y as a trademark. Also, we changed our company name to this, so that the advertising cost would not have to be split in two to advertise two names. In this way, all of our advertising funds could be spent on communicating information about our products.

It was quite a decision to change our company name Tokyo Tsushin Kogyo, a name that sounded good in Japanese, to a new name like SONY. When we did this, some Japanese thought that the Japanese company called Tokyo Tsushin Kogyo had been taken over by a foreign company called Sony Corporation. Today, however, we believe that the bold step we took was a good one. Marketing is something that I believe must be continued over many years in communicating the company philosophy and concepts. Customers will then become fully confident that any new products we would offer under our name can also be bought with a sense of reliability.

However, I believe that marketing requires investments for the future. Just as the manufacturer invests in the future by expending research funds for new products, and, in some cases, for basic science, so must investments be made in the sales area for future marketing. My experience tells me that this is often forgotten in the Western system. To understand this point, it may be helpful to consider the difference between the attitude of employees toward their companies in the United States and Japan.

## INVESTING IN THE FUTURE

In Japan nearly all the employees of a company stay in the firm for many long years. In our company, our managers and other key staff members have been with the firm for many years and will continue to cast their lot with the company for another 10, 20 or 30 years. For these employees it is not only important that the company business be good at present but also necessary that the company be healthy in the decades ahead. Therefore young, middle-level employees can clearly understand the need to make investments at present, even with some degree of sacrifice, to build for the future. It is, therefore, possible to establish long-range plans and invest to create future markets.

In contrast, those working in an American company are rated on the results they show every year. It is difficult for them to think of sacrificing today's profits for the sake of the company's well-being one or two decades from now. It is much more likely that they will want to cash in on all of the company's current possessions for the sake of profits today. However, very logical management principles have been derived from this kind of approach in the United States, and I have learned much from this American management method. Still, I cannot avoid the impression that the great attention given to making profits today causes a lack of willingness to sacrifice some of today's profits for developing markets in the future.

This is illustrated by the fact that, with the exception of a small number of companies, most firms in the United States are not export-minded. The development of export markets requires a great deal of investment, so that business can be conducted successfully in other countries having different customs and attitudes. This type of investment appears only as a negative figure in the business at the early stages. And this causes many American companies to regard exports as a nonprofitable business.

In order to gain trust in the United States we had to devote great efforts and invest money over a very long time. Even today we station many of our Japanese engineers in countries all around the world to study design preferences among customers, the attitude of such customers towards technology, and the many different regulations of those nations, so that our own designers and planners can be adequately aware of them. These efforts require a great deal of expense. But we believe that this expense provides us with the ability to produce products which will be appropriate for those nations five and ten years from now.

There are some companies in the United States that are like this. They are the truly multinational corporations that have accumulated a wealth of experience abroad. All such firms have invested considerably in the future. But while many companies are willing to spend research funds for future technology, very often they forget to spend money for marketing in the distant future.

A new product resulting from such studies may not at first be understood by even those inside the company. But the first step in marketing is to exert efforts to get these inside personnel to understand the new product. And I believe that the real marketing experts are those who approach the new product with a will to understand it and go out and sell it. This creating of markets involves efforts to increase further the trust of customers in the company and at the same time to communicate to the customer the benefits derived from new technology in new products. In this way the strength of the company is fostered every day.

For, marketing is not just marketing for today. An enterprise is not well off by being well off only today. To continue to be successful, there must be an adequate understanding of the need to invest today's profits for the future, not only in research and development but also in marketing.

# MELVIN R. GOODES

As CEO of one of the top pharmaceutical companies, Warner-Lambert, Melvin Goodes knows better than most how important marketing and image are; one false step in the drug-makers' world and it's years of corporate rehab. Fortunately, the Canadian native was tough-skinned and prepared for hardship. Growing up in relative poverty, he donated money from his newspaper route to the family coffers. Later, he was a grave digger and sorted blood-soaked laundry at the local hospital to fund his college education. Goodes studied business at Queen's University in Kingston, Ontario, Canada, and then earned an M.B.A. at the University of Chicago in 1960.

After working briefly for the Ford Motor Company and for a brewery in Canada, Goodes joined Warner-Lambert as a manager in new product development in 1964. At various times he held management positions responsible for European, Mexican, and Asian operations. He became president and chief operating officer (COO) in 1985, and then CEO and chairman in 1991. One of his first concerns was ensuring that management and employees were on the same page. "Much time is spent communicating with shareholders, the investment community, legislators and regulators," he said. "Yet, the most important audience is our employees." To capture their attention, in 1991 he introduced a stock options program for all employees. In 1999 more than 200 had become millionaires.

To increase sales, Goodes sought alliances within the industry, a once taboo practice. For example, to everyone's surprise, he cut a deal with rival Pfizer to comarket Warner-Lambert's new cholesterol drug, Lipitor. "Everyone gasped," he said, "but we couldn't market the thing on our own, and the 'not-invented-here' attitude in this business needed to go." Lipitor went on to generate record sales of $1 billion in its first year. Goodes, who retired in May of 1999, explains the importance of strong product and corporate brands in *How to Create an Internal Corporate Brand.* He provides a five-step process, which begins with speaking your mind. "We gave people the license to say what they really thought," he writes.

# How to Create an Internal Corporate Brand
## *Melvin R. Goodes*

Over the past five years, both individual product brands and corporate brands have been thriving. Firms such as IBM, General Electric, and Intel are unlocking and expanding the equity in their names to shore up their images—a remarkable turn of events given that at the start of the 1990s, brands were declared all but dead.

Warner-Lambert has also made an enormous effort to strengthen its image—not an easy task for a company that was mistaken for everything from a junk bond firm to the people behind Bugs Bunny. Our image was built from the inside out by winning the hearts and minds of 41,000 employees worldwide. It stems from a simply stated values set that is operative in all of the 150 countries where we do business. These values are understood and acted on by any colleague, at any level, anywhere in the company. The uptake of these values has built a global image that dovetails neatly with our brand equities. Spreading and sustaining these values, we expand an emerging corporate image and see the way to sustain our vibrant growth.

We did not introduce these values to forge a new corporate image. Rather, we introduced them to save a company that was in serious jeopardy. We made mistakes and continue to do so, but we also caught some good breaks. But luck is the residue of design. Our values made it possible to operate in new ways, strike novel alliances, attract and retain outstanding people, and build truly global product brands.

## PRESCRIPTION FOR FAILURE

In the 1970s and 1980s, Warner-Lambert consisted of well-balanced businesses set up to be safe, steady, international players. The company was considered a caring employer, but one where people were taught to show up for work, keep their heads down, and enjoy a job for life. Our corporate image revolved around our brands; people did not know the company behind the products. Although this positioning had its good points (it made crisis management considerably easier), our amorphous company image hurt us in the recruitment and retention of people. Many professionals came to Warner-Lambert to start a career, not to build one.

We compounded the drawbacks of a global scale by sticking too long with an arcane system of country management. In essence, Warner-Lambert was a confederation of 50 fully integrated companies. The country manager of Spain, for instance, had responsibility for marketing everything from ethical pharmaceuticals to bubble gum. Not surprisingly, this arrangement threw numerous roadblocks in the way of developing a distinctive corporate image as well as truly international global brands. In some nations, we operated as Warner-Lambert; in others, we operated as Parke-Davis or Capsugel or Adams. A fixture in many offices around the world was a collection of Listerine bottles—each one with a different shape and different ingredients.

In the early 1990s, Warner-Lambert ran into a number of serious setbacks on all fronts: The world's first Alzheimer's drug and our first major new pharmaceutical in more than a decade was a commercial disappointment; managed care and cost controls had reshaped healthcare; retailers like

Wal-Mart and Kmart hammered our margins; the Mexican peso crisis hurt one of our very large operations; and our manufacturing systems had fallen out of compliance with FDA standards—getting them back into shape cost us $1.5 billion.

---

Our amorphous company image hurt us in the recruitment and retention of people.

---

All of these factors significantly hurt our corporate image. The drumbeats of rumor about hostile takeover became louder. Every time a competitor took out a new line of credit at the banks, our colleagues (employees) assumed that the bullet was headed for us. There were almost times of paralysis in the organization as company after company of our size became victims of acquisition.

## FINDING THE ANTIDOTE

In the early 1990s, our priority was to stop our company's downward spiral. We focused on building an internal corporate brand by creating and installing a set of common values to change colleague behaviors. That initiative involved an intense five-step process.

### Step 1: Speak Your Mind
Our colleagues had no universal view of how they should do business. They were locked into silos and outdated behaviors. Ironically, the common values that did exist were the largest unspoken norms that got us into trouble in the first place. For example, Warner-Lambert had grown up to be a dysfunctionally polite company. Bad news was rarely discussed openly. Pre-meetings and even meetings before the pre-meetings were held to discuss who would say what and

what would be handled. It was like visiting someone's home when the kitchen curtains are on fire and your host is buttering the bagels.

---

We focused on building an internal corporate brand by creating and installing a set of common values to change colleague behaviors.

---

So the first step to building our internal corporate brand was to generate open and candid communication. We gave people the license to say what they really thought. They could talk about any problem, in any tone of voice, with any kind of reference as long as the reference and the discussion were based on achieving a solution.

*Step 2: Speed It Up*
It took a while to get people to understand that healthy debate was constructive. More openness and candor supported the next step in defining our internal brand: speed of action—to be fast and to be first to opportunity. Warner-Lambert is not the largest pharmaceutical company in the world, nor is it the largest consumer healthcare company. We have massive rivals in shaving products (Gillette) and confectionery products (RJR Nabisco, Wrigley). The question became: What was going to be our competitive advantage if we could not move faster and with more agility than anyone else?

The turning point for speed of action occurred in 1993, when we learned of an opportunity to acquire a French drug company. We had an initial meeting on Monday with all concerned parties, and by Friday of the same week, our president was negotiating the deal with the French counterparts. Two other companies had started negotiations with these people six months prior, and both their presidents and chairmen said they could not believe the speed with which we operated. At the closing, the leaders of the French drug company said they were not just impressed but astounded by the speed at which we could work.

---

Warner-Lambert had grown up to be a dysfunctionally polite company. . . . So the first step to building our internal corporate brand was to generate open and candid communication.

---

Another success story is our 1997 introduction of Lipitor, a cholesterol reducer. Its 1998 sales totaled $2.2 billion. In 1994, we were planning to introduce Lipitor in 1999. We decided that was not good enough; we needed speed of action. We had to develop a new model for drug development that maintains the highest scientific and medical standards as speedily as possible. As a result, we gained FDA approval in 1997—two years prior to the original schedule. Those two years saved us at least $3.5 billion in sales and probably more than $30 billion in market value.

*Step 3: Get Your Priorities Straight*
The next step was a relentless focus on what is important. The operating rule in the old Warner-Lambert was that everything was a priority. Buttering the bagels had the same urgency as extinguishing the flaming curtains. In the new Warner-Lambert, the cultural norm is to put effort into work that will do the most good. Moving quickly meant setting priorities and then working toward them. It meant getting everyone to understand that highly productive pharmaceutical R&D was going to be the fastest way to expand our company. That involved focusing further, divesting nonstrategic businesses, and changing our manufacturing strategy to create centers of excellence rather than to have plants manufacturing diverse product lines all around the world.

A few years ago, our values of openness, speed of action, and focus came together in a program called "Building the Bridges to Prosperity." In 1995, we visited more than 10,000 colleagues worldwide. Personally, I talked with 7,000. During that time, we told them and investors that we had a clear, credible plan to revitalize the company. We laid out a convincing case for staying with us. We explained that shared sacrifice was necessary in order to focus on products like Lipitor. Inherent in the "Bridges to Prosperity" program was the mandate that our new pharmaceutical programs and products had priority over virtually everything else. Every spare nickel we could get went into their development. We sold off some very good consumer lines so that we could spend the money to develop these drugs more quickly; we also reduced the number of our plants from 140 to 55.

---

> We needed to establish a culture where creativity is honored: Encourage the gadflies, the concept champions, the unconventional, even the eccentric.

---

*Step 4: Draft an Army of Creative Types*
With our new pharmaceuticals, we redefined our company as a product leadership company. Operational excellence and customer intimacy are important, but our central core competency is our ability to discover, develop, and market new products—products that drive the market, not simply reflect it. This new-found product focus hinges on our ability to find, manage, and develop the right talent.

So the next step was to develop talent with the vision of product leadership. To do so, we needed to establish a culture where creativity is honored: Encourage the gadflies, the concept champions, the unconventional, even the eccentric.

Get people passionate about new products and about the exploitation of their inherent values.

*Step 5: Reward Excellence in Successes — and Failures*
A company poor in dealing with bad news is also going to be poor in dealing with bad performance. So the final step was to reward excellence — to simply give bigger rewards to those who move us toward our vision than those who do not. Warner-Lambert managers dislike performance evaluations because they force them to clearly identify their best and worst performers. Our job here is not to be punitive but to be realistic, to channel the greatest rewards to the people who move the company ahead and to give the people who are not doing so well honest, candid feedback on how they can do better.

An important aspect is determining what constitutes true "success." At Warner-Lambert, it means honoring and rewarding those who reach for new ideas even if the ideas turn out to be ambitious failures. I have promoted a lot of people who ran failures because getting to the top tier means placing a lot of bets — some will be sure things, others will be long shots, and still others will clearly fail. If we do not have enough failure, we are probably not having enough success, and we will not get enough failure unless we provide incentives to try. We reward people who are bold but not reckless, people who thirst for good ideas and daring executions.

# A DOSE OF ALLIANCES

After a decade of studying globalization, we dumped our country management system and forged ahead. In only four months, we made a plan that got us 90 percent of the way to where we wanted to go. What emerged is a far better rationalization of resources, an understanding that the U.S. business is important but not the center of the universe, and that global development of talent in specific lines of business was required and implemented.

Most important, we gained a way to forge global alliances and a means to build global brands. These global alliances include partners like Pfizer and Sankyo. The combination of our values and our structure unleashed an incredible amount of focused energy and action in our company. That led to a rise in the value of the company, both in financial terms and in terms of patient and customer value.

---

> If we do not have enough failure, we are probably not having enough success, and we will not get enough failure unless we provide incentives to try.

---

Today, we are number one in value creation. Last year, we were the top creator of value in our industry group. We now have the opportunity to extend our corporate image. Other companies are coming to understand that being a partner with Warner-Lambert means that we can bring our values to the partnership and operate in a distinctive way. That brought us a number of new partnerships and alliances. For example, last year we formed a marketing alliance with Forest Laboratories for the antidepressant Celexa—a terrific win/win deal for both sides that is doing far better than we had planned. This deal was built because Forest Labs had confidence in the way we worked, saw what we had done with Pfizer, and came to us with the business opportunity.

## PROGNOSIS: A HEALTHY FUTURE

Today, Warner-Lambert has globalized businesses, emerging global brands, and alliances that are the gold standard in the industry. We have created thousands of new jobs world-wide, including more than 1,000 in the past year. We have broken the logjam in product development. Our pharmaceutical business, which analysts and many inside the company told us to sell in 1993, is now an incredible source of growth. Our market value has gone up sevenfold in four years. The drumbeat of takeover has ceased.

For Warner-Lambert, it was simple to state new values and tell people why they were needed. The trench work came in convincing 41,000 people worldwide that these new values could be their route to better, richer, and more productive careers. We had to win the hearts and minds of our colleagues, getting them to believe that Warner-Lambert was more than a collection of brands and a company flag. These values had to become a way of life, holding sway over all we do.

Our colleagues defied the cynics that surrounded them. They took up the banner of these values with astounding and delightful speed. They defined the 1990s by saving the company; they will define the next decade by cementing us firmly in the top tier. They will do this not only through global brands and new products, but also through a new tool—a company image that forcefully states the case for doing business with us wherever we go around the world.

# JENNIFER LAING

**B**ehind the eye-catching advertising campaigns for such venerable products as Cheerios, Tylenol, and Tide is Jennifer Laing, CEO of North American operations of Saatchi & Saatchi. The British native has been in advertising since 1969 and actually left Saatchi twice for other opportunities. The second time was to start her own firm, which was later bought by Saatchi's parent company in 1995. By then, brothers Maurice and Charles Saatchi had left to start another firm, so orchestrating Laing's return was a calculated attempt by management to reenergize the company. According to Laing, many thought that Saatchi was "an iceberg that was going to melt" without the brothers. Not so.

Laing took over the London office and after two years she signed a three-year contract to come to New York as CEO of North America, beginning in January of 1997. Upon arrival, she declared that "my first, second and third priority is the existing clients." Her schedule was hectic as she made the rounds; a one-hour meeting with a client can involve more than a day of travel time. One early coup was winning the Delta Airlines account, which turned heads and attracted others; at the time, Laing said, "It has made people go: 'What does Saatchi do? What have they got?' It's an opportunity for us to tell them." Unfortunately, not long after a new management team was installed at Delta, they dismissed Saatchi. "They wanted their own team," Laing said in response. "I've won and lost on those before; it's common in our industry. That's life on the fast track."

To inspire creativity, Laing consolidated her creative department, which was divided into five groups, so they could play off each other. "If new business is the lungs of an agency, then the creative department is the soul," she says. With the proliferation of the Internet and other media, she knows leading edge creativity is key. "More than ever before, brands need advertising that will carve a special, distinctive place in consumers' heart[s] and resonate long after the spot is gone," Laing writes in *Keeping an Endangered Relationship Alive.*

# Keeping an Endangered Relationship Alive
## *Jennifer Laing*

Have the traditional values of loyalty, partnership, and friendship—long considered part of a successful relationship between companies and their advertising agencies—become obsolete? A number of trends suggests this is true.

- The increasing number of consolidations and alignments are testing established partnerships, and the casual observer may think that a strong relationship is less valued than economies of scale, global reach, and infrastructure.
- The proliferation of consultants and advisors is having a profound impact: Design and brand consultants advise on brand essence and evaluations; media consultants check the budgeting and planning process; digital marketing experts talks about Web sites, banners, and e-commerce; and industry visionaries predict the future for our clients.
- Meetings have been replaced by conference calls and videoconferences; agencies and clients e-mail and voice-mail each other. It can take weeks to arrange a face-to-face appointment with a senior counterpart.

There seems to be fewer opportunities to build human bonds and get to know who is behind that e-mail.

Business life has certainly changed, and the softer values of a relationship do seem to be less valuable. So is it time for new rules of engagement? Yes and no.

## THE THREAT

The downsizing of the 1990s has left business more efficient and shareholders pleased by improvements in margins. However, not much cost remains to be cut, and investors are now looking for top-line revenue growth to increase earnings per share. This new urgency for top-line revenue means heightened pressure on companies to increase their investment in marketing and grow their brands. For many, mature brands in mature domestic markets will not deliver the growth they need, so they must increase their expansion abroad. Of course, international expansion is the war cry from many boardrooms, so the global marketplace has become a fiercely competitive battleground for brands.

This drive for brand growth is made more difficult by new technologies, which threaten brand differentiation:

- The speed of communication means that product innovations are being copied by competitors much more quickly than before.
- The proliferation of media channels and communication make it exciting for marketers to be able to reach consumers in new ways, but it also leads to a danger of fragmenting brand messages. How often do you receive a piece of direct mail that bears no relationship to the television spot, let alone the Web site?
- The Web itself is an extraordinary new marketing tool that presents an opportunity to advertise to new con-

sumers, develop dialogue with them, and even distribute straight to their homes. But for clients slow off the mark, it is a great way for competitors to steal their customers virtually overnight.

These are just a few of the events affecting clients' marketing as they strive to build their brands to new levels of consumer sales. All of this is happening when clients and agencies alike have depleted their labor forces to the efficient bare bones, so it is not surprising that they are turning to consultants, advisors, and digital experts for help. It makes sense for them to seek ideas wherever they can find them.

## THE POSSIBILITIES

What do these trends mean for advertising agencies? In many ways, the current situation is a bit like that of the 1960s and offers some of the same opportunities. Back then, the development of commercial television changed the way companies and brands communicated with customers. Agencies

---

Investors are now looking for top-line revenue growth to increase earnings per share. This new urgency for top-line revenue means heightened pressure on companies to increase their investment in marketing and grow their brands.

---

were energetic pioneers, adding real value to existing client expertise. We were central to the partnership—leaders, not followers. It was a time of confidence and experimentation when craft skills and judgment were valued and trusted. Our industry, our clients, and their brands prospered.

We have the opportunity to regain some of that excitement and extraordinary success. We have a fantastic chance to explore the plethora of new communications channels, to experiment and learn, and to be at the cutting edge once again. The time is right to regain initiative and become custodians of our clients' brands.

---

The proliferation of media channels and communication make it exciting for marketers to be able to reach consumers in new ways, but it also leads to a danger of fragmenting brand messages.

---

However, if we are to fully exploit this opportunity, we must make real changes to the way we work. We need to refocus on some of the best aspects of relationships from the past and develop new behaviors for the changed environment.

## THE METHODS

Saatchi & Saatchi encourages the following six behaviors for the future.

### Face Time
There is no substitute for quality, face-to-face time between an agency and its client to develop a shared vision for the brand. There can be no better investment than bringing the agency to the heart of the company's mission statement and its corporate plan. Clearly, there is no hope of producing distinctive, creative solutions if there is no meeting of minds between the company and the agency.

It is also vital to know and understand the extent of our clients' global ambitions and timetables so we can apply the right investment and resources.

All of these issues can be effectively communicated and built upon only if both members of the partnership institutionalize a high level of dialogue—with pagers, mobile phones, and e-mail turned off.

*Brilliant Ideas*
Once both companies are totally aligned, the principal task of the agency is to generate big, unique ideas for clients and their brands—and to keep doing it. Saatchi & Saatchi's mission statement demands that we be revered as a hothouse for world-changing creative ideas that will transform our clients' businesses, brands, and reputations. Like all mission statements, it contains ambitions and visions that stimulate and drive our culture. Ideas lead our mission statement because idea generation is the most important element in the client/agency relationship. Ideas are the lifeblood of brands, particularly in a world where product differentiation is short-lived.

---

Clearly, there is no hope of producing distinctive, creative solutions if there is no meeting of minds between the company and the agency.

---

We will not meet today's challenges if we believe that creative ideas are the sole responsibility of our art directors and copywriters; great ideas can come from anyone in an agency. Strategic ideas form the bedrock of successful relationships, and one of the smartest ideas is to bring the consumer to center stage. We work with university professors, trained psychologists, and anthropologists, and we talk to consumers when they are out shopping, in their homes, and on the Web, all in order to gain a unique consumer insight.

For example, for our Cheerios campaign, we talked about ingredients and taste, but we also worked with our partner, General Mills, to exploit the high-ground, nurturing benefits of the brand. In this campaign, we tapped into parents' deep-rooted desire to do what is best for their children and took Cheerios sales to new heights.

It should be self-evident that what is needed is to take a smart strategic thought and dramatize it with mold-breaking, creative executions. More than ever before, brands need advertising that will carve a special, distinctive place in consumers' heart and resonate long after the spot is gone. However, the diverse U.S. population, the demands for universally acceptable global copy, and a human tendency to stay in a comfort zone sometimes make it hard to do.

### Media Mania

As we move to the next century, media will increasingly drive brands and businesses and contribute to successful client partnerships. Amazon.com was a media-driven idea: The medium was the message, the distribution channel, and the backbone of the consumer relationship.

For Saatchi & Saatchi, investment in media has meant a significant investment in interactive experts. We recently brought in a new wave of marketeers to pioneer a new approach to the medium of the retail store. These investments enable agencies to build relationships with more depth and breadth in client organizations, which strengthens and extends our partnership. The industry is acquiring and creating a new breed of gurus to meet our clients' specialized needs.

### Integrated Thinking

Once we have developed these gurus, we need to plant them like seeds in the heart of our organization and let them influence our ideas. This form of integrated thinking means that our planners, account directors, and creative directors have to think beyond the confines of their traditional disciplines. We have to broaden our understanding of the communication weapons that are now part of our clients' armory. We need a process of osmosis between our traditional experts and the new gurus.

---

More than ever before, brands need advertising that will carve a special, distinctive place in consumers' heart and resonate long after the spot is gone.

---

Mixing together our teams has certainly influenced our work for Tide, for example. Our communications package now offers solutions to laundry problems—past, present, and future. One particular television spot for Tide drew upon real laundry problems that we have all experienced at some time or other. On the Web, we offer real-time solutions to problems as they occur: "Click here for more help to remove lipstick from your blouse and to order Tide with Bleach directly." Outdoors, we remind the traveler to buy Tide for laundry problems that are about to occur, probably in the very near future: sheltered from the rain, splattered by the bus; nice day, bad pigeon; 20-ounce soda, 6-inch pothole. All exploit the famous bull's-eye icon and speak with Tide's voice as a trusted friend.

*Speedy Delivery*
Instantaneous global communications enable products to be replicated at a stunning speed, so we need to get ideas into the marketplace faster. There are many opportunities to work smarter and faster and to eliminate waste, including:

- Eradicate processes that hinder big, brave ideas.
- Use digital systems to speed up communication and decision making, especially around the globe. We use our intranet, "The Brain," to transfer best practices around our network.

- Move away from traditional hierarchies. Create small teams empowered to make decisions.
- Experiment with new idea-generating techniques. We often invite consumers to our hothouses, which helps keep our thinking relevant.
- Embrace the smart consultants, enroll them in teams, and make magic synergies.
- Use research intelligently. Be intuitive and make judgments. Then get into market testing as quickly as possible.

*Balanced Performance and Rewards*

Clearly, the advertising industry is more aggressively focused on brand-building ideas and fully committed to growing top-line revenue for our clients. More of us are investing in new businesses, experimenting with new ways to communicate, and putting money into finding, growing, and training new talent around the globe.

In light of these imperatives, the old remuneration system of commission payments and the now popular method of cost plus margin seem somewhat inappropriate. The system is too focused on costs rather than the value of ideas. The time has come for us to be more accountable for the results of our work and to be more closely aligned with the clients' objectives for their brands. Moreover, we should be highly rewarded when we are highly successful. Win/win scenarios breed wonderful partnerships.

## THE OUTCOME

The old values of loyalty, partnership, and friendship are not obsolete. However, today's environment means that we have to change the way we work in order to warrant them. The industry has to get back to basics and evolve at the same time. We need depth and breadth to our understanding of clients' issues and vision. Then we have to work smarter and more collaboratively to bring brilliant, all-embracing, brand-building ideas to market—fast. And if we have and do all that, the outcome will be a healthy, long-term relationship for the 21st century.

# HOWARD J. MORGENS

**H**oward Morgens is the legendary leader who ruled over Procter & Gamble through three decades—the '50s, '60s and '70s—and made consumer research a top priority. In the first 15 years of his reign he tripled sales and quadrupled profits, and became the most sought-after executive in the United States. However, he never considered leaving the company, which has always had a reputation of being cultlike in developing loyalty. "I have been approached many times with offers that made my head spin," he said. "But I always felt that [at P&G] I was given more responsibility than I was prepared to handle and that I was growing. That feeling is more important than money." Morgens was a lifer.

After attending Washington University, and then graduating from the Harvard Business School in 1933, he joined P&G's advertising department. In the 1930s sales were poor in the rural south, so Morgens' first big assignment was to go door-to-door and find out why. He had to hire a local guide because the people he was attempting to visit for his market research feared he was from the sheriff's office and they were more interested in shooting him than talking soap. P&G was on the leading edge when it came to consumer research and marketing. Internal development of its executives was also paramount. Morgens kept a notebook in which he jotted down names of those with potential, and he pushed responsibility down the chain of command.

The company has been famous for launching products that compete with their existing products; that might mean dueling soaps, deodorants, cake mixes, and more. To prevent the company from becoming stale, Morgens preached that the best thing to do "is to hire and promote people that have varied backgrounds, with a constant emphasis on creativity." While an advertising advocate, in *Advertising from a Management Viewpoint,* he acknowledges, "Advertising cannot sell a poor product." He goes on to warn, "In fact, the quickest way to kill a brand that is off in quality is to promote it aggressively. People find out about its poor quality just that much more quickly."

# Advertising from a
# Management Viewpoint
## *Howard J. Morgens*

Ｗe in Procter & Gamble believe that *advertising is the most effective and efficient way to do it.* If we should ever find better methods of selling our type of products to the consumer, we'll leave advertising and turn to these other methods.

There are certain basic reasons for advertising's great effectiveness — reasons which go beyond mere dollars and cents calculations. They are fundamental to any appraisal of advertising from a general management point of view and they comprise my next few points.

### ADVERTISING CAN AND DOES
### CREATE NEW MARKETS

Advertising can and does create new markets. It can do this more rapidly, more intensively, and less expensively than any other method of selling the consumer.

In our own industry, the rise of personal cleanliness in every country in which we do business has closely paralleled the rise in advertising of soaps and detergents. In the United States, the social desirability portrayed by advertising of the daily bath, the daily clean shirt, and clean white teeth has produced cleanliness habits which are still relatively new in our society.

This is not to contend, of course, that advertising created a desire for cleanliness where none existed previously. Only small boys have ever contended that it was not desirable. What advertising did was to remind people of something they wanted and to tell them about products that encouraged and facilitated cleanliness.

---

Advertising can and does create new markets. It can do this more rapidly, more intensively, and less expensively than any other method of selling the consumer.

---

This general point about advertising's ability to create new markets does not need much positive documentation here. In fact, advertising is currently being criticized in some quarters for doing this job too well. It is said to force people to buy products that they do not want. I'd like to digress just a moment in an effort to clear up this misunderstanding.

I'll say categorically that no amount of advertising can force any large number of people to buy things they do not want. Advertising can only create a new market for products which fill a genuine—though often unexpressed or latent—consumer want. In other words, advertising cannot develop a consumer want except where the need or desire previously existed—even though it may have existed in unrecognized or dormant form.

This is more than just semantics. Some people may say that what people are unaware of, they don't want. In the same sense that "ignorance is bliss," that's true. But people certainly won't buy a great many things that they might be made aware of. The basic need or desire must be there to begin with.

This is also more than just a theory; let me illustrate how it works in actual practice. Before setting out to create a new market for a new type of product, most sophisticated companies go through a process of testing that product with the consumer. As part of this testing process, a group of people are asked to use the product "blind"—that is, without exposure to advertising, without a brand name, without labels or glamorous packaging.

---

Advertising can only create a new market for products which fill a genuine—though often unexpressed or latent—consumer want.

---

If the consumers so tested respond to the product favorably—if they recognize it immediately as "something they've wanted" or "would like to have"—then the company involved has a chance to develop a new market for it. On the other hand, if in the testing process consumers should not respond favorably to this new type of product when exposed to it without advertising, then the surest way to go broke is to spend advertising money trying to create a new market for it.

There may be exceptions to this. However, based on our own experience, it is about 99.44/100% correct!

## ADVERTISING, PROPERLY USED, LOWERS COSTS TO CONSUMERS

Another fundamental point about advertising is that, properly used, it does lower costs to the consumer. This is another point that seems never to be adequately understood.

It is true that advertising does, in itself, add to the cost of a product. However, it also results in savings that—in most instances—are greater than the cost of the advertising. It does this in many ways.

- *Advertising brings about savings in manufacturing costs.* This is well-known, of course. Advertising helps produce large volume on specific, standardized items, and this is what makes mass production methods possible.
- *Advertising brings about savings in other types of distribution costs.* The high volume which it creates lowers the salesmen's cost per unit. It also means rapid turnover for the retailer, which in turn makes lower retail margins possible—without reducing the dealer's profit on capital invested in inventories or shelf space. In this way, advertised brands have helped make the low cost supermarket operation possible. And dealer margins, as I said, are one part of the total cost of distribution.
- *Advertising brings about savings in buying, financing, and in many other business operations.* Properly used, it tends to produce more stable volume week in and week out. Stability of volume results in great efficiencies and economies in practically everything that a company does.

Time and again in our own company, we have seen the start of advertising on a new type of product result in savings that are considerably greater than the entire advertising cost. When we consider all types of production costs, all types of distribution costs, and all other operating costs, the use of advertising clearly results in lower prices to the public.

---

Advertising cannot sell a poor product. It might induce people to try it once. But it cannot build an enduring business on such a product.

---

Once a mass market has been created for a certain type of product—and once mass production equipment and techniques have been developed for that type of product—it is, of course, possible for someone else to take a free ride for a

112

time by selling the same type of product at a lower cost by not using advertising. However, it would be a great fallacy to go on from there to infer that all such products would be cheaper if there were no advertising on any of them. In fact, the contrary would be true.

## ADVERTISING SPURS CONTINUAL PRODUCT IMPROVEMENTS

Probably the most important point about advertising today, and one that is least understood, is its role in product improvement. It plays a tremendous part in the constant upgrading of consumer products.

Advertising cannot sell a poor product. It might induce people to try it once. But it cannot build an enduring business on such a product. That has been proven over and over and over again. In fact, the quickest way to kill a brand that is off in quality is to promote it aggressively. People find out about its poor quality just that much more quickly.

I'll go further. Advertising cannot sell a product for very long in a competitive market if that product stands still qualitywise! Advertising offers a quick, effective way for anyone to tell the world that he has improved his product. Assuming the improvement is genuine, the public is quick to notice it, and the return on the advertising expenditure is greatly enhanced. There is a constant struggle, as you know, to make one's marketing dollars work more and more effectively. This struggle acts inevitably as a spur to the development of better and better products.

## CONSUMERS BENEFIT FROM WORKING ALLIANCE OF RESEARCH AND ADVERTISING

Research people, of course, are constantly searching for ways to improve the things we buy. But believe me, a great deal of prodding and pushing and suggestions for those improvements also comes from the advertising end of the business. That's bound to be because the success of a company's advertising is closely tied up with the success of its product development activities.

---

The very essence of advertising is that it is an instrument of competition. If one believes in competition—and we surely do—it is hard not to believe in advertising.

---

Furthermore, when a company is confident of its ability to acquaint the public quickly with a product advance, it is more willing to invest dollars in the research which is needed to bring that improvement from the laboratory to the consumer. In this way, advertising and scientific research have come to work hand-in-glove on a vast and amazingly productive scale. No other form of consumer selling has yet demonstrated this ability to foster product innovation. The direct beneficiary is the consumer, who enjoys an ever-widening selection of better products and services.


## ADVERTISING FORCES COMPETITION

All of these points bring me logically to still another one which is so obvious to us who know advertising that it often goes unexpressed: Advertising increases competition.

Many of us can remember in the 1930's and early 1940's when advertising was frequently criticized in academic and governmental circles for being wasteful, ineffective, and parasitical. One of the purposes in starting the Advertising Council was to demonstrate the effectiveness of advertising to people in government by using it in public service causes.

Today, the pendulum has swung to the other extreme. Advertising is now being criticized for being too effective. It is so effective, we are told, that it may lead to monopoly and restraint of competition.

This criticism is most certainly based on a misunderstanding because one of the fundamental characteristics of advertising is that it *forces* one to be competitive. It seems to me that a recapitulation of what I've already said covers this point:

- Advertising will not work effectively if the product is not fully competitive in quality. This *forces* constant competition through product improvements.
- Advertising will not work effectively if the product — quality considered — is not fully competitive in price. This *forces* constant competition through cost reduction programs.
- Advertising will not work effectively unless the sales and other distributing functions are on their toes. This *forces* competition through vigorous competitive selling and merchandising.
- Through advertising, any company with a new product idea can tell the world about it in short order. This opportunity spurs competition through the creation of new products. This in turn means that established products must improve in order to live.

The very essence of advertising is that it is an instrument of competition. If one believes in competition — and we surely do — it is hard not to believe in advertising. To our mind it is completely irrational and certainly contradictory to be *for* competition and *against* advertising.

# PART IV

# Corporate Citizenship
# Brings Success

For those who ignore corporate ethics, think again: The Conference Board discovered in their 1999 research study, *Consumer Expectations on the Social Accountability of Business*, that in the last year 48.9 percent of consumers surveyed had *punished* a company they did not perceive as socially responsible by not making a purchase or by speaking critically of the company. On the flip side, in the last year 46.4 percent had rewarded companies they viewed as socially responsible by making a purchase or by speaking out in the company's favor. In the opening essay, Levi's chairman Robert Haas states, "Companies with strong corporate reputations have been shown to outperform the S&P 500, have higher sales, sustain greater profits, and have stocks that outperform the market." Simply put, commitment to ethical practices is good business, a message not lost on CEOs. According to another 1999 research report by The Conference Board, *Global Corporate Ethics Practices*, only 80 percent of the CEOs surveyed in 1987 were involved in formulating global business ethics codes, whereas 95 percent were involved in 1999. Anita Roddick, founder of The Body Shop and devout activist, has delved into ethical issues on a global scale; she preaches not free trade with developing countries, but fair trade so that communities in those countries can become self-sustaining and not have to rely on humanitarian aid for all their economic and social needs. Again, it makes good business sense. Katherine Graham, who was chair of the Washington Post Company for almost 30 years and one of the most powerful women in America, takes a more simple view of ethics that involves honest communication. She also has no tolerance for CEOs who view the world like the robber barons of old. All of the authors in Part IV make it clear that ethical practices don't cost the company money, they bring reward.

# ROBERT D. HAAS

Levi Strauss & Company has long been known for its progressive company culture. Even when forced to lay off thousands, as was the case in 1997, the company remained paternalistic. Robert Haas gave the workers, including seamstresses, eight months notice and spent $31,000 on each for retraining and job hunting assistance. His generous and practical management philosophy reflects the man who was a Peace Corps volunteer and earned an M.B.A. at Harvard University. While some have criticized his liberal style, Haas, who took the helm in 1994 and engineered a leveraged buyout in 1995, explained, "We are not doing this because it makes us feel good—although it does. We are not doing this because it is politically correct. We are doing this because we believe in the interconnection between liberating the talents of our people and business success."

Creating a tight-knit corporate family and teamwork have cut turnaround time from order to shipment in half in some factories. If the company makes certain financial goals in 2001, employees will receive a bonus equal to one year's pay. Unfortunately, business has been tough lately. The company was slow to adapt to the changing tastes of young people, such as the wide-leg jeans that became fashionable in the late 1990s. To recapture that market's attention, in San Francisco the company recently opened a four-story, 24,000-square-foot store with hundreds of speakers and a number of video screens to create a hip atmosphere.

Whether it is offering generous benefit packages or struggling to keep Levi's factories in the United States as opposed to using cheap labor abroad, Haas runs his business with a high ethical standard. In fact, he and the company were awarded the first Ron Brown Award for Corporate Leadership in 1998, which was presented by President Clinton and is managed by The Conference Board. Haas offers six ethical principles in *Ethics: A Global Business Challenge* and describes why good ethics equals profits. He warns, "In today's world, a television exposé on working conditions can undo years of effort to build brand loyalty."

# Ethics: A Global
# Business Challenge
## *Robert D. Haas*

What is most puzzling about most instances of business wrongdoing is that they clearly contradict both the values that are held by most of us as individuals and the collective standards we have established for appropriate business behavior.

In his famous essay on civil disobedience, Henry David Thoreau wrote that a corporation "has no conscience, but a corporation of conscientious men is a corporation with a conscience." I'd like to think that if Thoreau were writing today he would have spoken of both men *and women* with a conscience, though regrettably the corporate world remains more of a male enclave than it should be.

If Thoreau is correct, and I believe he is, how do we help honorable men and women confront and address the ethical challenges they face in the everyday world of work? This is the puzzle all of us must work to solve.

I'd like to conduct a brief quiz. By the way, these are the same questions I raise with my associates at Levi Strauss & Co. when I lead one of our ethics training programs. Do you:

- Consider yourself to be an ethical person?
- Believe that it's important for business to function in an ethical manner?

- Believe that you know an ethical dilemma when you see it?
- Feel there are clear answers to ethical problems?
- Believe that you always know an ethical dilemma when it arises and always know how to resolve it?

Clearly, all of us feel strongly about ethics in the abstract. But at the same time, each of us is keenly aware of the struggle we face as ethical dilemmas arise. It is a common struggle between our own desire to be ethical and the competing pressures of business performance. Like so many, we at Levi Strauss & Co. struggle every day with how to create a business culture that promotes ethical behavior.

## RISKY BEHAVIOR

When examining the ethics programs of companies it is useful to bear in mind the three very different approaches to dealing with ethical dilemmas. These are:

- Neglect—or the absence of any formal ethical programs;
- Compliance-based programs; and
- Values-oriented programs.

It is hard to imagine that any large company could rationally ignore the importance of ethics or fail to develop management policies and programs, given the effect ethical breaches can have on financial performance, sales, and corporate reputation. But some companies clearly don't get the message.

According to the Institute for Crisis Management, more than half of the news crisis stories filed in 1993 were crises brought on by the questionable judgment of management— firings, white-collar crime, government investigations, and discrimination suits. Coverage of these types of corporate misdeeds has risen 55% since 1989, while coverage of "operational" crises—chemical spills, product tamperings—has declined 4%.

Obviously, there are grave consequences for ignoring ethical problems. There is also increasing evidence from academic studies that shows positive correlations between responsible business behavior and return on investment, stock price, consumer preferences, and employee loyalty.

The companies that ignore ethics do so on the basis of assumptions that are false and never challenged. They seem to view ethics either as unimportant or as a costly and inconvenient luxury.

I think they're wrong on both accounts.

I believe—and our company's experience demonstrates—that a company cannot sustain success unless it develops ways to anticipate and address ethical issues as they arise. Doing the right thing from day one helps avoid future setbacks and regrets. Addressing dilemmas when they arise may save your business from serious financial or reputational harm.

---

The companies that ignore ethics. . . . seem to view ethics either as unimportant or as a costly and inconvenient luxury.

---

Many companies share this view, and a number of them have chosen a second approach to ethics—what Lynn Sharp Paine, an associate professor at Harvard, refers to as compliance-based programs. These ethics programs are most often designed by corporate counsel. They are based on rules and regulations, with the goal of preventing, detecting, and punishing legal violations.

Until recently, we were among the companies that took this approach. The centerpiece of our efforts was a comprehensive collection of regulations that spelled out our worldwide code of business ethics. In it, we laid out rules for hiring practices, travel and entertainment expenses, political contributions, compliance with local laws, improper payments, gifts, and favors. We addressed topics ranging from accounting practices to potential conflicts of interest. As you might guess, it was a long and weighty list of do's and don'ts for our people to follow.

---

Today at Levi Strauss & Co. we base our approach to ethics on a values orientation that includes six ethical principles: honesty, promise-keeping, fairness, respect for others, compassion, and integrity.

---

This approach didn't serve us well. First, rules beget rules. And regulations beget regulations. We became buried in paperwork, and any time we faced a unique ethical issue, another rule or regulation was born. Second, our compliance-based program sent a disturbing message to our people: "We don't respect your intelligence or trust you!" Finally, one of the most compelling reasons for shedding this approach was that it didn't keep managers or employees from exercising poor judgment and making questionable decisions.

## THE VALUES APPROACH

Today at Levi Strauss & Co. we base our approach to ethics on a values orientation that includes six ethical principles: honesty, promise-keeping, fairness, respect for others, compassion, and integrity. Using this approach, we address ethical issues by first identifying which of these ethical principles applies to the particular business decision. Then we determine which internal and which external stakeholders' ethical concerns should influence our business decisions. Information on stakeholder issues is gathered and possible recommendations are discussed with "high-influence" stakeholder groups, such as shareholders, employees, customers, members of local communities, public interest groups, our business partners, and so forth.

This principle-based approach balances the ethical concerns of these stakeholders with the values of our organization. It is a process that extends trust to an individual's knowledge of the situation. It examines the complexity of issues that must be considered in each decision, and it defines the role each person's judgment plays in carrying out his or her responsibilities in an ethical manner. We're integrating ethics with our other corporate values, which include diversity, open communications, empowerment, recognition, teamwork, and honesty, into every aspect of our business—from our human resource practices to our relationships with our business partners.

## ETHICAL GLOBAL CONTRACTING

I'd like to illustrate how we're linking ethics and business conduct with an area of increasing importance to many global corporations—the contract manufacturing of products in developing countries.

Because Levi Strauss & Co. operates in many countries and diverse cultures, we take special care in selecting contractors and those countries where our goods are produced. We do this to ensure that our products are being made in a manner that is consistent with our values and that protects our brand image and corporate reputation. So, in 1991, we developed a set of Global Sourcing Guidelines.

Our guidelines describe the business conduct we require of our contractors. For instance, the guidelines ban the use of child or prison labor. They stipulate certain environmental requirements. They limit working hours and mandate regularly scheduled days off. Workers must have the right of free association and may not be exploited. At a minimum, wages must comply with the law and match prevailing local practice, and working conditions must be safe and healthy. We also expect our business partners to be law abiding and to conduct all of their business affairs in an ethical way.

In developing our guidelines, we also recognized that there are certain issues beyond the control of our contractors, so we produced a list of "country selection" criteria. For example, we will not source in countries where conditions, such as the human rights climate, would run counter to our values and have an adverse effect on our global brand image or damage our corporate reputation. Similarly, we will not source in countries where circumstances threaten our employees while traveling, where the legal climate makes it difficult or jeopardizes our trademarks, and where political or social turmoil threatens our commercial interest.

---

In today's world, a television exposé on working conditions can undo years of effort to build brand loyalty.

---

Since adopting our guidelines, we've terminated our business relationships with about 5% of our contractors and required workplace improvements of another 25%. Likewise, we announced a phased withdrawal from contracting in China and exited Burma because of human rights concerns, although we remain hopeful that the human rights climate in these countries will improve and we can alter these decisions.

In the process of creating guidelines, we formed a working group of 15 employees from a broad cross-section of the company. The working group spent nine months formulating the guidelines, using our principle-based decision-making model to guide their deliberations. Drafting these guidelines was difficult. Applying them has proven even more challenging.

## FROM GOALS TO ACTIONS

When we were rolling out our guidelines—which included extensive on-site audits of each of our 700 contractors worldwide—we discovered that two of our manufacturing contractors in Bangladesh and one in Turkey employed underage workers. This was a clear violation. At the outset, it appeared that we had two options:

- Instruct our contractors to fire these children, knowing that many are the sole wage earners for their families and that if they lost their jobs, their families would face extreme hardships.

Or we could:

- Continue to employ underage children, ignoring our stance against the use of child labor.

By referencing our ethical guidelines to decision-making we came up with a different approach, one that we believe helped to minimize adverse ethical consequences.

The contractors agreed to pay the underage children their salaries and benefits while they went to school full-time. We agreed to pay for books, tuition, and uniforms. When the children reach legal working age, they are offered jobs in the plant. Thanks to these efforts, 35 children have attended school in Bangladesh; another six are currently in school in Turkey.

And how did we benefit from this situation? We were able to retain quality contractors that play an important role in our worldwide sourcing strategy. At the same time, we were able to honor our values and protect our brands.

## ETHICS COST MONEY?

Applying our sourcing guidelines has forced us to find creative solutions to vexing ethical dilemmas. Clearly, at times, adhering to these standards has added costs. To continue working for us, some contractors have added emergency exits and staircases, increased ventilation, reduced crowding, improved bathroom facilities, and invested in water-treatment systems. The costs of these requirements have been passed on to us — at least in part — in the form of higher product prices. In other cases, we have foregone less expen-

---

### PERSONAL RESPONSIBILITY

We learned that you can't force ethical conduct into an organization. Ethics is a function of the collective attitudes of our people. And these attitudes are cultivated and supported by at least seven factors:

- commitment to responsible business conduct;
- management's leadership;
- trust in employees;
- programs and policies that provide people with clarity about the organization's ethical expectations;
- open, honest, and timely communications;
- tools to help employees resolve ethical problems; and
- reward and recognition systems that reinforce the importance of ethics.

Ultimately, high ethical standards can be maintained only if they are modeled by management and woven into the fabric of the company. Knowing this, the challenge is to cultivate the kind of environment where people do the right thing.

---

sive sources of production because of unsatisfactory work-ing conditions or other concerns about the country of origin.

Conventional wisdom holds that these added costs put us at a competitive disadvantage. Yes, they limit our options somewhat and squeeze profit margins in the near-term. But over the years, we've found that decisions that emphasize cost to the exclusion of all other factors don't serve a com-pany's and its shareholders' long-term interests.

Moreover, as a company that invests hundreds of mil-lions of advertising dollars each year to create consumer preference for our products, we have a huge stake in pro-tecting that investment. In today's world, a television exposé on working conditions can undo years of effort to build brand loyalty. Why squander your investment when, with foresight and commitment, reputational problems can be prevented?

## ETHICS AS STRATEGY

But you don't have to take my word for it. There is a grow-ing body of evidence that shows a positive correlation between good corporate citizenship and financial perfor-mance. Studies by leading research groups such as Opinion Research Corporation and Yankelovich Partners, respected scholars, and socially responsible investment firms under-score the correlation. Companies that look beyond maximiz-ing wealth and profits and are driven by values and a sense of purpose outperform those companies that focus only on short-term gain.

Companies with strong corporate reputations have been shown to outperform the S&P 500, have higher sales, sustain greater profits, and have stocks that outperform the market. These are results that no bottom-line-fixated manager can afford to ignore.

Similarly, a recent study suggests that how a company conducts itself affects consumer purchasing decisions and customer loyalty. A vast majority—84%—of the American public agrees that a company's reputation can well be the deciding factor in terms of what product or service they buy.

These findings mirror our own experience. Our values-driven approach has helped us in many ways. We have identified contractors who want to work for Levi Strauss & Co. to achieve our "blue ribbon" certification, enhancing their own business stature. We have gained retailer and consumer loyalty. Retailers feel good about having us as business partners because of our commitment to ethical practices. Today's consumer has more products to choose from and more information about those products. A company's reputation forms a part of the consumer's perceptions of the product and influences purchasing decisions.

---

Companies that look beyond maximizing wealth and profits and are driven by values and a sense of purpose outperform those companies that focus only on short-term gain.

---

At the same time, we're better able to attract, retain, and motivate the most talented employees, because the company's values more closely mirror their own personal values. Because government and community leaders view us as a responsible corporate citizen we have been welcomed to do business in established and emerging markets.

## LONG-TERM INTERESTS

We are living in an environment in which ethical standards and behaviors are being increasingly challenged. Addressing these dilemmas becomes even more difficult when one overlays the complexities of different cultures and value systems that exist throughout the world. For example, in some cultures honesty will take precedence over caring—"tell the truth even if it hurts"—whereas other cultures find caring, or "saving face," the predominant value.

As you grapple with some fictitious ethical quandaries, I encourage you to ask yourself these questions:

"How much am I willing to compromise my principles?"

"Are there times when I'm willing to risk something I value for doing the right thing?"

---

We're better able to attract, retain, and motivate the most talented employees, because the company's values more closely mirror their own personal values.

---

For me and my associates at Levi Strauss & Co. I think the answers have become clear: Ethics must trump all other considerations. Ultimately, there are important commercial benefits to be gained from managing your business in a responsible and ethical way that best serves your enterprise's long-term interests. The opposite seems equally clear: The dangers of not doing so are profound.

Michael Josephson, a noted ethics expert, defined ethics this way: "Ethics is about character and courage and how we meet the challenge when doing the right thing will cost more than we want to pay."

The good news is that courage carries with it a great reward—the prospect of sustained responsible commercial success. I think that's what each of us wants our legacy to be. And I believe ultimately our key stakeholders—all of them—will accept nothing less.

# J. IRWIN MILLER

Irwin Miller, who received the Business Enterprise Trust Lifetime Achievement Award in 1992, was characterized as "a philosopher disguised as a businessman." His business happened to be the largest diesel engine manufacturer in the world—family-owned Cummins Engine Company. As for his philosophical side: He attended Yale, was a Rhodes scholar, studied Plato, enjoyed playing Bach on his Stradivarius violin, and taught Sunday school at church. Miller also donated an astounding 30 percent of his family's income to charity. Why so much? His answer: To "change things for the better. Else why are you taking up space?"

When Miller finished school, he had no background for business and had little confidence in his ability to run Cummins, among other family operations he had inherited. He feared failing the family's capitalist tradition that dated back to his great-grandfather, who founded the Irwin Union Bank and Trust Company in 1871. Yet, Miller was able to put his situation in perspective. "You can't copy what they did. What you copy is their spirit." Their spirit motivated him to turn around Cummins and the company even started selling engines to its competitors. The irony was not lost on Miller who observed, "We're in the business of selling engines to engine makers, which is surely not the smartest way to make a living."

In building his business, Miller never forgot the many ethical issues he became familiar with during his classical education. Ethical conduct became his company's centerpiece, not an expense to be reduced. For Miller, "Ethics cannot be a mere sub-discipline of public relations—a benign, conveniently vague creed that is too easily embraced by all." In *Company Social Responsibility—Too Much or Not Enough*, Irwin explains the importance of truly understanding the meaning of individual liberty and private property, two key concepts on which the United States is built, and how they relate to ethical behavior. For example, individual liberty doesn't mean "to heck with everybody else." We must protect each other's freedom, as should corporations.

# Company Social Responsibility — Too Much or Not Enough?

## *J. Irwin Miller*

O f those three words "Company Social Responsibility," two give us very little trouble. We know what we mean today by a corporation or a company; we also know what we mean by the word social—it's the society in which a corporation or a business finds itself conducting its affairs. It might refer to a local community, or to a regional area; it might mean the whole nation.

This word "responsibility" is the one that gives me trouble.

The English dictionary says it means being answerable or accountable to somebody for something. The closest I came to it in a Latin dictionary I found is a verb meaning to promise or offer something in return for another thing. Any place I turned, this word "responsibility" had the idea of some kind of contract implicit in it; that someone is supposed to give something of value because he receives something of value.

Now how do we make any sensible application of this to the relations between a corporation and society? The only legal contractual relation I know of is the legal obligation to pay taxes and to pay attention to existing ordinances. We must mean something more than that.

Perhaps we are referring to a contractual obligation of some sort other than legal. Let's ask ourselves a few questions. Suppose you are responsible for choosing a new plant location. After you have found that the various natural resources are there, do you simply pick the one with the lowest taxes and the cheapest utility rates, and look no further? Do you ever also say something like, "This is a good community, that is a bad community"?

You look for a first-class community—good schools, good recreational facilities, few slums, little crime—because you will have a great deal of difficulty operating a first-class plant, staffed by able people, in a run-down community. You look for what you call a good town—and by that I also mean a good state or a good nation or trade area.

Isn't a good town one whose citizens have a habit of voluntarily working for its welfare? Their spirit puts the interest of the whole community first; private interests come second. This kind of spirit is the result of the free and voluntary labors of past generations of concerned citizens.

---

**A loss of freedom or an impairment of rights or property for any man diminishes my freedom and my rights.**

---

The work of these past generations produced a good community—the kind you want to put your plant in. This benefit is a major asset to the business. It comes at no charge—for free.

There is an interesting sentence in Scripture which says, "Other men labored and you are entering into their labors," and this is what happens when we locate in a good town. As a businessman, you say: "Fine. But why should I have to pay for it?"

Legally there is no debt. There is no payment required for this asset. Morally there might be some kind of obligation. If there is, that obligation might consist of making a return toward the good of the community or society, a contribution in work or thought or money that is somehow comparable to the value of the asset which the corporation freely enjoys.

Two dominant characteristics of this free society are found in two phrases that we use a lot; one is individual liberty, another we call private property. Well, if individual liberty is intended to mean a single-minded concern for my own liberty, and to heck with everybody else's; if private property is intended to mean exclusive concern for my own property and things, then what we have is no different from the jungle. In a jungle, lives and property are constantly threatened; you really don't have very much liberty.

But if, in our society, individual liberty means a fierce concern for the liberty and rights of the other fellow; if our definition of private property means a dominating concern for the property rights of the other fellow, then everybody in that society enjoys the maximum of freedom. He can move around in safety. He can have opportunities that are known no other way.

A loss of freedom or an impairment of rights or property for any man diminishes my freedom and my rights. This is the lesson of the free society about which we are so concerned.

For its own freedom, for the maximum pursuit of its own true property interests, the corporation, like the individual, must make a free response to the society of its time. Its response must be aimed at the good and the improvement of that society. It is, therefore, in our desire for a free society that we begin to find the reason for the social responsibility of a corporation.

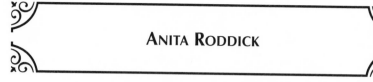

# ANITA RODDICK

Anita Roddick, founder of The Body Shop, has built a cosmetics firm with over 1,000 outlets in over 40 countries while defining herself as an activist. Growing up, Roddick imagined herself becoming an actress, but her mother convinced her that being a teacher was a more suitable profession. Toward that end, she won a scholarship to study children of the kibbutzim in Israel. After a teaching stint back in England, Roddick embarked on a voyage that included Switzerland, Tahiti, and South Africa, among other countries. "Everywhere I went I did my best to get to know the local people, to talk to them and eat with them and learn about their lives," she wrote in her autobiography.

In 1971 Roddick settled down, married, and then had two children. She and her husband were operating a restaurant/ hotel, but after a few years her husband, also a vagabond of sorts, decided to pursue his dream of riding a horse from Buenos Aires to New York City. To support herself and her children, Roddick started making shampoos, lotions, and creams from natural ingredients that were packaged in environmentally friendly containers. The first Body Shop was opened in 1976, next door to a funeral parlor, which created a stir and won her free publicity. Her strong ethical identity has also garnered attention and accolades.

Roddick, who has been a devout activist for environmental and other causes, first protested at age 12—the BBC filmed her campaigning for an ice rink. Today Roddick remains an activist; for example, in the fall of 1999 she attacked the Shell oil company for what she considered unethical advertising. Although she came under fire a few years ago for not always measuring up to her proclaimed high standards, it's clear she wants idealism on the agenda when it comes to measuring success: "We need to measure progress by human development not gross product." Her concerns are obvious in *Not Free Trade but Fair Trade,* in which she advocates developing fair business relationships with less-developed countries, not merely exploiting their resources and needs.

# Not Free Trade but Fair Trade
## *Anita Roddick*

Few economists are deluded by the fiction of global free trade. Real free trade has proven both elusive and illusory.

For The Body Shop International PLC, the issue of fair trade is vital. It means avoiding the direct exploitation of humans and animals and their habitats.

The center of this approach is our "Trade Not Aid" policy. Direct trading links are set up with producer communities in less-developed countries so that social development and environmental protection go hand in hand. We do not change the culture, the environment, or the ecology. Basically, all we do is sit down with them for a year and ask them how we can help make their lives easier.

Our trading arrangements hope to take some of the burden from conventional aid programs. If communities can finance their economic and social development through fair-trade prices obtained from their own trading efforts, then donor agencies can direct their dollars toward more-humanitarian ends. That is a good idea, but the big corporations and big donor countries do not always react that way.

In using the title Trade Not Aid, we do not mean to denigrate the concept of humanitarian aid. We are simply making a statement that fair trade is ultimately the only option for sustainable development in less-developed countries.

Our Trade Not Aid projects do not help just with social development; there is also a spin-off for environmental protection. A few years ago, a meeting was held in Altamira, Brazil. It was, I believe, the first time that Indian leaders got together in order to protest the construction of a dam. Faced with logging and mining in the area, the Kayapo invited The Body Shop to look for an economic and sustainable alternative.

In discussions between The Body Shop and the Kayapo, we felt that Brazil nuts could be sustainably harvested, and the oil used as an effective ingredient in a hair conditioner. We asked them to gather Brazil nuts for us. The Indians thought that the price of Brazil nuts was too low on the commodity market at $8 a kilo, so we talked with them to try to find ways of adding value. We brought in some simple technology so that the Indians can grind the nuts, cook them, and squash them until the oil comes through. This yields cold-pressed, virgin Brazil-nut oil. So instead of paying them $8 a kilo for the nuts, we now pay them $38 a kilo for the oil. These villagers now have independent dental, cultural, and health programs.

That is the responsibility of business. It is not to go into a community and say, "This is cheap labor; what can we get from it?" Business should ask the community what it needs to survive.

Another example of our work is in Nepal, one of the poorest countries in the world. We went into communities that make paper. The government had prohibited cutting down any more trees, so we told the people how to make paper from water hyacinths, a weed that is abundant there. This group of 150 people now have their own child-care facilities, eye-care clinics, inoculation programs, free food, free day care, and free education.

What characterizes these projects is respect for the environment, the people, their cultures, and their rights. There is also a political statement associated with Trade Not Aid projects. It is a statement of our belief that fair trade is the only ethical and sustainable way to do business, and that is why we are increasing our efforts in this area.

We have put in place a product-stewardship scheme that embraces the ecological ethics of our more conventional suppliers and the environmental impacts of our products from cradle to grave. We have also instituted a formal purchasing policy and environmental checklist, which buyers use on anything from computers to company cars.

Finally, we have a comprehensive scheme for ecological life-cycle assessments (LCAs) that takes into account a broad range of issues, including inputs and outputs from manufacturing, energy, raw materials, and wastes. In our LCAs, we also look at the potential impacts of our raw-materials sourcing on biodiversity, human and animal rights, and endangered species.

The overriding, long-term goal for business should be to forge an ethic of true sustainability. The phrase sometimes used is to "leave no footprints." My dream for The Body Shop is to put back into the earth more than we take out.

There is enough to do in the remaining years of the millennium, but I believe there is an essential link between good environmental housekeeping at local and global levels, and the establishment of a safer and more equitable world. Individuals, businesses, and governments need to recognize the link. Only by concerted action will we establish the conditions for globally sustainable development.

Let us be practical, but above all, let us be honest. The world has no real option but to elevate fair trade over free trade and conservation over consumption. These are the real ecological imperatives for business.

# KATHERINE GRAHAM

As president of the Washington Post Company for almost 30 years, Katherine Graham shepherded the company through the Watergate years, a tumultuous period because it was her reporters, Carl Bernstein and Bob Woodward, who broke the Watergate scandal. She has also been one of the most influential people in the United States for the last several decades. Her millionaire-banker father had bought *The Washington Post* in 1933, when it was financially ailing. Meanwhile, after attending Vassar and the University of Chicago, Graham took a job as a reporter for the *San Francisco News* in 1938. The very next year her father convinced her to join the *Post,* which she did, working in the circulation and editorial departments of the Sunday edition.

Nine years later Graham's father sold the newspaper to her and her husband; they proceeded to turn the company into a media powerhouse, adding *Newsweek* and other periodicals as well as radio and television stations. Unfortunately, her husband committed suicide in 1963, so Graham took the helm solo, where she remained until retiring in 1991. As chief of a media empire, ethics played a large role in her decision making as she, for example, supported Bernstein and Woodward's investigation of the Nixon administration. As Watergate unfolded, she was attacked for being unpatriotic and condoning bad journalism. One of Nixon's top advisers even made veiled threats. But she never dictated the direction her journalists should take. "You want intelligent, large-scale thinkers and writers," she explained, "and nobody for whom you have any respect would take an edict from on high."

In *Business Credibility: The Critical Factors,* Graham addresses ethics, paying particular attention to communication and language. She worries that too many business executives talk like robber barons from over one hundred years ago, when they need to be more accessible and open. She offers four steps for companies to improve their image, which includes injecting "more candor into all communications, and to be more willing to explain policies and acknowledge mistakes."

# If "Business Credibility" Means Anything
## Katherine Graham

"**B**usiness credibility" is a term that everyone, including me, uses too frequently and casually these days. Problems of credibility seem to be troubling everybody from presidential hopefuls to the Dallas Cowboys. It's become stylish to bemoan the loss of public confidence and trust in institutions, and everybody seems to have a poll that documents his or her own profession's low estate. My own favorite is a Lou Harris survey of some months ago that found that 51 percent had confidence in local trash collection, but only 30 percent had confidence in the printed press.

All told, the loss of credibility seems to have become a national malaise, as widespread and persistent as the common cold. But like the cold, the notion of "credibility" has become a barrier to clear thinking. For you can be sure that any word that is used so often, in so many kinds of situations, is being misused at least part of the time. Therefore, it's important to try to define more clearly what the problem is and what we might be able to do about it.

One source of difficulty is that when people plead for more credibility, they are really asking for more acceptance—and uncritical acceptance at that. That is a very human desire, but it ought to be couched in much more modest terms. Surely mature people, especially those who have or seek any power or influence, do not expect to be universally loved and supported. It was never thus, not in a free competitive society—and particularly not in a time of social and economic stress.

---

The loss of credibility seems to have become a national malaise, as widespread and persistent as the common cold.

---

It was Samuel Gompers of the AFL who once summed up what labor wanted in the blunt word: "more." There is nothing original or exclusive about that. When you get down to it, almost everyone wants more of something—money, power, protection or esteem. At minimum, they want to keep what they have. And those who have more, or who stand in the way of one's own ambitions, are bound to be the targets of a certain amount of resentment, suspicion and mistrust.

So every recession brings a new round of attacks on Wall Street, and if the oil companies and automakers feel maligned these days, they might recall the muckrakers' campaigns against the trusts 70 years ago. Such hostility to business is a constant theme in our history. It is, in fact, a fairly good index of the economic atmosphere.

Thus it is wishful thinking for many executives to expect public affection. But, you might say, they may at least desire to be believed—to have some credence given to their motives and their views. Yet this kind of "credibility," too, should be stated in modest and qualified terms.

For one thing, in most situations some people will not or cannot give credence to the other side. A champion of social change is simply not about to acknowledge the virtues of stability. Consumer advocates cannot afford to give businesses much credit for compassion or concern—not without undermining their own arguments and losing their hold on their constituencies. In the same manner, many corporate lobby-ists pay their rent by playing up the threats from what they paint as irresponsible citizens' groups and power-hungry bureaucrats.

Even if overstatements can be minimized, the fact remains that often nobody expects to be believed literally. That is the case with advertising, which is perhaps the great-est native American art. No one really expects that switching to a certain soft drink will produce instant world peace. Even under today's restrictive codes, the advertising game allows a large range for exaggeration, selectivity and dreams. The same is true in politics.

Or consider labor negotiations, a matter of special con-cern to me right now. Believability has a very complicated meaning here. The trickiest part of any negotiation may be establishing what each side recognizes that the other side is serious about. For instance, *The Post*'s management has had to take extraordinary steps, including publishing for over three months without most of our craft unions, to make the point that we really intend to regain control over our pressroom.*

Finally, then, believability depends on an intricate calculus involving words, performance and the standards that are being applied. And this, I think, gets us closer to the real source of difficulty today—for in many areas of our national affairs, something has gotten out of line. The gaps between words and actions and standards seem to be unreasonably large.

It is hard to have much sympathy for public officials who systematically lie or mislead the people and the press—and then complain about a loss of credibility. It's also easy to understand why large segments of the public automatically discount warnings from businessmen about the ruinous effects of environmental and safety rules. For instance, the makers of vinyl chloride claimed that OSHA's rules would be impossible to follow—and then found ways to comply. And so on.

---

*At the time of Graham's writing, *The Post*'s craft unions were on strike.

I don't mean to suggest that clean air and safe factories are cheap or easy to obtain. Nor do I think that industries are always wrong and regulators always right. Indeed, some regulations may be as costly and unreasonable as their opponents claim. Unfortunately, arguments to this effect have lost much of their force because executives have cried "wolf" too often.

At the same time, some business leaders have been crying "sheep" and there is little to say for them. In 1973, for instance, executives of a number of major corporations went before the Senate Watergate Committee to declare that they had made large, secret, illegal corporate contributions to the Nixon reelection campaign only under pressure so great it came near to extortion. Now it turns out that some of those firms and others have maintained secret political slush funds for many years. Similarly, during the go-go years on Wall Street, and even today, a number of high-flying firms gave investors and analysts very sunny reports—only to be caught later in very shoddy practices.

Some individuals and firms are now paying dearly for those mistakes. Indeed, some of the conduct now being condemned is unacceptable by any gauge. Much of it, however, has come under fire because the prevailing standards and values have changed. People are asking more of leaders and institutions, and tolerating much less. I think this has a great deal to do with the so-called credibility problems that now exist. So let's talk for a moment about changing standards—not in terms of their import for business or any other particular group, but in terms of their impact on society and the process of public debate.

Like everything else, the evolution of values has the defects of its merits. It is certainly not wrong to impose higher standards of morality and ethics in public affairs and in the marketplace. In fact, I think this change is overdue. But difficulties do follow, inevitably, when the new standards are not yet too clear—and when they are applied ex post facto in judging practices that evolved in a more lenient yesterday. The "everybody did it" defense does not excuse political corruption or account for frauds; it does explain why Spiro Agnew, for example, was so outraged and resentful when called to account.

On another point, it is certainly good to seek more safety for workers and consumers, and more protection for the environment. Yet these salutary campaigns have created many problems, not only because the changes involved may be costly, but even more because they often test the frontiers of technology and the ingenuity of managers.

Finally, it is certainly healthy to ask for more accountability and openness in public affairs, and to afford more groups better access to decision making and more ways to seek redress of grievances. But all these trends compound the time, paperwork and cost required to get anything done. Even worse, they abet the natural tendency of Americans to be litigious and to take every issue to Congress, a regulatory body, or the courts.

Incidentally, one of the most interesting developments in Washington is the opposition of many public-interest groups to proposed lobbying disclosure laws. For the first time, some of these groups are realizing why businesses complain so much about government's demands for reports.

---

The "everybody did it" defense does not excuse political corruption or account for frauds.

---

I am not suggesting that the side effects are so harmful that the prescriptions should be changed. Rather, I think the challenge is to find ways to reduce the difficulties without abandoning the gains. The passage of time will help; environmental laws are already becoming more familiar. But since endurance is no substitute for effort, we should ask what we can do to minimize hostilities and promote a climate in which communications will be easier and real conflicts can be worked out.

But if we ask what business can do honestly and specifically, I think the answer is that "business," as such, can do very little—any more than "Congress" or "the public" can. Even to think of "business" as a distinct, coherent group is to engage in the kind of generality and platitude that needs to be rooted out.

Professional and trade associations are better defined and can be effective forces—but we ought to fight the tendency to buck the hardest problems to committees, or expect special panels to relieve us of the burden of judgment. Thus I would focus on what individuals and companies can do—and several routes seem worth exploring.

The first is to define one's operating standards and develop better ways of policing oneself. Lawyers, accountants and broadcasters, to name a few, are wrestling with these problems now—as are the boards of Gulf and other companies.

The second step is to inject more candor into all communications, and to be more willing to explain policies and acknowledge mistakes. It seems almost too obvious to mention, but companies can avoid many problems by being more forthcoming with reporters, consumers and investors, and by volunteering information about products and practices. This applies especially to annual reports, which are most firms' major summary of their own view of themselves. . . .

The real erosion of public confidence occurs, I think, when a major breakdown takes place, catching the public by surprise, and it later turns out that warning signals were suppressed from public notice and remedy by good manners, personal friendships, habits of discretion, and very understandable human optimism. Such optimism is of course important. It can be the foundation of confidence in institutions whose stability and well-being in turn affect the well-being of millions of people.

And given the high public stakes in all this, it can be argued, and frequently is, that the press has an obligation to contribute to the maintenance of such confidence and the optimism on which it rests. But I would argue that while we must be responsible, our responsibility does not include a kind of blind Pollyanna reporting of business affairs and business conditions. On the contrary, our responsibility may on occasion point in a different direction. And that is because the other side of this optimistic bent of mind can be profoundly destructive of the very business soundness and general welfare it is intended to promote.

I would also enter a special plea about rhetoric. Too often corporate executives who are extremely up-to-date in other ways describe the free enterprise system, at least publicly, in terms that could have been plagiarized from the robber barons of the 19th century. The language about freedom from government control may never have been wholly true. It is certainly inaccurate now, when government is involved in most aspects of corporate operations, and when industries have encouraged regulation of everything from entry into the airlines business to official definitions of peanut butter and potato chips. It would be a remarkable advance if we could describe our economic system in terms that better reflect the real complexity of these relationships. It would also help to discuss deregulation the way we tend to lobby for it—selectively.

The third step, which grows out of the first two, is to show more hospitality to critics—to grant them, in short, the same legitimacy we ask for ourselves.

And the fourth is to seek substitutes for litigation as a way to work out conflicts. Though conciliation is not a panacea, it is certainly better than going to court. Another way is to set up an in-house critic or consumer advocate. For several years, *The Post* has had an ombudsman to investigate readers' complaints and serve as an independent critic of the paper's performance. There are many possibilities—but they all depend on a real commitment by top managers to listen to criticism and respond.

As you may have noticed, I have carefully avoided bringing up the role of the news media. I have done so for a reason: I don't want to encourage in any way the argument that the credibility problems of businesses or any other group would be reduced if the media would only do more to foster public confidence. Besides passing the buck, that line of thinking involves major misconceptions of the nature of news and the role of the media.

First, it assumes that there is a great mass of something called "good news" that the media aren't covering. The system doesn't work that way. By definition, news is the dramatic, the disastrous, and the unusual. When millions of workers go home at night without being poisoned on the job, or when new cars do not break down, that is important—but it is seldom news.

In fact, I doubt that you really want the ordinary to become a front-page event. That happened to *The Post* in October, when it was news that the paper came out at all, because our presses had been vandalized 48 hours earlier. That's not the kind of "good news" I would recommend.

Second, it is not the role of the media to promote, to ration bad news, or to feature an editor's idea of what is good or cheering for society. It is even less our job to try to compensate for someone else's mistakes. When the wheels fall off police cars, there's not much the media can do to help the company involved.

That is not to say there is nothing that news companies can improve. You can certainly ask—indeed, demand—coverage that is accurate, fair and grounded in real understanding of events. You can ask for much better economic coverage, an area in which much of the press has been quite superficial until recently. And you can ask news companies, even more than others, to explain their standards and policies, to acknowledge weaknesses and correct mistakes. But here, too, I would plead for fewer generalizations. Instead of grumbling about the media, take specific complaints to particular editors. Our performance will only improve if individuals apply higher standards and take specific steps.

Overall, I guess that my counsel on the subject of credibility adds up to this: don't think about it. Focus instead on honesty, perspective and performance. The gains that result may be modest—but they are likely to be real.

But because I would banish the word, don't think I feel the quality of credibility is dispensable. I see it as essential—and, obviously, so does everybody else. To permit myself one great generalization, "credibility" is shorthand for the basic level of trust and mutual regard on which our whole economy and democracy depend. It is that foundation which enables competition to thrive, arguments to rage, and accommodations to evolve, however inefficiently.

I happen to think that system is worth preserving. It is not as free or successful as its apologists may claim; but it is surely not as exploitive, repressive or rickety as its critics allege. It does face serious challenges. But it has provided, over two centuries, a greater measure of freedom, opportunity and prosperity for more citizens than any other social arrangement yet devised.

Further, I think the current anxiety about so many aspects of national affairs is in itself an affirmation of faith. Americans would not worry so much if we did not believe something important is at stake. So perhaps the definition I've been groping for is commitment—to certain basic principles and to the individual effort required to advance those principles. That is not a modest prescription at all, but I can't think of a better one for the Bicentennial.

# RAYMOND V. GILMARTIN

Ethics is of the utmost importance when it comes to drugs, especially drug manufacturing, and when Raymond Gilmartin took the helm of Merck & Company, ethics was one of the foremost issues on his mind. After all, the New Jersey–based pharmaceutical company, which develops everything from antidepressants to drugs that suppress AIDS, lives or dies with the success of innovative drugs and with the trust of their customers. Gilmartin earned a B.S. in electrical engineering from Union College in 1963 and an M.B.A. from Harvard University in 1968. He then went to work for the accounting and consulting firm Arthur D. Little, but departed in 1976 to join Becton Dickinson & Company as part of the company's corporate planning group. Eventually he became president in 1987 and CEO in 1989.

Gilmartin was recruited to become CEO of Merck in 1994. In the first years of his tenure, he cut overhead by hundreds of millions of dollars and put the savings into research and marketing. Battles between drugmakers is so intense, that research even includes studying physician prescription and purchasing decisions. To market their products, some companies join forces as Warner-Lambert and Pfizer have done, but Gilmartin prefers to remain independent: "The best use of our resources and time and attention is to grow through internal development rather than through mergers and acquisitions."

According to Gilmartin, the more competition the better: "Competition sparks innovation, creating powerful incentives for new, more effective, and more cost-effective medicines and treatments." He compares today's health care industry to the new corporations that appeared in the early 1900s; they were bulky and awkward and went through growing pains, but triumphed. He has the same confidence in health care. An integral part of the success formula is ethics. In *An Ethics Prescription for Success,* he declares, "High ethical standards create a sense of pride and a desire to achieve great things." To maintain those high standards, according to Gilmartin, a company must set clear goals and go heavy on the communication.

# An Ethics Prescription for Success
## Raymond V. Gilmartin

"Medicine is for the people, not for the profits. The profits follow, and if we have remembered that, they have never failed to appear. The better we have remembered that, the larger they have been." That statement, made by George W. Merck in 1950, still applies to Merck's business today. Our commitment to high ethical standards is part of who we are and what we want to be, and is reflective of ethics' growing importance: A recent Ethics Resource Center survey revealed that the number of companies with more than 500 employees that have internal ethics offices has skyrocketed from 11 percent in 1987 to 45 percent in 1997.

High ethical standards create a sense of pride and a desire to achieve great things. They inspire trust and confidence among employees, government officials, regulatory agencies, the medical community, and our customers and patients—all of whom are essential to Merck's success. But sustaining such standards is sometimes difficult, especially during uncertain times. For example, in 1994, Merck and the pharmaceutical industry were in turmoil. President Clinton's health plan was being debated, raising the possibility of price controls on prescription drugs. Intense competition and the emergence of large managed-care buyers had triggered the beginning of a series of mergers and acquisitions. Merck had fallen from grace in a survey conducted by *Fortune,* which had previously named Merck "America's Most Admired Corporation" seven years in a row. Merck stock was trading at $28 a share, down almost 50 percent from its previous high three years earlier.

Internally, departments were being reengineered and manufacturing plants were being closed. A voluntary retirement program had been completed the previous year, and rumor was that downsizings were imminent. Employees asked, "What is going to happen to Merck?" and, ultimately, "What is going to happen to me?" The opportunity for unethical behavior was ripe, yet we did not stray from our ideology.

## STAND BY YOUR MANTRA

Many of the factors contributing to Merck's ensuing turnaround involved new products that had been in the research pipeline and initiatives taken by Merck's management. But just as important as *what* we did was *how* we did it. As we implemented plans and strategy, we were clear that we care about results, but we also care about how we achieve them. From the start, our actions were firmly anchored in Merck's core values and high ethical standards, which can never be separated from our success as a business. Some initial actions included:

- Resolving the uncertainty surrounding Merck, especially among employees. A management team was formed so that everyone would know who the company's leaders were. This team had to inspire trust and confidence, and they had to be recognized instantly as being both highly competent and strongly committed to Merck's core values.
- Establishing a strategy for Merck with clear goals, priorities, and measures. Again, we wanted to ensure that

the strategy could be instantly recognized within the company as reinforcing Merck's high ethical standards.

- Communicating heavily across the company about future directions and the importance of our core values. As we communicated, one of the main messages was—and is—that, despite any changes in the marketplace, certain things at Merck would never change. Merck's values and ethical standards would be maintained and strengthened as we went forward.

---

High ethical standards create a sense of pride and a desire to achieve great things.

---

Today, the environment is very different. The threat of price controls on prescription drugs is gone, and choice and competition in the healthcare delivery system are providing new opportunities for innovative companies. Internally, we have become more productive, increased our investment in research and development, and strengthened our sales and marketing forces. Our 1997 worldwide sales total was more than $23 billion, and our stock price has more than quadrupled, increasing our market value by more than $100 billion. *Fortune* has named Merck one of the best companies to work for in the United States.

## FOSTERING ETHICAL BEHAVIOR

One core component of our business strategy is a recognition that, to ensure Merck's long-term success, we must respond quickly to change and opportunity. The only way to have that kind of organization is to create a working environment that helps Merck employees maximize their full potential. If they reach their full potential as individuals, then Merck will achieve its full potential as a company.

Developing people has clear ethical implications because, in the eyes of employees, a company's ethics are most often equated with how well it treats people. Over the past four years, our focus on values and respecting people has helped employees rally around our strategy and increased their trust and desire to build a strong future for themselves and for Merck. We have defined our standards and are backing them with education, training, and a variety of programs, including:

- An ethics office. Headed by an ethics officer, this office protects and promotes Merck's standards on a worldwide basis. We want people to know they should never compromise their personal integrity in the mistaken belief that they are helping to achieve company goals. Compromising integrity is not only inappropriate, it also destroys morale, so our approach on these issues reassures and motivates people, therefore supporting our overall goals.

---

Developing people has clear ethical implications because, in the eyes of employees, a company's ethics are most often equated with how well it treats people.

---

- Ombudsmen. As part of the Ethics Office, ombudsmen listen to employees, resolve problems, and take action on ethical issues when necessary. They are an outlet for employees to express concerns and seek advice regarding workplace problems, thereby creating a stronger organization by solving problems that interfere with workplace effectiveness.
- Interviews. We interviewed executives to assess where we stood on ethical issues. We conducted many internal focus groups worldwide to discuss our goals and

gauge people's reactions. Finally, we conducted an ethics survey among 10,000 employees to take the pulse of the organization and help set future directions.

- Global code of business conduct. When implemented, the code will apply to all our operations worldwide. It will serve as a valuable resource as employees strive to continue the ethical traditions of George W. Merck. The code will establish one standard of global conduct, based on our core values, for employees to follow in day-to-day interactions with customers, colleagues, stockholders, suppliers, and communities. It will pose a series of realistic questions and offer realistic solutions, all of which will deal with a variety of issues ranging from product quality to use of company resources.

---

We want people to know they should never compromise their personal integrity in the mistaken belief that they are helping to achieve company goals.

---

- Building leadership capabilities. We launched a company-wide leadership program aimed at achieving our goals and helping people reach their full potential. We clearly define "leadership" so that everyone has a clear blueprint for success. Merck leaders excel in four principles: they know and develop themselves; know and develop Merck's business; know, support, and develop Merck's people; and communicate effectively at all levels. From these principles we defined a wide range of behaviors that support and demonstrate leadership, such as setting clear objectives, recognizing employee performance, training and developing people, and supporting Merck's commitment to community responsibility. Heading the list of behaviors is the belief that people's actions should reflect a high degree of integrity and ethics, which means that leaders should be proactive in creating an ethical business environment in their business unit, help to ensure that others understand and act in alignment with Merck's business practices and policies, and take immediate action if they observe unethical behavior or situations. Last year we began giving employees a leadership rating in addition to their regular performance rating. Over time, this rating will affect employees' overall compensation, especially their bonus and stock options.

## SECURING A STELLAR REPUTATION

What has been the result of all the work Merck has done around ethics? Is there a pay-off in a business sense? At Merck, we emphatically believe that promoting ethics helps us meet our business goals, in addition to being the right thing to do.

---

Some people consider the term "ethical business practices" an oxymoron. Yet at Merck, we believe that ethical behavior is not just part of our culture; it is an important contributor to our corporate success.

---

Internally, our own people are the best judges of what we have accomplished. In a survey of 225 randomly selected employees:

- 97 percent said they were proud to tell others they work at Merck;
- 90 percent agreed that management is honest and ethical in its business practices; and

- 87 percent agreed that, taking everything into account, Merck is a great place to work.

Externally, our reputation for high ethical standards clearly contributes to our overall corporate image, which helps us recruit and retain top people. Even in the tight U.S. labor market, Merck received about 165,000 employment inquiries in 1997, so we are able to pick the best professionals available.

We have made much progress during the past four years, but we will never be finished; promoting and sustaining high ethical standards is a work in progress. But regardless of any changes in the marketplace, Merck's core values will not change. Some people consider the term "ethical business practices" an oxymoron. Yet at Merck, we believe that ethical behavior is not just part of our culture; it is an important contributor to our corporate success. When we invest in ethics, we are investing in our future as surely as when we invest in a new lab or plant. These investments reinforce our reputation and build the trust and confidence of Merck people, as well as physicians, patients, and payers.

We should never underestimate how inspiring it is for employees to embrace high ethical standards. Nothing is more motivating than a goal worth striving for and then pursuing that goal in a work environment where you are treated with dignity, honesty, and respect.

# PART V

# Conquering Technology

Technology, the computer, and the Internet have been driving the U.S. economy at a torrid pace in recent years and will continue to define the future. The importance of technology is reflected in The Conference Board's 1999 CEO survey as 25 percent of the responding CEOs said that "changing technology" was one of their top three marketplace challenges. For financial and professional services companies the numbers jumped to 38 and 39 percent, respectively. While technology can empower, it can also baffle. Charles Wang, cofounder of the third-largest American software firm Computer Associates International, warns in the opening essay that "an acute state of misunderstanding between corporate managers and their technology executives threatens American business." To resolve the issue, he says that everyone must first become techno-literate. Simon Ramo, who cofounded TRW and whose essay was written in 1974, recognized the very same issue: "The greatest remaining handicap to the fullest sensible use of the computer as an aid for senior management consists of the senior managers themselves." While technology does indeed empower and baffle, it also has the potential to dehumanize, which Arjay Miller warns of. Miller, who was president of the Ford Motor Company and then the revered dean of Stanford's business school, observes, "Some fear that the people who run things will be concerned only with problems that can be reduced to numbers, ignoring such fundamental but immeasurable values as individualism, freedom, and beauty." This section tackles technology from every angle and its importance can never be slighted, for as former Lotus CEO James Manzi poignantly promises, information technology is no longer a backroom operation—it's on the front lines.

# CHARLES B. WANG

Charles Wang is chairman and CEO of one the world's largest software companies, Computer Associates International (CA), which he cofounded in 1975. Born in China, Wang and his family fled their Shanghai home and emigrated to the United States after the Communist revolution in 1949. The family found themselves in a Queens, New York housing project. Fortunately, Wang was able to attend Queens College, where he earned degrees in both mathematics and physics. Wang then settled on becoming a computer programmer; because there were so many help-wanted ads for them, he concluded it was a growing industry.

When the company he was working for decided to sell their software division, he and friend Russell Artzt went for it. Artzt handled research and development while Wang became the consummate salesman. Artzt recalled, "He'd pick twenty pages out of the yellow pages, drink three cups of coffee, and not go to the bathroom until he'd cold-called every potential customer." Wang took CA public in 1981, and the partners have used the proceeds to gobble up some 60 other companies. CA even has merger/acquisition software that evaluates and ranks employees. Within seven days they are either brought on board or fired. "We tell them the truth, so they can get on with their lives," Wang explained, although he has come under fire for what some call ruthless merger tactics.

Interestingly, the techno-evangelist admits, "I like the idea of sitting in bed flipping through the *Sunday New York Times* magazine, because I see things that interest me, an article, an ad, the crossword puzzle." Ultimately, Wang believes in the power of information technology. He writes, "I cannot be clearer than this: Give up any idea you may have about how information technology can support your business. Your business is information and information is your business." In *What CEOs Don't Know,* he writes that if CEOs (and all managers for that matter) don't educate themselves on information technology "they will deny themselves access to the fundamental driving force of the modern global economy."

# What CEOs Don't Know
## *Charles B. Wang*

**A**n acute state of misunderstanding between corporate managers and their technology executives threatens American business. Caused by differences in training, temperament, and tradition, this disconnect takes a serious toll on productivity and quality. Both groups agree on the problem but, rather than seeking to solve it, continue to blame each other. Such accusations are, in fact, further signs of the disconnect.

Assessing fault is not the issue. I believe that it is the responsibility of CEOs to repair the rift. Once they accept responsibility, a new partnership can be formed. The following three steps are a way to begin.

## OVERCOME TECHNO-ILLITERACY

CEOs, who already know how to speak the technical language of accounting, finance, and law, must become familiar with the language of information technology. Why do CEOs—who know that AR means accounts receivable, that IPO stands for initial public offering, that SEC spells trouble—take perverse pride in rolling their eyes at the mention of LANs (local area networks) or BPR (business process reengineering)?

Not that information technologists have gone out of their way to make discussion of their field accessible to others—is there another profession with more acronyms, abbreviations, and buzzwords? Recently, while browsing in a bookstore, I found myself more chagrined than surprised to discover no fewer than eight dictionaries dedicated to information technology.

It is no surprise that CEOs, most of whom come from finance or marketing backgrounds, are familiar with certain buzzwords and not others. Nevertheless, it is vital for them to be conversant with every discipline that contributes to the success of their companies. In this last decade of the 20th century, CEOs need to be at least as comfortable talking about GUIs (graphical user interfaces) as they are about TDAs (tax-deferred annuities).

---

Recently, while browsing in a bookstore, I found myself more chagrined than surprised to discover no fewer than eight dictionaries dedicated to information technology.

---

Fortunately, techno-literacy can be achieved by bypassing buzzwords and concentrating on integrating information technology with traditional business practice. The goal can be reached by using technology to solve business problems.

One way or another, CEOs must acquire sufficient knowledge about information technology to do their jobs, and it doesn't matter how they get it—through special training sessions or on the job. If American business leaders remain at their current level of ignorance, they will deny themselves access to the fundamental driving force of the modern global economy.

# CIOs Must Participate in Strategic Planning

At a recent convention, attended by more than 100 chief information officers, I asked a simple question: "How many of you will be considered for a CEO job or are in the upper echelons of executive management where you deal directly with the CEO?" Three hands went up.

I couldn't believe it. To what do these technology managers aspire? I concluded that they all had professional careers but few had business careers. Under such conditions, CIOs have very little stake in the long-range success of their corporations. They must, therefore, believe their only option for career improvement is to move on to another company, another learning opportunity.

Many CEOs, on the other hand, tell me CIOs are not ready for the challenges of leading modern enterprises. They complain that their CIOs have neglected to gain business experience and perspective. Unfortunately, for the most part, they are correct. But to the extent they blame their CIOs, these CEOs are dead wrong.

Correcting the disconnect is the CEO's responsibility. A prime HR task facing every CEO is to break down the information-technology ghetto. To do so is not an option but a requirement. If technologists continue to be shut out of the strategic-planning process, the corporation suffers in two ways: It won't utilize information technology fully, and its technologists will leave for organizations that do offer real partnership.

The way information technology fits into the organizational chart speaks volumes. It's expected to take a supporting, tactical, or strategic role. I believe that the CEO-CIO reporting relationship should be as direct as possible. Companies in which the CEO and the CIO have a close working relationship are typically the first to develop sophisticated and powerful business applications.

## INTELLIGENT EVOLUTION, NOT REVOLUTION

Revolution both perpetuates and feeds on the disconnect between CEOs and CIOs. It applies pressure to abandon the status quo in favor of new systems and architectures—an example of the technology-for-technology's-sake type of thinking that is inimical to the enterprise's best interests. Simultaneously, the dizzying pace of technological change challenges CEOs and CIOs alike to distinguish between change that is fundamental and change that is peripheral.

Evolution is the answer. Unlike revolution, evolution keeps people accountable. It demands that CIOs justify the changes they recommend this quarter in light of the changes they suggested last quarter. Evolution also leverages investments already made. Because the pace of evolution is more manageable, CEOs have the time to evaluate technology recommendations in the context of their enterprises' strategic objectives. Evolution also limits risk by allowing new technologies to be introduced without imperiling the smooth functioning of day-to-day business.

Conversely, revolution is destructive. It demands that we replace our existing technology simply because some new technology has come along. We all know that something new will always be coming along, but only rarely will it be in your business's best interests to abandon that which is working well in favor of something untried that may, or may not, work at all.

Instead, consider what I call intelligent evolution. Intelligent evolution takes today's effective technology and builds on that foundation with new technology. This approach makes financial sense, too, because it utilizes investments already made.

Of course, it's hardly surprising that few CIO candidates are enthusiastic about embracing the status quo: They have accepted without question that revolution is the byword of information technology. Without a doubt, there is a place for revolutionary products—but the thoughtful CEO must ask whether this company, at this time, is that place.

162

I recall one CEO who shared with me his CIO's recommendation to abandon an existing technology infrastructure in favor of a compelling new one. This CIO had promised that the new architecture would help the company become proactive and thus anticipate the needs of tomorrow. What, this CEO asked, did I think?

Be careful, I warned him. Whenever I hear the term "new architecture," my skepticism meter goes into the red zone. This was revolution, but revolution in support of what? I told the CEO that, while gambling on what will happen tomorrow may be interesting, it may be more profitable to determine what happened yesterday. Perhaps, as a result of our conversation, the CEO selected an evolutionary process that could achieve solid results without enormous risk and expense.

Clearly, business does not need more instability; an immense shakeup has already transformed corporate America. In the 1990s organizations are being restructured around information access. Until a few years ago, most centralized organizations relied on research and development and marketing to stimulate growth. Today, with an increasing emphasis on decentralized business units and a high rate of technological change in a global economy, access to information has displaced R&D and marketing as the key business tool.

Companies with a track record of successfully using information technology are usually led by CEOs who have come to terms with it. These CEOs have not become information-technology experts—the field changes too rapidly to allow that—but they have committed to three management practices:

First, they have decided to become as familiar with information technology as they are with finance, marketing, sales, and other critical business processes. They recognize that a change of attitude is necessary.
Second, they are determined to forge new relationships with their CIOs, insisting that they report directly

so as to involve them fully in the decision-making process at the highest level. Once the CEO accepts the leadership role and the CIO acknowledges that his or her role is to deliver solutions that meet the needs of the business, the partnership—and the enterprise—will flourish.

Third, they are committed to embrace a course of intelligent evolution in information favoring the pragmatic over the pie-in-the-sky.

These three steps are merely a beginning, but they set the stage for decision making that can benefit from technology and not be frustrated by it.

## A Disconnect Checklist for CEOs

How disconnected are you from your CIO? Answer the following questions to measure the health of what should be a working relationship. Based on the rating scale below, you may find the need for action.

1. Do you trust your CIO's judgment? (If your answer is no, skip this exercise. You have a different problem altogether.)
2. Does your CIO report directly to you?
3. Does your CIO proactively meet the business challenges of your organization?
4. Has your CIO drawn up a clear technology plan for the 1990s? (Give yourself one bonus point if you have actually read the plan; give yourself another if you understood it.)
5. Has your CIO tried to brief you and the board of directors on this plan? (Give yourself one bonus point if you actually held the meeting.)

6. Has a complete cost/benefit analysis of the plan been done?
7. Does the technology plan leverage off existing information-system resources?
8. Does your CIO consider outsourcing companies a benchmark against which to measure the company's own performance?
9. Has your CIO built a robust network infrastructure that can reliably handle the workload of distributed computing?
10. Has your CIO made a defensible case for downsizing to smaller platforms to reduce dependence on the mainframe? (If not, give yourself one bonus point if the CIO has made a defensible case for retaining the mainframe.)

*Rating System*
Score one point for each "yes."

*Total Points Analysis*
11–13 You're very lucky and should immediately invite your CIO out to lunch. He's probably being actively recruited by the competition.
7–10 Your CIO is squarely in the tradition of most contemporary CIOs.
4–6 Your CIO is struggling. Consider looking for a new CIO.
0–4 Get a new CIO. Today.

**B**rilliant inventor and entrepreneur, Simon Ramo was awarded the Presidential Medal of Freedom by Ronald Reagan. Although a man of science, it was the violin in particular, that paved Ramo's way. His parents owned a clothing store in Salt Lake City and hopes for college were slim. So in 1929 Ramo spent all his savings on a top-of-the-line violin for playing in a competition he hoped to win—the prize would pay for college. "Many years passed after that first deliberate gamble before I realized I had become a hybrid of scientist, engineer, and entrepreneur. Risk-taking, I understood well by then, was a major factor in my life." Needless to say, he won the prize and went on to earn a Ph.D. in electrical engineering and physics from the California Institute of Technology.

Ramo's first job was in research with General Electric (GE), and by age 30 he was considered the preeminent expert in microwaves and had been awarded 25 patents. The GE bureaucracy, however, was stifling, so in 1946 Ramo joined Hughes Aircraft, owned by the eccentric millionaire Howard Hughes. Since Hughes was a recluse, Ramo had free reign as chief of operations and recruited a high-powered group of scientists and engineers. "We would have a weekly 'town meeting' where the scientists and engineers could voice their ideas about how to cut administration red tape and maintain close communication and mutual stimulation to achieve the full benefit of each other's talents," he said.

Unfortunately, Hughes's increasingly bizarre behavior worried the U.S. Government; they weren't too keen on a madman owning a top defense contractor, so Ramo and his good friend Dean Woolridge left in 1953 to form the Ramo-Woolridge Company, later to merge with Thompson Products and become TRW. Technology has obviously played an important role in Ramo's growth as an inventor, but he also incorporated the computer into his management practices years before many others. In *The Computer in Management* he describes the importance of combining intuition with analysis, the qualitative human, and the quantitative computer.

# The Computer in Management
## *Simon Ramo*

Until almost the present moment, the computer as a tool to extend management's brainpower has generated confusion and doubt. Its potential for major management improvement often has been oversold. Foolishness, flimflam, and cost ineffectiveness have accompanied unfounded fears that the computer would soon replace management, at least middle management. And computer programmers, a breed unto themselves, have had as little knowledge of management principles and requirements as the typical manager has had of the computer's capabilities and limitations, causing the generation of little-used and only slightly useful data with little impact on the key decision-making processes of management.

Today, a sudden emergence from this jumble is occurring because the right things are happening simultaneously on several fronts. New generations of managers who understand the computer, and of computer specialists who understand what management needs, are taking over. Computer modeling of operations is changing quickly from a curious side issue to a practical, real-life portrayal. New information-handling technology is permitting the man-machine partnership to bring data, assumptions, analysis, and creative speculation into harmonious working ensembles. The universities are producing management-computer specialists whose zeal is now matched by a pertinent and applicable intellectual discipline.

Good management involves a combination of hunch and analysis; the qualitative and the quantitative; the imponderable, vague and incomplete, on the one hand, and the deliberate, clear and thorough, on the other. It is not one set of considerations, one kind of thinking, to the exclusion of the other.

The human manager must be the one to make the assumptions and check computer results against his intuition, common sense and experience. He uses the computer to ensure consistency and logic and to mix, according to his selected rules, all of the key parameters of his management problems with proper weights. The more the manager understands his business, the better his assumptions will be; but the more he removes inconsistencies in his thinking and tests his assumptions against facts and logic, a process in which the computer shines, the better will be his management decisions and his understanding of his business. It is a reinforcing process. . . .

## THE MANAGER AS BOTTLENECK

The greatest remaining handicap to the fullest sensible use of the computer as an aid for senior management consists of the senior managers themselves. It is still common to hear: "The computer is not better than the assumptions, and I make those," or "I'm not going to let the computer run my business, because there are too many subtleties, unknowns, sudden, external impacts and unpredictable, competitive phenomena that the computer can't take account of," or "The computer tells me how A would change with B, but it is C that's the important thing, and if I knew that, I wouldn't need a computer."

All of these commonly heard comments are evidence of a failure to assign the right role to the computer—namely, to assist the manager in some aspects only, still leaving him full scope to manage as he chooses as to these and all other aspects. If a manager has not yet found a computer useful to him in management, it means that he has not yet a competent team and that he does not yet understand how to obtain the benefits.

Failure to use the computer fully in management often traces back to a bias by management against the whole idea of planning ahead. No one can predict the future. It is much too complicated for that. So the practical, pragmatic manager wants to be sure to keep planning in its place, a minor tool in the background. Moreover, planning (as with the USSR's series of five-year plans) smacks of an attempt to obtain a controlled society where everything is tied to a plan and variations are considered sinful. In this sense planning is totalitarian; it is anti-free enterprise; it is anti-freedom. It is also anti-real life where flexibility must exist to permit one to move in the best way regardless of plans made earlier when the real happenings were not foreseeable.

There is, however, a difference between the truly unpredictable and the merely unpredicted.

We can't predict everything, but we can predict some things. We can't make foolproof or complete plans and shouldn't try to. Possibilities, clear or not, probable or improbable, can be listed. Where the consequences, should these events occur, are seen to be very serious or to offer outstanding opportunities, then it behooves us to consider them ahead of time even if they never occur.

In today's complex management situations, planning without the computer is bound to be very superficial and to consider only a fraction of the usually available facts and useful assumptions. With the computer, the manager has a much better chance in the decade ahead than at any time in the past to make a huge step upward in management competence. He can cause more of the future to happen *because* of him rather than *to* him.

# ARJAY MILLER

In September of 1945, a 28-year-old Henry Ford II was forced to seize the ailing Ford Motor Company from his senile, but legendary grandfather. At the conclusion of World War II, he was savvy enough to hire a group of 10 brilliant ex–air force men, who were experts in statistical analysis and manufacturing and who sold themselves as a team. A key member of that group, which became known as the Whiz Kids, was Arjay Miller. After studying at the University of California, Los Angeles and earning a Ph.D. in economics at the University of California, Berkeley, he went to work for the Federal Reserve Bank in San Francisco, honing his financial skills.

World War II interrupted Miller's career with the government, and after a stint in the air force he joined Ford in 1946, bringing with him the rigors of statistical analysis and financial planning. He and his cohorts saved the company; he became president in 1963 and spent his tenure focused on product planning and marketing. At the time Henry II was CEO; and although their relationship was tumultuous (as most of Henry II's relationships were), years later it came out in court that if Henry II was ever kidnapped, all negotiating was to be handed over to Miller—the man Ford forever had confidence in. In the winter of 1968, however, Miller became vice chairman and the presidency was handed over to a General Motors recruit. Later that year Miller was tapped by Stanford University to become the school's dean of the graduate business school.

Miller sought to improve the management talent the school was sending forth, so he moved the program away from being lecture oriented to the more hands-on study of actual cases. His other goal was to give students a broad education: "Up-to-date training for management, construed in its broadest sense, is vitally necessary, not only in meeting the traditional business goals, but also in helping to resolve broad social problems." In *Human Values in the Computer Age,* his long-founded belief in statistical analysis as well as his progressive views are clear; however, he also argues that individualism and the human factor must not be lost.

# Human Values in the
# Computer Age
## *Arjay Miller*

One of the penalties of rapid technological change is its unsettling effect on large numbers of people who view it as a threat to their well-being and to the established order. This has been true, we are told, from the very beginnings of industrial history. It is especially true, I believe, of that shining symbol of modern technology — the computer.

In our eagerness to exploit the new technology, we have been looking at the trees and failing to see the forest. In our adulation of the computer and other new devices and techniques, we have dwelt too much on the amazing technological capabilities of new electronic hardware and have done far too little to demonstrate its equally amazing potential for advancing human welfare.

As a result, we are witnessing what might be called a human backlash — a perfectly understandable anxiety as to what will become of the individual in a society that makes increasing use of highly sophisticated machines and large organizations to do its work. Mixed with human awe and admiration of the new technology is a vague, disquieting fear that, because of the computer, man has somehow lost position in this world — has become less important in the scheme of things.

## "DON'T PUNCH ME IN"

The manifestations of this anxiety are not hard to find. Most of us, I'm sure, feel a strong bond of sympathy with the university student who carried a sign reading, "I am a human being; do not fold, bend, or mutilate."

And I'm sure most of us share some apprehension at the knowledge that computers make it easier for the government to move into more and more phases of our personal affairs. There is always the suspicion that George Orwell's "1984" might not, after all, be a piece of literary fantasy.

Mixed with human awe and admiration of the new technology is a vague, disquieting fear that, because of the computer, man has somehow lost position in this world.

In the course of constructing urban freeways in various parts of the country, engineers have sometimes relied too much on computers and have failed to make proper allowance for such factors as beauty or esthetic value. In some cases, a technically correct freeway network has threatened to lessen unnecessarily the attractiveness of the communities it is meant to serve.

These examples could be multiplied, but I think the lesson is clear: if technological progress is to have real meaning and human significance, it must be made to serve man in ways that he can understand and appreciate. As John W. Gardner reminds us:

"The basic American commitment is not to affluence, not to power, not to all the marvelously cushioned comforts of a well-fed nation, but to the liberation of the human spirit, the release of human potential and the enhancement of individual dignity."

172

Part of our problem is a widespread misconception of the purpose and uses of the computer. Some observers see a future in which decisions will be made not by men, but by computers — or at best, by a handful of men who are in tune with computers. Some fear that the people who run things will be concerned only with problems that can be reduced to numbers, ignoring such fundamental but immeasurable values as individualism, freedom, and beauty. This obviously must not be allowed to happen. Our task is to focus on man and his needs — not on technology itself.

The computer is only a tool — an electronic device that is completely subject to human will. It is essentially a tool for problem solving. It can provide decision information that previously was too costly, took too long to process, or was literally beyond human capabilities to obtain. More importantly, it enables us to grapple with problems that are too complex and contain too many variables for the human mind to handle unaided.

But the choice of problems to be solved, the establishment of priorities and the broad outlines of the attack on these problems are decisions for men, not for computers.

## SYSTEMS ANALYSIS

It is largely because of the computer that we are able to undertake the broad-scale approach to problem solving called systems analysis. Speaking very broadly, systems analysis is simply a way of looking at problems and deciding how best to attack them. First, we set forth the objectives we are trying to attain. Next, we set forth all the elements or factors that influence our ability to achieve those objectives. Then, with a full picture of alternatives and the likely consequences of each, we can choose the course of action that offers the best combination of benefits and costs.

This is one of the most valuable developments of our time. Traditional methods of problem solving are just not equal to the complex problems we face. We now are able, thanks to the computer, to take a "total" approach—to see all elements of a problem in proper perspective.

Used in this way, the computer is an aid to thinking, not a substitute for thinking. It extends brainpower in much the same way that machine tools extend muscle power.

As a matter of fact, one of the best things about the computer is that it forces us to think through our problems logically before we can even turn it on. In order to program a computer, we must have clearly in mind what it is we are trying to accomplish and the various means by which we can achieve our goals.

Thus far, the new technology—systems analysis, computers and the rest—has been used mainly to serve private ends. It has been used also, of course, for military purposes and for space activities, but these uses are for the most part highly technical and far removed from the everyday experience of the average person. The tangible benefits that the average man has gained are primarily in the form of greater choice of products, higher quality, lower costs and prices, elimination of much heavy or repetitive work and greater freedom to enjoy leisure-time activities.

---

> One of the best things about the computer is that it forces us to think through our problems logically before we can even turn it on.

---

Our success in meeting private needs and wants is a matter of proud record. More people enjoy more material advantages than was thought possible even a generation ago. Economic man has been well served in our society.

But what about our social needs, both old and new?

## New Social Problems

In the wake of rapid technological and economic progress has come a wave of new social problems—urban decay, air and water pollution, highway safety, to name a few—that we must learn to deal with effectively. And even our fantastic economic gains of the past 20 years have failed to eliminate such perennial, deep-rooted problems as poverty, crime, ignorance and chronic unemployment.

Until recently, it made little difference whether or not we recognized these problems because we felt powerless to solve them. When problems are that big and complicated, the tendency is to ignore them, hope that someone else will find solutions, or simply throw up our hands and admit defeat.

Today our mood is different. Rapid progress in some aspects of life has led us to anticipate equally rapid progress in all aspects. As our standard of living rises, we are less willing to accept the prevalence of ugliness, dirt, congestion, and crime. As affluence grows and education spreads, poverty and ignorance are no longer tolerable. As our vision of the future expands, we find it difficult to reconcile ourselves to the fact that as many as one-sixth of our fellow citizens are not sharing adequately—or, in some cases, at all—in our progress to date.

Today, as a matter of fact, there is no longer any excuse for inaction or ineffective action. We have the resources to attack our social ills effectively. Science and technology are giving us the means both to analyze our problems and to point out solutions. It is no longer a question of whether or not we can meet our social needs, but whether we will make the necessary effort to apply our capabilities to social as well as private goals.

Systems analysis can be a powerful tool for the solution of social problems. It forces us to consider new possibilities, new opportunities, and new choices of many kinds. It enables us to discard old methods and old limitations on thought and action. In this sense, with more freedom of choice, we can be more human.

What is required first is that we as a people establish our national goals and our priorities. This must be a conscious and continuing effort on our part. In producing for private consumption, the setting of goals and priorities is no problem. Output is automatically determined by the market place as millions of individuals satisfy their own private needs and wants. In seeking to shift emphasis from private goods to "public goods," however, we must consider carefully what will do the most good for the most people.

---

The effective organization must take advantage of the fact that human talents are not homogeneous and interchangeable.

---

This involves, among other things, a set of moral or ethical judgments—a philosophical re-examination of our scale of values. And as we make our choices through normal political processes, we must face the fact that, even in a society as affluent as ours, there are simply not enough resources to meet all of our needs at the same time.

Within the broad framework established by popular choice, we should be able to tackle specific problems in an organized way, breaking them down into manageable pieces and setting realistic timetables for corrective action. From there, we can look at our resources and match them against the cost-effectiveness of each of the alternate approaches available. Where there are trade-offs involved, we should be able to choose intelligently what we will sacrifice in one area in order to achieve another, more desirable goal. Only in this way can we arrive at some sensible understanding as to how much we can do, how best it can be done, at what speed and at what cost.

As we develop new plans for social action, we should recognize the advantages of large-scale organizations in handling the large-scale tasks required of us. The massive problems and opportunities facing our society must be matched by massive resources working efficiently toward common goals.

Does all this mean that the individual will somehow be submerged or lost in the shuffle? Not at all. On the contrary, there will be greater need and scope for individual effort than ever before. Large organizations, by their very size and complexity, offer a wide opportunity for utilization of an incredibly broad range of talents. Far from reducing the individual to the least common denominator, the effective organization must take advantage of the fact that human talents are not homogeneous and interchangeable.

The premium, as always, will be on smarter and more creative people — men and women with broad, well-balanced knowledge and skills.

## CREATING CREATIVITY

One of the special tasks of big organizations is to create an environment favorable for creative people. It is no accident that those organizations which place great emphasis on computers and systems analysis are usually also dedicated to what is known as "free form organization" — a concept in which people and ideas take precedence over traditional departmental or divisional patterns. Because these groups recognize that *change* is the overriding characteristic of our time, they seek to encourage innovation and constant self-renewal through giving the greatest possible rein to the creative talent of individual managers and employees.

Technology becomes an invaluable aid when it is linked to this spirit of innovation and new enterprise. It can give form and force to sound ideas for human betterment. In the same sense, to fail to make the fullest use of all the new tools and techniques at our command would be to limit unnecessarily our human response to human needs.

# James P. Manzi

While the software company Lotus Development Corporation was founded by Mitch Kapor, it was James Manzi who built it into a prized billion-dollar firm. Manzi was a native New Yorker whose father was a dentist in Yonkers. Preferring a good story to a good crown, Manzi chose to study the classics at Colgate University, graduating in 1973. His first job was as a $140-a-week newspaper reporter in Port Chester, New York, but after several years he became disillusioned when asked to interview the parents of someone who had committed suicide. Manzi went back to school and earned a masters in economics from Tufts University in 1979. Next stop: McKinsey & Company where he was a consultant from 1979 to 1983.

In 1982 Manzi was consulting for Lotus and loved the excitement surrounding the start-up so much that he joined the company in 1983 as vice president of marketing and sales. He then became president in 1984, adding the titles of CEO in 1986 (Kapor left in 1986) and chairman in 1989. Not long into his tenure, Manzi earned a reputation as a tough boss. "I expect results from everyone who works at Lotus. If that makes me an SOB, then fine," he said. Certainly, battles with software giants like Bill Gates can test one's temperament. But he liked having fun, too, dressing up as Aretha Franklin at the company's 10th birthday party and lip-synching "Respect."

In his first nine years with the company he grew revenue from $156 million to $1 billion with such hits as Lotus 1-2-3 and Lotus Notes. But in 1995 IBM made a hostile takeover bid for Lotus. Not wanting to lose control of his baby, Manzi searched for a white knight, including Oracle and Hewlett-Packard, but none wanted to vie with the deep pockets of IBM, which had offered $3.52 billion. Manzi was to stay on as CEO of Lotus and as a senior vice president of IBM, but after three months he resigned. In *Beyond Strategy: A View from the Top,* Manzi provides a glimpse of how he created a company that would so attract IBM's attention. One key: He recognized that "information has moved from being a stock item to being a flow item."

# Beyond Strategy: A View from the Top
*James P. Manzi*

S trategy at Lotus is about constant battling and getting a grip on changes that are going on in our company or the marketplace. Constant vigilance is required. In the past 10 years, we have all experienced that whatever we are doing is harder to do now than it once was, largely because of the megaforces at work in the business world. The globalization of markets is driven in part by the technology industry; the creation of the global marketplace is as much a result of the invention of the microprocessor and increased telecommunications speed as it is anything else. Those twin forces—global markets and new, rapidly changing technology—are making all our lives much more complicated.

For years, people have said that information technology plays a key role in the strategy of the organization and that we should think of information as a strategic asset. Not only has the role of information technology changed, but also what you are able to do with it and how it will impact industries and companies. This is what Lotus is all about.

Lotus is largely built around personal computers being grouped into small-, medium- and large-scale networks, new communications technology, and particularly a new class of software for collaborative computing software known as "groupware." As a result, information technology is moving from what was the back office—the transaction processing operation—to the front lines of the organization. It is no longer going to be used just for counting money in the transaction shop, but also for making money or changing the way you compete. No one in management can afford to ignore what information technology is doing to markets and the opportunities it provides.

## REDUCING CYCLE TIME

The hot buzz in the business press is around cycle time reduction and speeding up time to market. There has been a change in the rate of change. In the early 1970s, market cycles were between three and seven years at a minimum. But now, those cycles have shrunk to the point where 12 to 18 months is often the length of the window of opportunity. The idea that this compression exists is driving much of what goes on in the marketplace; and it will also feed back into the discussion of the importance of information technology. Time-based competition is not a vehicle for strategy; rather, it is potentially an ingredient in formulating a strategy in differentiation and in defining a different value proposition in the marketplace.

---

The creation of the global marketplace is as much a result of the invention of the microprocessor and increased telecommunications speed as it is anything else.

---

About four years ago, whenever Lotus shipped a product in the United States, it took 12 to 15 months to fully translate and feature the same product in the Japanese market. But through new technology, we have been able to cut that cycle. In June, we shipped a new version of our spreadsheet in the United States, and two weeks later, we shipped it simultaneously in Japanese and four other major languages around the world. The opportunity there was to compete for a different class of customers that wants to have synchronized versions in all their product subsidiaries around the world. We also wanted to compete more aggressively in the Japanese market.

---

Information technology is moving from what was the back office—the transaction processing operation—to the front lines of the organization.

---

About 10 years ago, one of the founders of Intel invented Moore's Law, which essentially predicted that the rate of growth in processing power of microprocessors would double every 18 months. That is pretty much what has happened. The microprocessor has been widely viewed as the miniature miracle that is driving most technological change.

---

Time-based competition is not a vehicle for strategy; rather, it is potentially an ingredient in formulating a strategy in differentiation and in defining a different value proposition in the marketplace.

---

Even more interestingly, the rate of growth in bandwidth (a measure of how much information and data you can send down a pipe) is now growing faster for the first time than the rate of growth of microprocessors. These twin forces are what is reshaping the business world and will do the same to education, entertainment and other areas.

---

The traditional, hierarchical organization, which was really a construct for the vertical processing of information within and between organizations, is now too slow, too inflexible, and too inward-looking.

---

One result of this growth spurt is the attempt by businesses to position themselves to take advantage of a powerful information flow that has been unleashed by microprocessors and bandwidth. In a sense, over the last 10 years, information has moved from being a stock item to being a flow item. The traditional, hierarchical organization, which was really a construct for the vertical processing of information within and between organizations, is now too slow, too inflexible, and too inward-looking. Businesses are looking to new structures to more effectively mobilize their knowledge, their information and their expertise, both internally and externally. The key point is that nonhierarchical organizations are being created, which means that they will depend on new forms of communications technology to do what the old, hierarchical structure used to do.

## KNOWLEDGE IS KEY

Increased specialization in everything that is going on in the world is largely a function of information volume. There is so much information out there that specialization is required. It is demanded by the doubling of information every six years. Shorter cycle times, new technologies and the resulting increase in specialization is making everybody in every industry rethink what is inside and outside of their company, what their strategy should be, and what their point of differentiation is. We are now contending with all these forces.

---

Mobilizing the intellectual capital of the company is the critical ingredient for going forward.

---

Specialization poses a unique problem to management. How do you coordinate all of that unique knowledge and specialized expertise that is scattered across your organization, when one group of experts is geographically or organizationally dispersed from another group of experts, when the coordination that was traditionally supplied by hierarchies is no longer available because of the information volume or the information specialization? On the one hand, companies must deal with increased specialization, but on the other hand, increased information volume and information flow make it even more difficult to achieve differentiation in the marketplace. The key is making that knowledge available internally, accessing remote or customer sources of information or expertise, and increasing the mobility and velocity of the information or knowledge within your company.

## LOOKING TO THE FUTURE

As we go forward, fewer and fewer companies are going to want to compete solely on the basis of cost. The lesson in our industry is it's better to compete on value because cost-based strategies in the future are likely to be much more inwardly focused. You will be thinking much more about your own systems and missing the opportunity to compete in the marketplace, particularly as market cycles get increasingly shorter and the need to be externally focused increases.

Mobilizing the intellectual capital of the company is the critical ingredient for going forward. It is changing the way companies think about their business and how they relate to their customers. Customers can help themselves to everything we know about our technology and every technology in the marketplace. It is defining a new way of working with customers that both we and customers find rewarding.

# PART VI

# The Drive for Quality and Profits

Quality is the most important factor to consumers when it comes to judging a company. In The Conference Board's 1999 research report, *Consumer Expectations on the Social Accountability of Business*, 54.6 percent of the responding consumers said "brand quality, image/reputation" was the most important component in evaluating a company and its products. Yet, in The Conference Board's 1999 CEO survey, 48 percent of the responding CEOs tagged downward pressure on prices as one of their top three marketplace concerns. So, how does a company resolve the seeming conflict of offering higher quality at a lower price? Joseph Juran, the guru whose name is synonymous with quality, explains that one of the dictionary "definitions of quality is 'freedom from trouble, from errors, from defects, from redoing, from field failures.' This is a cost-oriented definition; the more trouble you have, the more it costs your organization." The message couldn't be clearer: Investment in quality processes ultimately reduces costs that can be passed on to the consumer. But still, CEOs find that their people resist quality initiatives; Michael Bonsignore, CEO of Honeywell, writes that "leading a large organization is like trying to turn a supertanker—up on the bridge, you sometimes wonder if the ship's wheel is connected to anything." His solution to driving the quality message home is to play both head coach and cheerleader, as well as to create a vision that centers on delighting customers. The authors in this section provide concrete examples for improving quality and for the more arduous task of rallying the troops around quality.

# JOSEPH M. JURAN

The name Juran is synonymous with quality; no other management expert has influenced the drive for quality on the factory floor like Joseph Juran, who has been consulting companies and governments since 1945. Quality is not a word one would use to describe Juran's childhood in Rumania, where he was born. His father, a shoemaker, left for the United States in 1909 and it was three years before he saved enough money to bring the rest of the family over. That year Juran sold newspapers, his first of many jobs to help the family. He excelled at math and at age 11 he was hired as a bookkeeper for an icehouse. Homelife improved when his father became a bootlegger in 1919, and the next year Juran entered the electrical engineering program at the University of Minnesota.

After graduating Juran took a job with Western Electric in what the company called the Inspection Branch at the Hawthorne Works factory in Chicago. The factory made equipment for AT&T and was considered a working laboratory in dealing with issues faced by large industrial organization. Juran learned early on that quality does not cost the company money, failure does: "If things fail internally, it costs the company. If they fail externally, it also costs the customer. In these cases, quality costs less." As he moved up the corporate ladder, however, his management skills were less than satisfactory and he later admitted, "When I got to be manager, starting to have power . . . I started getting even with the world."

During World War II he took a leave of absence from Western Electric to help the federal government set up the Lend-Lease Program, which funneled supplies to allies. During that period he realized that he could go no further within a corporate structure, so Juran struck out on his own in 1945. By the early 1950s he was lecturing around the world and was the preeminent voice on quality. Age 90 found him still active as the chairman emeritus of The Juran Institute. He is still amazed by companies that develop "quality initiatives without clarifying the meaning of the word quality," and in *Strategies for World-Class Quality,* he provides his own definition for the word.

# Strategies for World-Class Quality
## *Joseph M. Juran*

**I**n recent years, winners of
the Baldrige Award have achieved stunning results in many
activities. This proves that achieving world-class quality is
feasible in American culture. We should not attempt to change
our culture but build on it, as these winners have done.

## What Is Quality?

I am dismayed, however, at the number of companies that
are developing quality initiatives without clarifying the
meaning of the word quality. Two of the many dictionary
definitions of "quality" should concern managers. One is
"oriented to income." Here, quality means those features of a
product or service that make customers willing to choose it
rather than a competitor's. This generates income.

The second definition of quality is "freedom from trouble, from errors, from defects, from redoing, from field failures." This is a cost-oriented definition: the more trouble you
have, the more it costs your organization. If trouble occurs in
the purchaser's organization during use, it also costs them.
This affects your company's income because the user is less

willing to buy that product or service again even though it may have wonderful features.

Many managers debate whether or not higher quality costs more. Two managers discussing quality might not understand each other if one is thinking of the first definition of quality and the other is thinking of the second. Of course, they are going to reach different conclusions.

## NOT A DIFFERENT WAY OF DOING BUSINESS

Until the 1980s, most CEOs and senior officers avoided the issue of quality, leaving it strictly to the quality manager. Then the crisis appeared, drawing the CEO into the arena of quality. This required quality managers to spend time explaining basic principles to senior executives. Here, an analogy with finance is useful.

---

Too many top executives have said the right words but have not taken any action themselves; that's cheerleading, not leading.

---

Financial managers make use of three processes to manage: financial planning (creating a budget), financial control (assuring that goals are being met), and financial improvement. We can explain to managers that they can manage quality with the same three managerial processes, changing the names to quality planning, quality control and quality improvement. An executive is halfway there if he or she is able to use the same conceptual approach in managing for quality that was always used in managing for finance.

It is very important for senior executives to understand their non-delegable roles in the quality process. You cannot demand upper managers to be committed or involved. We have to establish what they must do personally. These expectations include:

- personally serving on the quality council, which signals that quality has high priority in the company;
- having the last word in establishing the quality goals and providing the needed resources;
- personally conducting reviews of progress; and
- giving recognition publicly for work well done.

In addition, senior executives must revise the reward system—the basic contract between the employee and the company—which influences progress at the annual rating. It must be changed because every time we assign somebody to a project team we are adding to his or her workload and function. If the reward system is not changed, it sends a signal to the rest of the organization that nothing has really changed.

Upper managers should understand what they are asking their people to do. It is useful for them to serve on some quality improvement teams to get firsthand experience. True leadership requires setting an example. Too many top executives have said the right words but have not taken any action themselves; that's cheerleading, not leading.

## SETTING QUALITY GOALS

Quality improvement should be tackled first when undertaking a quality initiative. For example, in Company A, quality is defined in terms of income. The firm is a leader in quality, getting better every year, and is profitable. However, a competitor is improving at an alarmingly rapid rate, and soon Company A will be in trouble. If you want to be in the quality vanguard, your rate of improvement must be at least equal to that of your most aggressive competitor.

In U.S. companies, we find a striking difference in the success of achieving the two kinds of quality. In the case of generating new features and products, U.S. companies are well structured. They often have a committee that oversees decision making for funding products, that reviews progress periodically and that decides whether to continue funding, abort or change direction. A separate, funded department works full time to provide the technology. Some companies may not do this well, but at least the right structure is in place.

By contrast, most business plans fail to include goals or guidelines to reduce errors, trouble or redoings; there is usually no infrastructure for this. Responsibility is vague and improvement voluntary, despite the fact that wastes are huge. This must change. The stakes are as large in this area of quality improvement as they are in sales.

TQM cannot be understood unless you identify the actions and decisions that differ from the way you are currently working. TQM is a collection of actions. Setting up the management councils can aid in identifying the required actions. The next step is to include quality goals in the business plan. Here we can take a lesson from the finance area because total financial management has existed for a long time.

---

Most business plans fail to include goals or guidelines to reduce errors, trouble or redoings. . . . Responsibility is vague and improvement voluntary, despite the fact that wastes are huge.

---

One type of quality goal which should be included in the business plan is hurdles for improving product performance. Companies should know how well products meet customer needs, if the company is performing better than competitors. Specific goals should be established, such as to reduce field failures by 50 percent in the next three years, improve the reliability of order fulfillment, or to bring down invoicing errors by a specific amount. These goals are basically a wish list, however, if we do not identify what needs to be done in order to meet those goals, who is going to take action, and what resources are needed.

Setting corporate quality goals optimizes company performance rather than departmental performance. However, responsibility for attaining these goals rests within the business units. For example, if we set a goal to reduce field failures, we may allocate that goal to particular business units. In the end, teams or sometimes individuals are ultimately responsible for reaching the goals.

A quality improvement process is a series of steps that involves setting up a presiding group—a quality council. This temporary group is needed in order to get moving. It typically comprises the CEO's immediate assistants. They address the quality agenda on a regular basis. Quality improvement should be mandatory, not voluntary. It is not an addition to the regular job; it becomes a part of the regular job. Responsibility has to be set out formally and adequate resources must be provided.

Many companies use facilitators trained in the improvement process to help cross-functional teams with their first few projects. The need for such facilitators, however, diminishes as people gain experience in making improvements.

## THE ROLE OF EMPLOYEES

Employee apprehension often relates to the costs side. For many people, reducing errors and subsequent redoings means losing jobs. They are correct in that assumption; those whose work consists of fixing errors may well find themselves unemployed. If we do not address these fears, rumors take over and make matters worse.

Part of what the world-class companies have done is to include empowerment of the work force. Since the beginning of the 1900s, the Taylor system of separating planning from execution has dominated U.S. business. This method had its day, enabling the United States to become the world leader in productivity. But, at the same time, it damaged human relations and quality. It is now obsolete because the premise on which it was based—assuming low levels of employee education—is no longer valid. Today, we are in a position to far outstrip the successes of the past by making use of a largely underemployed work force. Most people have much more education, creativity and experience than they are given credit for.

---

For many people, reducing errors and subsequent redoings means losing jobs. They are correct in that assumption; those whose work consists of fixing errors may well find themselves unemployed.

---

One way to more fully utilize the work force is to make individuals completely responsible for their jobs. Workers should know what they are supposed to do, if they are doing it, and if they are not performing. Self-control takes a big load off managers and supervisors. There are many benefits from this practice: A shorter feedback loop and a sense of ownership are but two. We know of no better way to expose quality problems and get them fixed than actually involving the employee. This empowerment process, particularly the use of self-supervising teams, is the wave of the future.

We have done a lot of training in the past two decades, most of it misdirected. Training should be oriented primarily at changing behavior. For example, if we want to teach someone quality improvement, we should not start by training them in the tools and then leaving them on their own.

Instead, we should assign them to a team which is given an improvement project. This way, they learn by job-related experience and will not forget. Furthermore, they will have the exhilaration of being on a winning team and enjoy both self-respect and the respect of others.

---

The quality journey will take years because there is a great deal of cultural resistance and skepticism.

---

## A LOOK TO THE FUTURE

In the future, quality departments will have to pay more attention to achieving concrete business goals. The role of the quality manager will be much more like that of the financial controller: to help the council formulate the quality goals, supply information on progress, and provide a basis for quality audits.

The quality journey will take years because there is a great deal of cultural resistance and skepticism. It takes time to establish a strategy and begin to implement it. Implementation should be done at pilot sites and, if successful, the results should become the means of convincing others of the benefits of quality.

Companies that have achieved world-class quality have taken at least six years to get there. Understand, too, that there is a price to be paid. The new procedures will increase the workload and upset the organization. Know at the outset that you will be stirring up trouble.

# JON C. MADONNA

When he served as chairman and CEO of the venerable consulting firm KPMG Peat Marwick, Jon Madonna saw his share of client problems and became an expert on quality by observing and helping to fix others' follies. After college and serving in the army, Madonna went to work for KPMG in 1968. He was elected partner in 1976 and eventually became the managing partner of the San Francisco Bay area practice. In 1987 he was elected to the board of directors and in 1990 he became the chairman and CEO of KPMG's U.S. operations. Madonna added the titles of chairman and CEO for KPMG worldwide five years later.

During his tenure, he focused on transforming KPMG from a classic accounting firm to a global consulting powerhouse, and in the process, he hung his hat on giving the customer quality.

According to Madonna, little attention was paid to quality in the consulting industry until the mid-1980s when global competition became fierce: "We felt during the sixties and seventies, as we saw foreign competition coming in, that quality was not what it was all about. What it was about was price, we said. If we could draw the cost down, that would make us successful." Not until Baldrige Award–winner Motorola insisted that all of the company's vendors (which included KPMG) apply the Baldrige principles to their own company, did Madonna focus on quality. For example, KPMG started a client survey process, unique then but commonplace now.

Changing KPMG's culture required a grassroots movement. He said that first "we learned that leaders cannot dictate quality. It cannot be a top down program; it's got to be a grass roots, bottom up program." Madonna, who retired in 1996 when his term as chairman and CEO expired (and is now president and CEO of Carlson Wagonlit Travel), warns that if you don't monitor quality, you don't hear about problems until the customer is walking out the door. Needless to say, quality is the major theme in *Measure, Monitor and Improve Quality*. Madonna relates his experience at KPMG and concludes that quality "rests on teamwork and on the 'little things.' "

# Measure, Monitor and Improve Quality

*Jon C. Madonna*

The quality movement is an issue not only in the United States, but worldwide, and one by which we have all been touched. It has become a global concern, and the reason is that in business today, we are going through a period of unprecedented change.

On the subject of quality and why it has become so crucial to the issue of competitiveness, three observations stand out in my mind from business travels all over the world. My first observation is that we now live in a world where we do not have guarantees. In the 1960s, 1970s and 1980s, many things seemed obvious and even predictable to us. But today, every morning when we pick up *The Wall Street Journal,* some company is going through streamlining or rightsizing, or is merging or going bankrupt. Just a few years ago we would have said to ourselves, "*That* company should certainly do well."

My second observation is that we are dealing with a true global economy. Last week I heard economist John Naisbitt speak about the global marketplace and how we're now all competing with each other, not in a domestic world but everywhere in the world. One of John's examples was McDonald's Corporation, which is about as American as you can get; yet its largest, most successful store is in

Moscow. Before leaving for Japan recently, I visited one of our clients in New Jersey—Minolta Corp., a Japanese company. While there, I talked to both Japanese and Americans. Minolta is being run as an American company, but it is clearly a Japanese company. Two days later, I was in Tokyo meeting with Motorola Inc., a great example of the few success stories of American companies in Japan. Motorola has been so successful in Japan because there they have operated essentially as a Japanese company. We are dealing in an environment today where our competitors are not next door but are around the world, and the best ones are taking on the motto, "When in Rome, Do as the Romans Do."

The third observation deals not only with the amount of change, but also the speed of change. People predicted the events in the Soviet Union and in Eastern Europe, but no one predicted that these events would take place so rapidly. The speed and magnitude of change are clearly affecting the business world, and that has a great impact on our economies.

Putting these three elements together, one can say that we are competing in a marketplace that is unprecedented in history; that competition has driven us to the total quality movement.

---

We are dealing in an environment today where our competitors are not next door but are around the world, and the best ones are taking on the motto, "When in Rome, Do as the Romans Do."

---

During the 1960s and 1970s, as we saw foreign competition coming in, we felt that quality was not "what it was all about." What it was all about was price, we thought, and if we could drive costs down, we would be successful. So in the United States, quality lagged. But we woke up to the fact that good quality was ultimately cheaper, more efficient, and was what our consumers wanted. That pushed us into the total quality movement during the 1980s, when I believe it really started.

A recently issued Congressional report said that the service sector has lagged and has not been as quick to get on the quality bandwagon as manufacturers. Quality is as important for a service firm as it is for a manufacturing enterprise; still, it is not surprising that the service sector is not keeping pace. As professionals, we have always believed that the only thing that mattered was the product—that is, the operation performed by the surgeon or the report issued by the accountant. What mattered was the product that consumers received, not the process of getting it to them. We have learned by now that the consumer is becoming much more demanding, and the process is every bit as important as the product.

Today, our clients want both a good process and a good product. Professionals are not yet as concerned as they could be about deadlines, about responsiveness, about what the customer thinks. Those are exactly the issues that we are trying to attack through our quality program.

## GOOD AND GETTING BETTER

Our quality program started three years ago and was designed to make service better for our clients. We call it the Constant Improvement Program, because although our product was already good, there were many elements that we could continuously improve. Today it has three major components, the first of which is our product. We have always taken great pride in that, and it is as important today as it has ever been.

The second is our clients. We realize that if we're going to have a first-class firm and a first-class quality product, we should be quite concerned about the clients we're dealing with. In fact, we have taken a hard look at our evaluation standards for new and current clients and have actually walked away from some clients over the past year. That is very different from the way we looked at the world in the 1970s and 1980s.

---

We asked each of our clients their opinion on how we were providing service. In short, we asked them to rate us, and it has caused a major change in the way we look at the world.

---

Finally, the most important part of our quality program is service: the process of getting our product to our client. Or to put it another way, how we deliver. There are two major parts to that. First, in each of our 139 operating offices we have formed Quality Councils so that everyone — from our administrative staff to our most senior partner — can meet on a regular basis to talk about how to become more efficient and responsive in serving our clients.

The second and more important part started three years ago, when we asked each of our clients their opinion on how we were providing service. In short, we asked them to rate us, and it has caused a major change in the way we look at the world.

We asked our clients to rate us on a scale of 1 to 10, with 10 being best; we received 12,000 responses. A year ago, our rating was 8.2; this year it was 8.4. Another question asked of our clients is, "Are we exceeding or at least meeting your expectations?" A year ago, 94.9 percent said that we were meeting or exceeding them. This year, we gained an entire percentage point — something we're very proud of. The program has had a great impact on our people and on our organization in how we see our clients.

We have learned some important lessons. For one thing, our quality program has resulted in a major change in behavior. One requirement for that change is leadership. We've learned that as leaders we cannot dictate quality; it cannot be a top-down program but rather a grassroots, bottom-up process. But if we as leaders don't set the standard, don't provide the enthusiasm for the program, don't constantly show that it is being invoked and that we're measuring it, we won't have a quality program because it is much easier for employees to conduct business as usual. So we must keep the pressure on.

But the real strength comes from empowering the people. When we empowered our people and said, "Take pride in what you're doing and try to do a better job in serving your clients," that's when the program really took off and became successful. However, we are still learning what does and doesn't work. The more you learn about quality, the more you feel you need to learn.

## THE SINGLES AND DOUBLES

The bottom line in our experience is that quality rests on teamwork and on the "little things." It is especially true today in this tough economy in which people want us to hit home runs. They are constantly looking for a cure-all for problems in the economy.

---

We've learned that as leaders we cannot dictate quality; it cannot be a top-down program but rather a grassroots, bottom-up process.

---

But it is not home runs that lead to winning; it's the singles and doubles. October is World Series time, and this year marked the 40th anniversary of Bobby Thompson's "shot heard 'round the world"—his home run that gave the New

York Giants the National League pennant. Ever since, people have been talking about that one home run as the hit that won the pennant. But that one home run by Bobby Thompson didn't create the "miracle of Coogan's Bluff" that brought the Giants from 13.5 games back in mid-August. There were a lot of singles and doubles every day by the whole team that brought the Giants from mediocrity to excellence. It is that need to hit singles and doubles every day that is the essence of a corporate quality improvement program.

---

It is not home runs that lead to winning; it's the singles and doubles.

---

Here are eight reasons it's important to strive to be better every day in the service business:

1. It costs four times as much to gain a new account as to keep one.
2. Premium profits come from the most satisfied accounts.
3. For each complaint you hear, there are 50 you don't hear.
4. Most clients don't like to complain; many staff members don't pass along problems.
5. If you don't monitor clients' satisfaction, you may find out about their dissatisfaction as they walk out the door.
6. Clients expect to have problems; they become dissatisfied only when problems go unrecognized and unresolved.
7. Negative comments from dissatisfied clients outnumber positive referrals by more than four to one.
8. Clients evaluate your technical competence by your service performance.

Every organization today needs some type of constant improvement program. Whereas a year ago I thought that such a program was designed to make us better and more profitable, I now believe that every organization needs a quality program just to stay on the playing field. A successful program is one where both the leaders and all employees are involved. The leaders lead, not manage, and the people are empowered to make it happen.

In 1997, Peat Marwick will be 100 years old. Our goal for 1997 is to be the best professional service firm in the entire world. The way we are going to measure that is by how our clients feel about us. Our ultimate goal, in terms of survey responses, is to have 100 percent client satisfaction.

# PAUL A. ALLAIRE

Xerox is a high-profile company, forever under the watchful eye of consumers and business analysts alike. Today the company's leader is Paul A. Allaire who has his work cut out for him in the Digital Age as copiers, printers, scanners, facsimile machines, and even document storage products blend together. Allaire earned an electrical engineering degree from Worcester Polytechnical Institute and a masters from Carnegie-Mellon University in 1966. That year he joined Xerox as a financial analyst. In 1986 he was named president, adding the titles of CEO in 1990 and chairman in 1991.

In the mid-1980s Xerox was a lumbering copier giant with products of questionable quality. "The importance of quality was brought home to Xerox in the early '80s," Allaire reflected. "To put it mildly, Xerox was in deep trouble. Foreign competition had cut our market share in half." Allaire initiated several programs to improve quality and to make the company leaner and more profitable. At the start of his tenure he went outside the firm to replace three of his top eight executives, and then eliminated tens of thousands of jobs. To those who survived the cuts, he preached TQM—Total Quality Management. The company won the Baldrige Award for Quality in 1989. Allaire explained, "We did not go into the Baldrige Award expecting to win. In fact, the reason we went after it was to have outside, independent confirmation of where we were good and where we were weak."

The company has even taken the drive for quality to their suppliers: "We will help our suppliers develop quality processes and we will work with them so we can validate their process for providing us a product that gives us the quality we need." Allaire concludes that "quality improvement is a race without a finish line." In *Leadership through Quality at Xerox,* Allaire points to six elements needed for the race: "Tools and processes; reward and recognition; communications; training; employee involvement and empowerment; and senior management behavior."

# Leadership through Quality
# at Xerox
## *Paul A. Allaire*

Xerox embarked on the quality journey for its survival: After a few amiable decades of tremendous growth and expansion, we were faced with intense competition in the shape of some formidable U.S. and Japanese competitors. Once we entered this environment, we started to engage in competitive benchmarking to discover who the competitors were and what they really focused on.

We went through a familiar process: The first reaction to competition is denial. We looked at the Japanese at the low end of the market and didn't really believe they were that good or capable. But we started to realize they were selling products at what it cost us to manufacture them at that end of the market.

Our reaction to this was that their product couldn't be very good. We were wrong again. We then thought they probably weren't making any profit selling products so cheaply, but we were wrong once more. Finally, we faced the truth: We had a real competitive threat which we had to focus on. We realized it was taking us twice as long to develop new products and that our design costs were about three times as high as the Japanese companies'. We had some administrative difficulties in the form of numerous billing errors. Our service was not quite up to the standard of some of our U.S. competitors, and our customers noticed it.

---

### The first reaction to competition is denial.

---

These problems were reflected in our results: Our market share started to slip significantly and our profitability was substantially reduced. In the early 1980s, our return on assets was reduced to less than 8 percent. Survival was at stake; we realized we had to change dramatically from top to bottom: the way we managed and worked, our reward and recognition systems, the way we communicated, and our entire corporate culture.

Fuji Xerox, our joint venture in Japan, facing some of the same competition, had implemented a quality management approach and had started to turn their businesses around. So we decided to follow a similar approach learned from our Japanese partners, adapted to our culture. We implemented a strategy we call Leadership Through Quality, which has six elements:

- tools and processes,
- reward and recognition,
- communications,
- training,
- employee involvement and empowerment, and
- senior management behavior.

The entire corporation focused on meeting customer requirements. We defined this as our quality process and, in essence, made it the job of every Xerox employee. We have used this process for nearly eight years, and the result has been clear and gratifying: Quality works.

# THE RESULTS

Customer satisfaction has improved significantly and currently is rated at 90 percent or more. Our customers now rate Xerox number one in the industry in product reliability and service. Independent agencies like Dataquest have rated our products number one, in five out of six of our market segments. Buyers Laboratory, an office products testing lab, just named our product line the best in the industry. We have substantially improved the product, reduced our average manufacturing costs by over 20 percent despite inflation, reduced the amount of time it takes to bring a new product to market by nearly 60 percent, corrected our billing errors by a factor of 10, and increased our return on assets from 8 percent to 14 percent.

---

Senior management must embody the quality strategy; this can't be delegated to another employee or relegated to a staff function.

---

We believe we are the first company in an industry targeted by the Japanese to regain market share. In addition to achieving the hard results in profitability and customer satisfaction, we also feel the "soft" results—those concerning people and corporate culture—are equally impressive and probably the true reasons for our success.

What has quality really meant to us? I believe the following answer this question:

- We are now truly customer-focused. It is a reality, not a slogan.
- We have substantially improved our achievement of objectives from the top down and, therefore, have clarified the corporation's direction.

- We have involved all our people in quality and in the subsequent achievement of our business objectives.
- We have substantially improved our business and work processes; they are now controlled and customer-oriented.
- We have a common language with which to work.
- We use data and facts more precisely to get at the root of issues and to rectify problems instead of symptoms.
- We've greatly increased our ability to learn from our failures as well as our successes.

## FROM THE TOP DOWN

The point is that this process is not easy and doesn't happen overnight; it depends on senior management's behavior and leadership. Leadership from the top is absolutely essential and takes three principal forms.

First, senior management must embody the quality strategy; this can't be delegated to another employee or relegated to a staff function: Quality is in the line, by the line. It must start at the very top of the corporation. We spend a lot of time benchmarking companies not only in Japan but also throughout the United States, and the common denominator among companies who have successfully implemented a TQM approach is a deep understanding and commitment to quality among the company leaders.

---

Quality improvement is a continuous, never-ending battle to meet increasingly tough expectations and competition.

---

Second, senior management must lead by example; commitment must be active as well as theoretical. Quality is so deeply integrated in our company that senior management spends all of its time on it. It's the way we manage. This is necessary because people look for signals from the top. If the signals aren't there, then quality has no chance. Although this is tough for most of us who are used to being above the fray, the CEO particularly must be a role model.

Third, senior management must make it happen. It starts with a vision of what you want to accomplish, coupled with the belief that quality can help get you there. At Xerox, we knew where we were headed, we had a strong belief—a vision—and we knew quality was a key to success. This enabled us to go forward.

Quality improvement is a continuous, never-ending battle to meet increasingly tough expectations and competition. Customers are more demanding; no matter how good your service or product, they expect you to do better. Quality has become the key force driving business. It enabled Xerox to survive the 1980s and, in my view, will allow us to be truly successful in the 1990s.

# MICHAEL R. BONSIGNORE

In the wake of Honeywell's agreed 1999 merger with AlliedSignal to create one of the largest defense contractors in the country and AlliedSignal CEO Lawrence Bossidy's retirement in 2000, Honeywell CEO Michael Bonsignore has his work cut out. But he is more than qualified.

Bonsignore, whose father was an army surgeon, considers himself an army brat who learned to adapt. "The best training I had was being an army brat and the leadership training at the Naval Academy," he said. He joined Honeywell in 1969 and 13 years later was named president of European operations. Bonsignore, who speaks French, Italian, and Spanish, reflected, "Running Honeywell Europe was from a unique perspective like running a miniature Honeywell. All the lines of business were there, all the policies and procedures, the tax issues, human-resource issues, and cross-border operations."

Bonsignore was named COO in 1990 and CEO and chairman in 1993. One of his tenets is to make sure he's accessible: "Making proclamations isn't good enough anymore. CEOs must be perceived as real people." He has spent most of his tenure streamlining operations and attempting to boost profits, not an easy task considering that Honeywell's core business is in the mature industry of controls for heating and air conditioning. Part of his strategy has been to divest money losers and to acquire new companies to fuel growth; for example, in his first five years at the helm they purchased some 50 companies in Europe alone.

Whether it be a computer room that needs to remain at a certain temperature or a satellite system, Bonsignore recognizes that quality is crucial because a breakdown spells disaster. He decided one way to improve quality is to tie compensation to it. In 1997 he said, "More than 50 percent of U.S. employees— including those at the factory-floor level—are now under some type of pay-at-risk program that ties pay increases to value creation, product cost, working capital, or profit." Bonsignore shows how to jump the hurdles on the road to quality in *The Quality Experience at Honeywell.*

# The Quality Experience at Honeywell

*Michael R. Bonsignore*

Honeywell is the world leader in control technology. Honeywell temperature controls are in more than 100 million homes and 5 million buildings worldwide. Its industrial process controls are used by 24 of the world's 25 largest oil refiners, 7 of the top 10 pulp and paper companies, and 15 of the 20 largest chemical companies. Honeywell flight management controls are found on board virtually every aircraft.

In the mid-1980s, however, Honeywell was not this visible or this stable. In order to focus on its controls competence, the company underwent major divestitures, spin-offs, acquisitions, and consolidations. These actions reduced staff from 94,000 in 1985 to 52,000 by 1993. Sales hovered around $6 billion. Increased revenue growth was imperative, but we could not grow the company with the existing culture. Nor could we be satisfied with financial performance that still trailed the best among our peer companies. We had to demonstrate Honeywell's intrinsic value at the bottom line.

## THE QUALITY MOVEMENT BEGINS

Honeywell began to work toward its goals with a guiding framework—total quality management (TQM). When I

209

became CEO in 1993, I knew I had to be both head coach and cheerleader in the quality arena. But leading a large organization is like trying to turn a supertanker—up on the bridge, you sometimes wonder if the ship's wheel is connected to anything. We can make sure that the wheel is in fact connected to the rudder and that the entire crew knows what is expected of them if we do not stray from the quality framework.

The tools of quality include vision, mission, and values; continuous learning; performance improvement processes; recognition and feedback; and compensation and rewards. These five points are the primary tools that connect the CEO's office to the rest of the organization.

*Vision, Mission, and Values*
Our vision is to delight our customers; achieve undisputed global leadership in control; grow profitably; and reach our full potential for our customers, investors, employees, and communities. Delighting customers has been my personal crusade; it is not enough to just satisfy them anymore. That gives everyone a simple, personal benchmark that connects to the company's larger goals (see Exhibit 1).

---

Leading a large organization is like trying to turn a supertanker—up on the bridge, you sometimes wonder if the ship's wheel is connected to anything.

---

Our mission is to create value for shareholders through leadership in advanced control solutions that help customers achieve their goals. Even as the operating priorities of the business inevitably change, people at Honeywell see this mission as constant. But getting the message to sink in takes repetition, unfailing consistency, and a commitment to removing

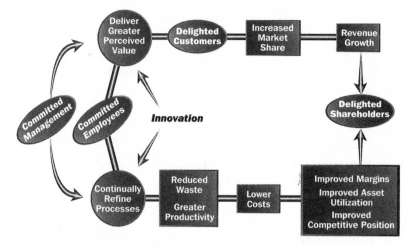

**EXHIBIT 1:** Value Creation — What a Business Aims to Achieve
Source: *Baldrige for the Baffled*, Honeywell Inc., 1996.

barriers. Most of all, it takes leaders who uphold the vision, mission, and values by their daily actions. Few leaders could have reached the upper levels of management without a thorough grounding in marketing or finance. Until recently, understanding quality was not part of most executive development plans. We do not have to be quality experts, but we cannot run a company if we are quality illiterates. And we cannot expect our operations to apply TQM principles if we are not doing the same.

*Continuous Learning*
Honeywell has taken numerous initiatives to train its employees. Each corporate employee receives five days of quality training. We have benchmarked work products and processes both inside and outside the company. All functional groups and many cross-functional teams hold sessions to remove non-value-added work. For example, we have streamlined our billing paperwork and reporting requirements, which will save us about $1 million per year. Last

year, total productivity savings at our corporate headquarters exceeded $3 million. This kind of improvement could not have happened without training. Honeywell's training budgets will not be cut when profit-and-loss pressures occur because training is an investment in improvement, not a cost.

---

Delighting customers has been my personal crusade; it is not enough to just satisfy them anymore.

---

Every February, we hold a two-and-a-half-day business retreat that brings together all our senior managers. We devote one day to quality-related matters. This year's agenda included an annual report on quality, a series of workshops on best practices from Honeywell operations worldwide, and a presentation by C.K. Prahalad on creating value through global leadership.

*Performance Improvement Processes*

The annual management meeting sets the leadership tone, but how do we push that tone deeper into the organization? Perhaps our most important means for institutionalizing a quality culture is the Honeywell Quality Value (HQV). Based on the Baldrige criteria, this process provides an annual benchmark for each operation. Each business assesses its current performance and develops a road map for future improvement.

The HQV serves as a:

- value-creating management system;
- way to integrate valid management practices from a variety of sources;
- vehicle to communicate about important issues;
- mechanism for continual improvement; and
- framework for ongoing learning.

*Recognition and Feedback*

Honeywell has a number of techniques to provide recognition: the Delighted Customers Award, which goes to the top-scoring units in the customer satisfaction section of the HQV; the People Award, which is based both on a human resources score and on consistency with Honeywell's values; and the Chairman's Achievement Awards, where employees play a role in recognizing their co-workers.

---

Eighty percent of our employees say that customer requirements drive their work. This embrace of a customer delight ethos is wonderful proof that culture can change.

---

We also have a new tool: the Honeywell Insights survey. Modeled after the HQV and Baldrige criteria, it represents a fundamental shift away from polling employee attitudes. Instead, it asks employees to gauge how well we are doing in keeping with our vision and values, and to identify barriers to their success. Honeywell Insights tracks five core issues: customer focus, business results, leadership, process management, and people.

Eighty percent of our employees say that customer requirements drive their work. This embrace of a customer delight ethos is wonderful proof that culture can change. In terms of business results, employees see a strong commitment to quality in their business, and they receive regular feedback on financial results. That is essential if our employees are to think and act like owners. Employees say they believe that senior management is committed to Honeywell's vision and values. At the same time, they identified weak spots in our cross-functional processes, and they see room for improvement in our teaming effectiveness. Clearly, we can unleash the potential of our people only if we address the barriers they encounter (see box).

*Compensation and Rewards*

Compensation is a powerful way to encourage specific quality objectives and direct people toward certain goals. We have made major changes in our reward systems to align them with our vision. More than 50 percent of our U.S. employees are now under some type of pay-at-risk program that ties pay increases to value creation, product cost, working capital, or profit. We are encouraging increased stock ownership among employees as another way to tie employee interests more closely with those of the shareholder. Today, our employees own 6 percent of Honeywell; our goal is to increase their ownership to 15 percent.

For the past two years, part of senior executive compensation was geared to encourage the creation of world-class customer satisfaction measurement systems. Now, our need is to reinforce long-range planning. So a portion of compensation will reward executives for their total performance over a three-year period.

---

Compensation is a powerful way to encourage specific quality objectives and direct people toward certain goals.

---

## THE PAYOFF

In 1995, sales and orders were up by 11 percent. Earnings per share increased 22 percent. Stock price rose 54 percent. In fact, we ranked first among our 20 peer companies in total shareholder returns. We also won quality awards in four states; awards in the United Kingdom, France, and Australia; and numerous "supplier of the year" awards from customers. We had our third Baldrige site visit, and in 1996 another Honeywell business [will try] for a Baldrige.

## HURDLES ON THE ROAD TO QUALITY

*Thinking we're better than we are.* Honeywell has long been a product and technology leader, but today we compete for customers and investors. We must continually survey them and benchmark against our competition, or we will be overtaken. Those complacent with where they are will not be there for long.

*Whose fault is it?* When quality is not at the desired level, it is tempting to point fingers. Once we adopted the process thinking that comes with a quality mindset, we could see that there are very few bad apples. The bigger problem is "bad barrels," or root causes, which encourage or even compel unproductive behavior.

*This time, we really, really mean it.* To lead a quality process, you have to be committed to quality as a fundamental value. The business world has always been subject to passing management fads that promise new cures. This creates tremendous cynicism and resistance to change because people believe that this, too, shall pass. At Honeywell, we hoisted the quality banner several times before we really got under way. Only when we linked the quality process to customer delight were we finally able to integrate TQM into our culture.

*For whom are we working?* One of the key revelations of a quality process is how much work is unrelated to customer satisfaction. Confusion exists about who the customers really are. Many of Honeywell's products are installed by contractors, sold through distributors, or purchased by original equipment manufacturers. We call all of them customers, but none of them use our products. In reality, they help us deliver products to our true customers—home owners, airline crews, and the people who run commercial and industrial enterprises.

*How do we measure results?* Quality principles can provide the framework for how performance ought to be measured. If we believed that distributors were our customers, then we might measure our quality based only on the things distributors care about: Are products in stock? What are the discounts and payment terms? We have to understand who our real customers are, what they expect, and what they value.

*Don't ask us to do more with less.* Quality improvement initiatives can be controversial because they are seen as something extra—or, worse yet, as a way to pass off cost cuts. For quality to take hold, people have to understand that quality and continuous improvement are a part of their job. At Honeywell, quality provides a guide for evaluating how we allocate resources so they provide greater returns.

*Cooperation in a fragmented world.* How do we run an effective organization while involving as many people as possible in the decision? Our quality model helps Honeywell's stakeholders see the process, what they contribute, and how common goals can be addressed as they work across cultures, languages, and functional disciplines.

We have also turned around our return on expectations internally and externally. Externally, customers, investors, and the media are taking note of the new Honeywell. In fact, we jumped 67 places on Fortune's "Most Admired" list. Internally, we feel a real sense of pride in what we have been able to achieve, and an appetite to improve even more.

After all this, one may wonder how a leadership role in quality differs from leading a business. They really are not different—except that an executive who takes a leadership role in quality will be doing a better job of leading everything.

# PART VII

# Strategic Growth

Growth is the lifeblood of a company, but if not managed effectively, it can just as easily spell doom. Jim Koch, founder of the Boston Beer Company and master brewer of Sam Adams beer, has walked that fine line in guiding his company through explosive growth of 30 to 60 percent annually in their first 12 years. The philosophy he presents in the opening essay is very direct: "If you want to grow, you must officially set goals and then drive the organization backwards from that. Determine what you need to do to get there." Setting aside financial considerations for a moment, the relevant question that then arises is, what are the best criteria for benchmarking nonfinancial goals that will ultimately drive growth and income? In The Conference Board's 1999 research report, *Aligning Strategic Performance Measures and Results*, responding companies listed the following top four strategic measures: customer satisfaction, market share, new product development, and quality. Once the goals for each criterion have been determined, the next key issue is inspiring people to achieve them. A number of authors in this section recommend tying compensation directly to performance. James Kelly, CEO of United Parcel Service, has made sure "employees at all levels have a personal stake in the success of our business." But what about entering new markets, such as developing nations, where concrete goals are difficult to define? Rebecca Mark, chair of Enron International, eschews any attempt to quantify a strategy. "Instead of relying on studies and economic analyses," she writes about a particular project, "we visited everyone who had an opinion to offer." She seeks to grasp a qualitative feel for how to grow the company. Being out in the field, visiting with employees and customers alike, is as important in developing a strategy as putting together numbers back at the office.

Jim Koch, founder and CEO of the Boston Beer Company, has been brewing the award-winning Samuel Adams beer since 1984, and as far as he's concerned, no European import can compare in quality. Before becoming a brewmaster, he worked at the Boston Consulting Group. "When I was a consultant I used to tell people you've only got a business if your product is better or cheaper," he said. He chose to make something better. The company uses the antique method of brewing small batches of each of its beers, whereas the big brewers will make a huge amount of a concentrated base beer and then dilute it differently to create several different beers.

Back in 1984 no one gave Koch much of a chance. "When I started, craft brewers were the lunatic fringe of American brewing," he reflected. "You had to be obsessive and passionate about beer to start when I did. Nobody ever thought it would be profitable." As accolades and distribution grew, the company came under attack from the larger brewers such as Anheuser-Busch, which at one point tried to buy Koch's entire hops crop out from under him. Fortunately Koch had a long-term contract with his supplier. "I felt like Luke Skywalker at the end of *Star Wars,* when there's about to be another saga called *The Empire Strikes Back,*" he said. Sure enough, Anheuser-Busch later tried to convince beer wholesalers to stop selling specialty brews.

The marketing and sales organization behind Samuel Adams has been crucial to the company's success. Salespeople must first work at a brewery so they understand the process inside and out, and then they must get to know the distributor's business. "I try to remind everybody that the Golden Rule of distributor relations is very simple: Never ask a distributor to do something that's not in the long-term interest of his business," said Koch, who claims to taste one of his products every day. In the beginning the beer was sold at one bar or distributor at a time; now they're able to use television to garner a greater market share. In *Brewing Up Growth: An Innovator's Tale,* Koch explains why in the beginning growing the company was more important than profits.

# Brewing Up Growth:
# An Innovator's Tale
## *Jim Koch*

**G**rowth has been a defining characteristic of the Boston Beer Company since it began in 1984, when the whole company consisted of two people—my secretary from my previous job and me. Today, she has 150 people working for her (only two-thirds of the company)—a true sign of Boston Beer's growth. Over the past 12 years, we have grown between 30 and 60 percent every year, which has catapulted us into the top 10 breweries in the United States. But that is the equivalent of being the seventh or eighth largest U.S. car company—it is sort of like being the tallest pygmy.

When I was a consultant, I used to tell my clients that they only have a business if one of two things is true: Either their product is better or it is cheaper. If it is not one of those, they may make some money, but they do not have a business. That was my theory when I started the Boston Beer Company. I knew I could not make a better beer for the mass market than the large U.S. breweries were producing. For example, Coors is good at making and marketing clean, consistent, inexpensive beer. It has a very delicate, subtle flavor that cannot hide any mistakes. Thus, a home brewer should never start by trying to make a light beer. Rather, he should try to make a stout because he can hide his mistakes and defects behind the flavor.

On the other hand, my family have been brewers for 150 years; I know how to make beer and what makes a quality beer. I did not look at the 97 percent of the beer business that the big companies controlled, but at the 3 percent controlled by imports that was open for competition. In that 3 percent, I could make a product that was better. Ultimately, if I could grow, I could make a product to economies of scale that was less expensive. I could get a cost advantage over Heineken,

---

When I was a consultant, I used to tell my clients that they only have a business if one of two things is true: Either their product is better or it is cheaper.

---

Beck's, and other imports because even though I would spend more money on the ingredients, they would have an inherent disadvantage in their shipping costs. They also have an inherent quality disadvantage. Beer is supposed to be fresh; it does not improve with age. Beer should be consumed within four months. The imports cannot get beer into this country as fresh as I can. And the big brands that we drink in the United States—Heineken, Beck's, and Corona—are not considered great beers by anybody except U.S. beer drinkers.

## FROM THE GROUND UP

Knowing I could make a better beer less expensively and spend more money on the brewing process, I sought a very small niche—1 out of 1,000 drinkers, maybe. Money for television advertising would have been wasted because the niche was so small. Instead, we went directly to the bars where people drink imported beer and want something better, even at a higher price. Originally, we priced about 30 percent above Heineken; now, we are slightly below Heineken in those same markets. Our economies of scale have enabled us to hold our price back—we have not raised our price (except for excise tax increases) in 12 years.

We wanted to reach 30,000 beer drinkers in Boston. They probably went to one of a limited number of bars as least once or twice in a 30-day span. My partner put together a list of 150 bars to visit—that was our marketing plan. We went to those 150 neighborhood bars, not chain bars. It took us two years, but we got to every one of them. They were willing to experiment with new things and build a rapport with us and, thus, our business.

---

I still spend two days a week going to bars and stores and talking to the consumers because that is a key thing for us—to understand the market in a very hands-on way better than anybody else.

---

So the core competencies that built our business were better quality beer and an intense sales force. We now have about 150 salespeople—the third largest sales force in the brewing business.

As we got bigger and we paid more attention to costs, we ended up being the low-cost producer in our category even though we spend about 40 percent more on ingredients than virtually any other brewer. When I started the company, I said that it did not really matter how much it cost to make the beer. For the big brewers, ingredient costs are about 75 cents per case. Even though our ingredients cost about $2 per case, we sell our beer for $4 or $5 more per case, so we get the cost back. We went to breweries and used their excess capacity. That gave us some production efficiencies, so we get more of the cost back. Basically, we can put more money into the beer and give consumers a better product.

> My partner put together a list of 150 bars to visit—that was our marketing plan.

## UNDERSTANDING THE MARKET

We are in a very stable market, but it is not flat. A market like that is not one you can figure out with traditional marketing people who look at research and assemble focus groups. Rather, you figure it out by being in the market, by frequenting bars, by seeing the retailers. I still spend two days a week going to bars and stores and talking to the consumers because that is a key thing for us—to understand the market in a very hands-on way better than anybody else. As a result, we have been able to bring out a succession of new products: For example, our Samuel Adams line now has 15 beers in total.

> If you want to grow, you must officially set goals and then drive the organization backwards from that. Determine what you need to do to get there.

We started creating independent companies to exploit market niches that build off of our production and logistics system and our brewing capabilities. We have eight full-time brewmasters at our brewery—probably more than any other beer except Budweiser, Miller, and Coors. We have the capabilities to make great beer at a high-quality level and deliver it to markets efficiently. We understand the markets that enable us to start up new companies.

Those are some of the capabilities that we have had to generate. I created value by growing the company, not by making profits. The Boston Beer Company recently went public and got a market valuation of about $400 million. We built revenues with a business system that had the capability of generating profits.

## WORKING BACKWARDS

When we plan our budget, we look at it from a growth target backwards. We want to produce two million barrels by 2000; that is a given. Then we work backwards because everything else is flexible. We would like to post good earnings per share numbers, but we are not going to sacrifice growth in order to do that. We need to continue to generate the economies of scale and ultimately to build a sustainable business position when the growth stops in my category and it becomes more competitive. We need volume at a level high enough to support our bigger sales force and the efficiencies in manufacturing and production.

---

We started creating independent companies to exploit market niches that build off of our production and logistics system and our brewing capabilities.

---

If you want to grow, you must officially set goals and then drive the organization backwards from that. Determine what you need to do to get there. Then try to find a way to make it profitable and to make it fit within the other constraints.

# CHARLES D. MILLER

Charles Miller is the highly respected CEO of Avery Dennison, the premier maker of adhesive labels and the same company that developed and manufactures the self-adhesive stamps for the U.S. Postal Service. After graduating from Johns Hopkins University, Miller worked for a lock manufacturing company from 1949 to 1959 and then with Booz, Allen & Hamilton as a consultant from 1959 to 1964. He joined Avery in 1964 and became CEO in 1977. In the mid-1980s the company attempted to take on 3M's Post-It notes and Scotch transparent tape, but failed miserably. Miller realized the company needed to focus more on the customer.

Miller's first move was to trim headquarters staff and to empower low-level managers to roll out products. For example, one assistant product manager was able to convince Microsoft and other software companies to incorporate Avery label codes into their software's printing standards, which was a major marketing coup. To fuel growth, the company purchased their arch rival Dennison in 1990. Shortly thereafter 3M dropped out of the office label business and Avery Dennison found itself with 85 percent of the market. The merger, however, was not easy. Dennison was financially weaker than expected and even unable to track product-line profitability.

Time-based management became Miller's rallying cry: "Time based management requires a focus on the entire business, because customer service is not just a function of the marketing department. . . . Teams should be used to ensure a continuous work flow and to relieve downstream problems. Eighty percent of the time problems are controllable because they occur in the front end of the business, such as order entries and salespeople's mistakes." It meant radically cutting delivery times and inventory costs. To institute changes, time-based management was carefully explained to every employee. Miller discusses his role in the planning process in *Using Strategic Planning to Lead the Corporation*. To make plans come alive, according to Miller, the CEO must meet face-to-face with every manager and give them a sense of urgency.

# Using Strategic Planning to Lead the Corporation
### *Charles D. Miller*

Six months ago, Avery merged with Dennison Manufacturing Company. Our combined 1990 sales were about $2.6 billion. Our core businesses are office products, pressure-sensitive adhesives and materials, and product identification and control systems used principally in durable goods, health care and retailing.

When I joined Avery as the corporate planning director, I set out to push planning responsibility down to profit center management and to inject a sense of urgency. Now the real planners are the division general managers and the group vice presidents — the people close to the market and customers.

## OUR STRATEGIC PLANNING PROCESS

Our planning system has three parts: development of key issues for a single division or a group, documentation of the strategic plan itself, and face-to-face discussions between senior officers and operating management. The third part is the most important, especially for the top divisions which total 80 percent of the corporation's economic value. Each year, these divisions develop a five-year plan; other divisions prepare their plans less frequently.

Developing key issues is done primarily by the CFO and the planning department with group and division management. Examples of these issues are: a change in market position, a major decision (e.g., to divest a major operation, double capital investment, or price more aggressively), and a need to run a certain business differently.

Our documentation is short and simple. It consists of about 10 pages, which emphasize strategic direction rather than numbers. The documentation is to spread understanding of each division's direction and to stimulate discussion.

## THE LEADER'S ROLE

It's in the face-to-face discussions that I, as CEO and chairman, can make a contribution. These meetings are normally held at the operating division. They are intense and decision-oriented, not just a recitation of facts and figures already submitted. Being an attentive listener during long days for weeks at a time is extremely demanding but for me, most rewarding. My involvement makes the planning come alive. Division managers know they're going to come face to face with the CEO. These interactions bring a sense of purpose and urgency to the process: operating managers know they're going to be heard; they can argue and get a reaction.

My hope for these sessions is more effective leadership of our operating divisions. In a decentralized company, interaction between the CEO and operating managers is critical. The larger the company, the greater the danger of the CEO being isolated from operating divisions. These planning meetings are the main way for me to understand their strategic direction. It can take a full day to review the key issues and to understand the alternative actions, costs and probable outcomes. Division managers tell us what they need and we try to make decisions right then. Sometimes we have to ask for a further meeting when we're not satisfied. I explain my perspective, giving the division manager and group vice president the opportunity to argue. Our managers have the right—and the responsibility—to argue with the president and with me. And they do, sometimes more often than I'd like, but I go along with it as part of my involvement.

As a CEO, you cannot manage change by sitting in your office and reviewing plans with corporate staff. You have to be there. I believe the planning process is the single best vehicle for a CEO to demonstrate his leadership of the corporation. Our managers have to hear for themselves that I care about the environment, product quality, service reliability, employee communications and, of course, about profits.

## IMPROVING THE PROCESS

Our general managers used to complain they needed written confirmation of what direction to take as a result of the meetings. So now we designate a planning officer to confirm the final outcome for each division. Whatever the results, they are put into writing immediately.

We continue to improve our process. For example, in the last five years, we set out to understand economic value and how to create and calculate it. It has been an eye-opener. We're now convinced that a company's stock price is directly related to its ability to generate real economic value. Defining economic value as the sum of sales growth, margin improvement, and asset turnover, we're amazed at how much management time typically goes into businesses with negligible economic value.

I take strategic planning seriously. I think about it, plan my calendar around it, and participate in it. Yet I hold operations managers accountable as the real planners. The line manager who balances day-to-day operations with managing for the long term is a candidate for promotion. An understanding of strategy and an ability to handle operating responsibility are the essence of leadership. This results in a dynamic, successful organization. Another result is an irreplaceable sense of personal satisfaction.

# REBECCA P. MARK

**R**ebecca Mark is a power player in an industry dominated by men; she is chair and CEO of both Enron International (a global energy company) and Azurix (a global water company), both subsidiaries of Enron Corporation, where she also holds the title of vice chair. Mark was named chair and CEO of Enron International in 1996 and has managed the building of power plants in China, the Philippines, Columbia, and India, among other countries. Her projects take her a long way from where she was born and raised on a Missouri farm. Mark worked her way through college, earning a B.A. in psychology from Baylor University. However, she found clinical psychology depressing, so she went on to earn a masters in international management. In 1978 she joined a Houston-based bank to assist companies that sought funding for high-risk projects.

Mark's career took a fateful turn when she joined a natural gas company in 1982, bought by Enron four years later. Although now part of a dynamic management team, Mark elected to earn an M.B.A. at Harvard University, which she did in 1990. She also continued to do work for Enron and convinced top management to establish Enron Development Corporation, a division that would focus on international opportunities. Of course, she was named CEO of the new subsidiary. (In 1989 international operations was 2 percent of earnings, in 1998 it was 40 percent.) But not all came up roses. Construction of one power plant in India was halted after a new regional government was elected. Unwilling to give up, Mark spent five months renegotiating with the new government and triumphed.

Reflecting on her unique career path, Mark said, "Opportunities and challenges define your career. You just have to follow your instincts." She prefers instincts to raw analysis: "Because we are deluged with information, we could spend all day at our desks just reading the paperwork piling up, when what we really need are people who are politically savvy." In *Risky Business* Mark relates how she explored and conquered unknown territory with a straightforward strategy. Her number one credo throughout is simply: Stick to what you know.

# Risky Business
## *Rebecca P. Mark*

In 1996, *Fortune* named Enron the most innovative company in the United States. How did the $16 billion energy company achieve this distinction? By constantly evaluating the business it is in and redefining itself accordingly. Enron strives to always be a visionary and a leader—both inside and outside the company—so it can create new business opportunities and remain the leader in its industry.

Enron is the product of the merger of several large U.S. companies in the 1980s. It is one of the largest natural gas and electric companies in North America and the second largest in the world. Its international business began in 1990 with a power project in the United Kingdom. The following year, it ventured into the rest of the world with no market presence, no name recognition, and only a vague idea of what it wanted to be internationally. Thus began Enron's strategic journey of global innovation and risk-taking.

## ENTERING A NEW ENVIRONMENT

When Enron began international operations in 1990, we suffered from limited information and knowledge about how to enter the global marketplace. At the same time, a major shift occurred in the environmental focus of how countries pursued their energy strategy. Gas became more important, as did environmental safeguards and controls. Countries became concerned about large-scale capital budgets and government investment in what had been seemingly inefficient utilities. Interest in admitting private, efficient, foreign investment into the energy field mushroomed. Suddenly, we found ourselves in an entirely new world.

---

Instead of relying on studies and economic analyses, we visited everyone who had an opinion to offer. We wanted to personally know how opportunities looked and felt.

---

Most of the growing economies today were not even on the radar screen in 1991. India, for example, was virtually bankrupt and had no foreign reserves. We opened offices in countries ranging from Argentina to Indonesia and started spending development capital because we felt these would be the places where the market economy would grow most quickly. We have since invested about $5 billion in a series of infrastructure projects around the world.

## A SAVVY STRATEGY

Having completed this initial investment, we are now moving to the next phase of our evolution—offering our core products and services to third parties. We no longer have to build, invest, and conduct all the capital work ourselves; instead, we can offer services to others that are already doing that. This strategy is supported by the fact that we have enough tangible investments to prove we have handled emerging markets in a credible way as an investor. In fact, we are the single largest foreign investor in several nations. Such developments stemmed from four key actions:

*Sticking to what we know.* We specialize in power, pipelines, and natural gas.

*Gathering information first-hand.* Instead of relying on studies and economic analyses, we visited everyone who had an opinion to offer. We wanted to personally know how opportunities looked and felt, how we might take advantage of them, and what government officials were saying about them.

*Creating the demand for energy and then providing it.* We constructed several large-scale power stations and then looked for the gas to fill them rather than store large amounts of gas and look for somebody to buy it.

*Thinking big.* Very early on, we had to think small and took any opportunity that we thought was a credible investment in a promising location. Then, in 1992, we started targeting several large-scale opportunities and markets, many of which have resulted in strong businesses. But when we first took on many of those large-scale activities, people questioned our strategy of assuming large risks.

## THE GAMBLER

Trying new things in unfamiliar places was a huge risk for Enron. No one could tell us how to conduct our business in such locales because no one had done it before. Markets were changing rapidly because of increased consumer knowledge and access to information. Many barriers to access capital disappeared so that people could more easily transcend prohibitive boundaries. To overcome these hurdles, we decided to constantly reevaluate our business and decide where we were and what business we were in. Thus, risk became acceptable.

---

That process of thinking about how we divide our company and how we arrange ourselves organizationally will continue to evolve. It will always be a process of change.

---

One of our more notable risks was when we went into India in 1992 to build a large-scale, 2,000+ megawatt power plant for a total investment of about $3 billion. The total foreign investment in India over the previous 15 years had not totaled $3 billion; for one company to spend that amount on one project was considered hazardous. About one-third of the way through the construction, the Indian government publicly canceled our contract. Patiently, we practiced our negotiating and diplomatic skills and eventually the contract was resurrected. We are extremely pleased with that investment, as are the state of Maharashtra, where we are doing business, and the politicians who canceled the project in the first place. Today, we are completing the second half of construction and will have the plant operating by early 1998.

## BLOCKING STUMBLES

Taking risks was not the only obstacle we faced. Many diverse challenges exist in terms of how we grow the business and how we think about ourselves internally. But well-defined strategies have helped us prevent any new falls.

## The Organization Challenge

At one point, we thought about our business as functional and divided it into business units. We also looked at it from a business-line viewpoint—we were a power company, a pipeline company, a gas company. Now we have combined all those business lines and functions into a unit that has responsibility for holding everything together, initiating projects, selling customers the services they may want through merchant services, operating assets, and running joint ventures on a day-to-day basis. Our business unit is run by general managers who are responsible for finding opportunities that exist in the market at any given time. That process of thinking about how we divide our company and how we arrange ourselves organizationally will continue to evolve. It will always be a process of change because as we grow and as our business evolves, we must change the organization to match it.

## The People Challenge

Enron is basically a midwestern and southern U.S.-based energy company, long characterized by white males. But this homogeneity has changed over the last five years. We began selecting unique individuals from the military, consulting firms, widespread international organizations, and the top MBA programs. We aim to hire people who bring a multitude of talents to our company.

---

It is important for us to always think about the marketplace and the opportunities around us, not in terms of what everybody is doing, but where we think the industry is going.

---

We also pay close attention to the values these people bring. Honesty and integrity are very important, and we remain mindful that we work in environments with different rules. As a U.S. company, we are subject to regulations such as the Foreign Corrupt Practices Act; in other countries, we are subject to their rules and regulations as well. Careful attention to these differences will prevent us from conducting an illicit or illegal business transaction.

*The Partner Challenge*

If possible, we partner with a company only when we are well into a business plan so that we can see what the arena looks like. We try to develop our partnerships slowly and with as much information as possible.

When we do develop partnerships, we create joint ventures. We often run the business for the first few years, but it

---

> If possible, we partner with a company only when we are well into a business plan so that we can see what the arena looks like.

---

is important to respect the partner. That means we pass information to others in economies where we work to create value, create jobs for the people around us, and give local people the chance to learn and let them run that business over the long term.

## PEERING INTO THE CRYSTAL BALL

In 1996, 40 percent of our earnings were from businesses we were not involved in 10 years earlier. By the year 2000, 40 percent of our earnings will be from businesses we were not involved in in 1990, so we must constantly examine our business to determine what our customers are going to require next. For example, we recently started a major branding campaign because of the opportunity to provide retail energy services directly to customers who will want choices

234

as electricity and gas industries continue to deregulate. Simply, we are going to transform ourselves from a wholesaler to a retailer. Although this will not occur as rapidly in the international marketplace because of lagging environments and infrastructures, we plan to realize this opportunity to the maximum extent possible in highly developed markets.

In sum, it is important for us to always think about the marketplace and the opportunities around us, not in terms of what everybody is doing, but where we think the industry is going. We then have to be willing to take the risks, supply the money to support them, and pursue them wholeheartedly. For Enron, this strategy has enabled us to become America's most innovative company.

# JAMES P. KELLY

On January 10, 2000 *Forbes* magazine declared United Parcel Service (UPS) the company of the year for 1999, and gracing the cover was UPS CEO James P. Kelly. Not bad for a guy who, while earning a business degree from Rutgers University, started as a package delivery driver for UPS in 1964. Like all of the company's top management, he worked his way up through the ranks. Kelly became CEO in January of 1997 and now oversees 330,000 employees in 200 countries that help the company deliver 12.5 million packages a day.

Since taking the reins, Kelly has had two major battles on his hands. The first was the 15-day teamsters strike in the summer of 1997, when 185,000 union members walked off the job. Kelly's nemesis was Teamster's president Ron Carey, himself a UPS driver for 12 years. The result: 75,000 managers and nonunion workers were able to move only about 5 percent of the 12 million daily packages and customers rebelled. "Certainly the strike has had a devastating impact on our customers and our people," Kelly admitted. He called for President Clinton to intervene, which the president has the power to do if he warrants a strike to be a danger to the nation's economy (President Clinton declined to intercede). Kelly's second battle involves the U.S. Postal Service, which in the last few years has been pushing into UPS's market. "There's no reason for a government agency to have a competitive area," he argues.

Since the strike, the picture has become much more rosy for Kelly. In 1998 UPS delivered 55 percent of all goods sold over the Internet—just consider that e-commerce was about $80 billion in 1998 and is forecasted to grow to $3 trillion by 2003. In November of 1999 the company went public. Traditionally, all stock was held by managers, but after 92 years the company decided to put 10 percent up for public sale ($5.5 billion worth). The initial public offering (IPO) is part of the company's growth strategy, which Kelly details in *Growing a Global Delivery System*. Most important: Making all of the employees owners to deepen their personal commitment.

# Growing a Global Delivery System
## *James P. Kelly*

**W**alter Wriston, former chairman of Citicorp, summarized globalization as "suddenly meeting a person you never heard of, who comes from a place you can't locate on a map, and who's eating your lunch in your own home town." United Parcel Service (UPS) views the growing global business not just as a strategic imperative, but as a matter of future survival.

Open trade has provided much of the opportunity to expand our business worldwide; we have addressed this opportunity in two distinct ways. First, we made a full commitment to globalize. Second, we have aggressively executed our global expansion. These are the two most important elements in our entire global growth strategy.

## No Fear of Commitment

UPS's commitment to global expansion has required large investments in powerful information technologies, new facilities, and the personal involvement of thousands of people throughout the organization.

*Developing a Technology Network*

UPS established a long-term investment plan to expand and extend the company's information infrastructure. For example, in 1983, we had a total of 90 people in our information technology group whose activities revolved around generating reports for the accounting and operations group. Today, more than 4,000 people are devoted to information technology. We have 12 mainframes, 90,000 PCs, 80,000 hand-held computers, and the world's most extensive cellular communication network. We have been cited as one of the leading information technology companies in the world.

UPS needs such a massive technology backbone because information about the package is just as important as the package itself. As our former chairman and CEO, Oz Nelson, commented in 1982: "One of the most critical services we can provide is the management of information on customer distribution. The leader in information management will be the leader in international package distribution."

---

For decades, our company had been owned by about 23,000 managers. That gave us and continues to give us some uncommon freedom to pursue long-term strategies, such as global expansion, without being overly concerned about quarterly results.

---

Because UPS has always placed itself at the intersection between the buyer and the seller, the rise of electronic commerce has huge implications. But the conduct of commerce via electronic bits and bytes does not eliminate the need for physical distribution of goods. In the electronic world, UPS can become the only physical connection between the buyer and the seller. We become a critical link in the supply chain; we take the place of wholesalers and distributors. Companies will rely on UPS not only to ship goods, but also to provide information about those goods so they can better manage their businesses.

Over the past several months, we have launched a number of electronic-commerce initiatives, including partnerships with such industry leaders as IBM and Yahoo. Most recently, we have teamed with Deloitte & Touche to secure a UPS-branded global electronic delivery service. It is both a secure e-mail delivery service and a global verification service so that people who are doing business online can know with whom they are dealing within the virtual word and that they really are who they say they are. It is a marriage of UPS's trusted reputation of delivery with Deloitte's trusted image in auditing.

Electronic connectivity also allows UPS to coordinate complex supply chains from pre-sale activities like facility planning and warehousing to post-sale functions like order processing and fleet management. Our worldwide logistics group is doing that with leading companies around the world. For example, we are working with Gateway 2000 to consolidate computer parts while they are in transit. We are bringing together keyboards from the Philippines, monitors from Mexico, CPUs from Malaysia, and other customer-specific features so that Gateway can offer customized products with short delivery times at low prices around the world.

*Building the Infrastructure*
Technology, as powerful as it is, is only part of our global growth story. Being committed to global expansion also requires an ongoing investment in physical infrastructure, which UPS has made around the world:

- In 1996, we rolled out a $1.1 billion plan in Europe for new vehicles, facilities, and information networks.
- We recently opened our new Asia-Pacific hub in Taipei as part of a $400 million air network that will be one of our top three gateways in the world. It also positions us

in the nerve center of one of the world's most lucrative markets.

- We opened a technology-driven customs clearance facility in Miami that will help expedite packages and documents traveling from Latin America.
- In Chicago, we are completing a new $150 million ground-consolidation hub. At full capacity, the super hub will be able to process three million packages per day.

*Employee Dedication and Ownership*
Our global infrastructure investments in technology and facilities have been accompanied by a deepened personal commitment by our employees. Their skills, imagination, and teamwork are the invaluable element in our global transition. UPS employees are the custodians of new ideas, cutomer loyalty, and quality—the things that will determine our future.

---

UPS employees at all levels have a personal financial stake in the success of our business. That is an important asset for any company swimming in the sometimes hazardous seas of international competition.

---

The ownership of UPS has changed since we began our global expansion. For decades, our company had been owned by about 23,000 managers. That gave us and continues to give us some uncommon freedom to pursue long-term strategies, such as global expansion, without being overly concerned about quarterly results. Last year, we expanded the eligibility for ownership of UPS shares to include all employees with at least one year of service. To date, more than 84,000 people have joined the UPS employee stock-purchase plan. About two-thirds of our shareowners are now in nonmanagement positions. More than ever before,

UPS employees at all levels have a personal financial stake in the success of our business. That is an important asset for any company swimming in the sometimes hazardous seas of international competition.

## EXECUTE THE PLAN

Having made the commitment to grow globally through technology, physical investment, and employee ownership, we established and followed some key guidelines for our execution. Some of the elements include partnering with successful locals wherever possible in order to establish a UPS presence quickly in new markets and offering a broad menu of global products and services.

*Profitable Partnerships*

Through a series of alliances, mergers, and acquisitions with local carriers, we were able to grow from 3 countries in 1985 to more than 200 countries in 1988. When we first ventured outside the United States and established start-ups in Canada and Germany, we made some mistakes. We thought we could go it alone and applied our reliable domestic formula to new and different cultures. We learned an important lesson very quickly: Doing business globally is not simply a matter of grafting a rigid set of operations from one country to another. What works well in the Netherlands could easily fail in Italy and vice versa.

UPS learned that in some countries it would be faster, better, and cheaper to either acquire companies or form alliances with established delivery companies rather than build our business from the ground up. To date, UPS has acquired more than 16 companies in Europe. We launched our Asian service in 1988 by acquiring Asia Courier Systems.

But acquisitions are not always the answer. Traditional joint ventures often make more sense. To establish a presence in Japan, we created a 50/50 joint venture with Yamato, Japan's oldest, largest, and most respected package delivery company. We aligned ourselves with a partner who knew the business and Japanese culture. The product of our venture is a subsidiary called Unistar, which carries express and custom freight daily between the United States and Japan, and between Europe and Japan. In addition to Yamato, we now have more than 20 service agreements with Asian delivery companies. Working with a local partner, Sinotrans Pekair, UPS currently serves 75 key markets in China.

---

Doing business globally is not simply a matter of grafting a rigid set of operations from one country to another. What works well in the Netherlands could easily fail in Italy and vice versa.

---

Similarly, in Latin America, there was no UPS business operation prior to 1989. Today, we are aligned with more than 50 service partners and have 180 flights daily throughout the region. For example, we recently concluded an agreement with Challenger Air Cargo to expand our service into Latin America strategically matching UPS's aircraft resources with Challenger's preexisting air rights.

*Expanding Into New Products — But Not Too Much*
Not every alliance relationship has worked out well. In our attempt to aggressively grow our international business, we made a few mistakes along the way, such as aligning ourselves with companies that did not share our strategic focus on the small package or express business. In one country, instead of generating additional small package revenue, we found ourselves becoming the largest movers of cemetery gravestones and mattresses — not exactly UPS's core competency. It was not long before this began to drain the efficien-

cies of our operations network, which was designed for small packages and documents.

To help us refocus on small packages while still being able to offer freight solutions to important customers in Europe, we formed an alliance with Danzas, a freight-forwarding company based in Switzerland. Through Danzas we can move large freight to our customers while picking up new revenue streams in the process. Danzas will collect, transport, and deliver pallet-sized shipments and freights that exceed our weight and size limitations. By the same token, UPS makes available to Danzas our extensive European and worldwide express document and package delivery network on behalf of their customers. It is a classic partnership, the kind that will help us grow our business globally in the years to come.

## THE PROMISE OF FREE TRADE

Free trade is pivotal to the future of many companies, including UPS. Although many trade agreements have been forged around the world in the past decade, there are no guarantees that those doors will remain open. Local economies in many industrialized nations and certainly in the United States have endured some job losses and downturns that can produce political pressure to slam doors shut again. This is understandable, but certainly short-sighted. We are in a period of adjustment that is painful for some. In the long run, however, a free, borderless economy will benefit the entire world. As the 21st century begins, global growth is something that concerns every company of every size in every corner of the globe. UPS plans to be there when they arrive.

# PART VIII

# Breaking through Bureaucracy

As companies seek to best the competition by cutting prices, increasing productivity, and getting closer to the customer, eliminating bureaucracy remains a top management issue: Consider that in The Conference Board's 1999 research report, *Organizing for Global Competitiveness*, 85 percent of the responding companies had reorganized since 1990. To be meaningful, programs aimed at cutting red tape and flattening the organization must have substance. Lawrence Bossidy, revered CEO of AlliedSignal and former General Electric vice chairman opens by ridiculing those who deliver "gaseous sermons about empowerment and liberation." He demands action, but even when it comes to action, he warns, "An autocrat can walk around in shorts and still be an autocrat." He recommends starting on the factory floor, mapping the various processes, and truly listening to hourly workers to identify wasteful practices. Empowerment is crucial, but making it a reality is not always easy. To do so, British Airways chairman Lord Colin Marshall of Knightsbridge espouses self-management, which involves setting up "cross-functional checks and controls among internal suppliers and customers"—the troops police themselves. Management guru Tom Peters concurs with Lord Marshall, stating, "We need to give up 'control,' and lots of it, to stand even a chance of gaining control in these tumultuous times." If management insists on reviewing every issue, he argues, not only are important decisions delayed, but as information travels up the hierarchy, it becomes distorted. As for a successful example of information-flow, Peters cites General Motors's installation of a hotline between a management team and an assembly plant to ensure direct communication. By eliminating management layers, everyone joins the fray, feedback loops are shorter, and companies respond far more quickly to customer needs.

# LAWRENCE A. BOSSIDY

As vice chairman of General Electric, Lawrence Bossidy was one of the most highly recruited executives in the United States. The winner was AlliedSignal, where he became CEO in 1991, and quickly established a reputation as tough as his old boss's, Jack Welch (and to think Bossidy was an altar boy growing up in Pittsfield, Massachusetts). Beginning at the age of 12 he worked in the family shoe store, and while attending Colgate University he sold shoes out of his car to fellow students. He reflected, "Running AlliedSignal is like running Bossidy's shoe store—only multiplied hundreds of times." When he came on board, the company was a sluggish, mature conglomerate of aerospace and auto parts, among other products.

First came the cost-cutting as it had at GE in the early Welch days. In the following six years 30 factories were closed and 43 sold, the workforce was cut 23 percent, and 75 percent of the company's top 125 executives had been replaced. Bossidy admitted, "Restructuring is a negative. You get a frightened workforce. Eventually you need to maintain or create jobs, not destroy them." The company, however, needed to eliminate bureaucracy, beat competitors to market, and get closer to the customer. "Business leaders who were used to calling the shots are now being forced to dance to the customer's tune," Bossidy reflected. "But the dance steps are intricate, and they can't be mastered in a one-hour lesson."

To reduce dependency on the company's traditionally cyclical businesses, he went shopping for other companies. In 1998 the company failed in a $10 billion hostile takeover of AMP, but Bossidy found a merger partner in Honeywell in 1999. The strong leadership and the corporate makeover are reminiscent of GE in the 1980s and the following essay is from 1991 when Bossidy was still with GE. The lessons remain poignant as he provides insight into what motivates employees. He begins by stating: "The American worker is not docile. He refuses to sing company songs. He makes fun of pompous fools in high places—but he possesses a curiosity, a free-form creativity, and an intensity of response when challenged . . ."

# Why Do We Waste Time
# Doing This?
## *Lawrence A. Bossidy*

The American worker is not docile. He refuses to sing company songs. He makes fun of pompous fools in high places — but he possesses a curiosity, a free-form creativity, and an intensity of response when challenged that in my view is absent in the regimented cultures and hierarchical corporate structures of most of our offshore competitors.

After a decade of reading a seemingly interminable series of books on how to become Japanese, it is gradually dawning on us that what we must do in the '90s is become more American.

But transferring the kind of creativity, atmosphere, and culture that is normally found only in a garage shop or in Silicon Valley to a company such as General Electric, with 292,000 people in 13 businesses all over the globe, is no mean feat. No one our size has ever even tried it, much less succeeded.

People have been delivering gaseous sermons about empowerment and liberation for decades. But merely talking about it accomplishes nothing. A total, long-term commitment and massive action is required. The device we at General Electric Company are using to change our corporate culture is called "Work-Out."

When we decided to launch Work-Out in the latter part of the '80s, we sat down over a period of a year or so and tried to describe the characteristics a winning enterprise would require in the '90s. There were several. But the one that kept recurring was speed—speed in product development, in market penetration, in customer service, in globalization. From there we tried to home in on the obstacles to gaining speed and we kept coming up with complexity as the culprit—whether it be the more egregious manifestations of bureaucracy or the more accepted practices in business, such as the custom of marketing, finance, engineering, and customer service each having its own fiefdom, jargon, and procedures. We concluded that to be faster, we had to be simpler.

We found that complexity is often a by-product of insecurity. People who are unsure of their worth in an organization tend to surround themselves with complexity to make their functions seem more difficult and sophisticated than they are—and themselves more valuable because of their ability to penetrate the fog that they themselves generate. Those who know their worth because of their visible achievements in the real world, rather than on the artificial turf of bureaucracy, act and speak with simplicity.

Brand-new lieutenants strut and swagger and place high value on the trappings and badges of rank. Those who have distinguished themselves on the battleground rather than the parade ground act with the quiet confidence of those who have nothing to prove and much that is worth learning from.

What General Electric is trying to do is to create an environment in which each individual can make a connection between what he or she does each day and winning in the marketplace.

What we call Work-Out is something of a chameleon in that it assumes the cultural flavor of the 13 businesses in General Electric. But it does share one central institution: regular New England-style town meetings. The Work-Out town meeting is kicked off by the leader of the particular business and, in the early years, some outside consultants, and includes people from every function in the business and all levels of rank.

The first activity of a typical Work-Out town meeting is what can be described simply as a bitch session, with questions that run along the lines of: "Why do we waste time doing this?" "Why do we have to fill this out?" "Why do we need all these approvals?" The early sessions focused on easy targets — bureaucratic barnacles that grow on any organization — and many of them were simply abolished right on the spot.

At one session that I recall, an employee questioned the necessity of a long-standing work practice that made no sense to him. It apparently made no sense to the business leader either — who had never even heard of the practice — because he turned to the head of the local union who was present and said, "You got any problem with getting rid of that?" The union guy said, "No," and it was killed on the spot.

Such actions were absolutely essential to getting Work-Out off the ground. When workers accustomed to being ignored see their views accepted — not just with patronizing nods but welcomed and, above all, implemented — ideas and views come in a torrent. Action is the key to allaying the natural cynicism that always greets an effort like this. Veteran middle managers have drawers full of T-shirts and coffee mugs imprinted with the slogans of long-forgotten campaigns and long-departed managers. Only sustained successful action can convince the doubters.

At our appliance business in Louisville someone wanted to know why management had to wear suits and ties — one of the key delineators that separates "us" from "them" in a manufacturing business. No one had a good answer. Today, the whole place dresses casually. That's fine as far as it goes, but we've found that you have to be careful not to confuse style with substance. An autocrat can walk around in shorts and still be an autocrat. People must see and feel real improvements in the way they work.

Rewards are obviously critical as well and they must be experienced in the wallet and not just the ego. Four hundred people in General Electric used to get stock options—5,000 now do, including secretaries and foremen, and 10,000 will. People who never paid attention to the stock prices now study the business pages in the morning and are beginning to feel a personal connection between their efforts, the company's success, and the rewards that result.

The examination of some of our processes at the Work-Out sessions has begun to yield some interesting results. At our electrical distribution and control business we found that one of our least sophisticated products, a circuit breaker, was being built on a 20-week cycle with a 15,000 mile pipeline. It was built in eight plants and was on the road between those plants for 10 weeks. The most astonishing thing was that no one knew this. Now this implies that we have Rube Goldberg and the Three Stooges running our manufacturing operations. I assure you we don't. But the point is that until you take the time to examine your processes and listen to the people who actually run them on a daily basis, you have no idea of the wasteful horrors that exist in the way you do things or how many opportunities there are to make those processes more productive.

One of our business leaders who has spent the most time examining processes inside and outside General Electric swears that the mapping in detail of how any given process works will lead to a quick 20 percent productivity increase.

---

We've found that you have to be careful not to confuse style with substance. An autocrat can walk around in shorts and still be an autocrat.

---

We're not used to focusing on processes. The successful leaders of the '80s typically did the General Patton routine— threatening, cajoling, and rewarding people for meeting goals—and through deference or fear or ambition, by God, they met those goals. We're now trying to examine processes, fix them, and make them better—and in doing so meet not just some number, but radically improve the way we do things.

The leader of the '90s has got to immerse himself in the processes, listen to people rather than harangue them, empower them, and give up a lot of control. But tell this to a 45-year-old general manager, or middle manager for that matter, and you get a cold stare. So the education, the conditioning for this new way of working has to start at the top. The business leader must be totally, visibly, and continuously involved in the process. Turning it over to the human resources people is a formula for failure.

And I'd be less than candid if I told you we had all the answers on how to go about changing the corporate culture. We still have autocrats—highly successful '70s- and '80s-style people—and we're not sure what to do with them. But I can tell you they won't be leading General Electric businesses very far into the '90s unless they can change.

We've learned to have patience as well. There are no quick fixes, no instant cultural changes. What we have set out to do will take years—maybe decades. A year or two ago we came up with a new label, "the cement layer," and applied it to middle managers because they weren't jumping on the bandwagon every time we gave a speech. These are the people who take the brunt of change—the first to get shot when some hill has to be taken and often the last to share in the rewards when it is taken. It is critical that we court them, inspire them, empower them, and convince them of their value. We don't use the term "cement layer" anymore because we are aware that in many cases it's the result of outdated business leadership.

Convincing middle management and the organization at large means sending out signals that are absolutely consistent. We believe utterly in the value of partnerships, bringing the vendor into our processes at one end and our customers at the other, a boundaryless continuum of productivity and added value. But when cash flow falls short of target, payments to vendors are sometimes delayed at one end and customers are badgered for collection at the other. That is where employee cynicism stems from.

The ultimate false message, in my view, is any that implies that productivity and customer service are part of a zero-sum equation. The implication that satisfying customers is anything other than the number one mission of any business is crazy—and yet it has not become embedded in the national business culture. One of our vice presidents from GE Plastics who's been in Japan for several years recently came back to the United States "spoiled," as he put it, by customer service levels in Japan and was appalled by what he saw here. He told us that he went to one American retail store and asked an employee, who turned out to be the store manager, if he could have some help locating a few things. He was told they don't help customers—and, "We have low prices so people who come here shouldn't expect help." Low prices in lieu of service is a malignant trade-off that is killing American business with its customers—or at least the ones that are being "spoiled" by the Japanese.

I say this self-righteously. Yet we at General Electric measure our businesses on cash flow—even though that sometimes leads to an unintentional squeeze being put on suppliers and customers. We also measure our businesses on head count—even though that sometimes causes us to ignore or penalize customers. We have to find enlightened ways to measure key performance results, ways that do not kill the new corporate culture we are trying to midwife.

All over General Electric, Work-Out meetings are becoming a routine part of business life and the results are becoming visible. I believe, however, that the degree of improvement possible in these sessions is limited without constant injection of fresh thinking and new ideas from the outside—in General Electric's case from among our 13 businesses as well as from the outside world. To foster new ideas we have developed teams of operating people who study the very best practices and processes of companies around the world and then work with our businesses to adapt them. The constant upgrading of our processes by using as our standard the world-class best is, in my view, where the potential lies for enormous productivity growth.

It has been my belief for a year or two, and remains so, that as the year 2000 approaches there will be fewer than 25 megacorporations in the world, about equally divided in number among the United States, Europe, and the Far East. At the other end of the scale there will be hundreds of successful moderate-size niche players. Those that remain in between—the medium-to-large-size generalists with no particular high cards, who view low prices as a substitute for serving customers—have a date with oblivion.

It is sobering to contemplate that of the companies that constituted the original Dow Jones Industrial Average only General Electric is still in existence—and that of the top 500 American companies in the mid-1940s, more than 250 have disappeared. I believe that productivity, more than any other factor, will decide who wins and who winds up in the dustbin in the '90s.

American business has a challenging decade ahead of it: Growing customer demands, unpredictable regulatory bodies, and environmental legislation will combine to punish companies that are not productive, customer focused, and receptive to change.

Work-Out is General Electric's big bet for winning in this decade and beyond. The program is very expensive in terms of resources, time, and management attention, and there is no guarantee it will succeed. But we are deeply encouraged by what we are seeing: we have stirred the imagination and excitement of our people. The game is ours to win—and if we do the rewards will be enormous.

# Edgar S. Woolard Jr.

As DuPont's CEO and chairman from 1989 to 1997, Edgar Woolard is credited with revitalizing the once decrepit chemical company. His accomplishments were recognized by the entire industry when he was awarded the 1998 Chemical Industry Medal from the Society of Chemical Industry. The North Carolina native earned an engineering degree from North Carolina State University in 1956 and then joined DuPont as an industrial engineer. After stints as a product supervisor, plant manager, marketing director, and in corporate planning, Woolard was named president and COO in 1987, and then two years later was made CEO and chairman.

At the time DuPont's costs were high, market share eroding, and profit margins squeezed. United States sales growth had been sluggish at a mere 1 percent annually for the 1980s, and the pressure was on as he had to operate under the critical eye of the powerful Bronfman family, who owned one-fourth of the company's stock. Woolard set some immediate goals such as zero waste generation and 3 to 5 percent U.S. sales growth, solid targets for a very mature company. To achieve his plans, he initiated a $1 billion cost-cutting program from DuPont's $11 billion fixed-cost base, and a $2 billion program to streamline operations—at one point DuPont had 40 accounting systems.

In the restructuring, each business was evaluated on whether it could exceed the cost of capital throughout a business cycle— the chemical company has been notoriously cyclical. If a particular business did not have a competitive advantage, it was spun off or a partner was found. Woolard understood that "we were not competitive, not bringing out product fast enough." He reenergized the company with an entrepreneurial spirit by declaring, "We can act like good business managers and focus on the markets and customers we know best, or we can act like entrepreneurs and leaders and go after new markets and customers who don't exist yet." Woolard takes that message home in *Did You Ever See an Elephant Charge?* The first question he had to answer: Was DuPont really ready to act in an entrepreneurial fashion?

# Did You Ever See an Elephant Charge?
## *Edgar S. Woolard Jr.*

As we talk about reviving a spirit of entrepreneurship in our companies, we should keep in mind that even as we speak, people halfway around the world are embracing a new spirit of entrepreneurship with fierce intensity.

Recently, in China, I had lunch with the chairman of a firm in the Guandong Province. The firm's leadership comes from old economic-planning groups in the Communist Party. When given the freedom to move to Hong Kong and develop trade and business for their province, they built a $1.5 billion business in 14 years from scratch. They claim it is very profitable, and the shares they issued increased 10 times in the past few years. I asked the executive to describe his company's areas of business. He responded, "Anywhere we can make money." I came back from that trip convinced that China will grow and profits will be made.

These new entrepreneurs have an advantage. Their companies are, in a sense, new organisms adapting without hesitation to the global business environment we face because they have never known anything else. They don't have to unlearn old ways of operating. They don't have to transform or reengineer themselves. If I had to say where the advantage lies—with our business experience, technology, and innovation or with their raw energy and drive—I'd say we could be looking at a dead heat early in the next century.

---

The choice is clear: We can act like good business managers and focus on the markets and customers we know best, or we can act like entrepreneurs and leaders and go after new markets and customers who don't exist yet.

---

By contrast, right now it's very easy for U.S. and European-based companies to reduce their focus on emerging markets because business is strengthening in the traditional markets where we're more comfortable, where the risk is lower, and where a spirit of entrepreneurship does not seem quite so essential to success. I would not be surprised if many companies choose to do that rather than position themselves strongly on the economic frontier in Asia.

But it stands to reason that if we want employees to act like entrepreneurs, there is no better way than to turn them loose on that frontier. The choice is clear: We can act like good business managers and focus on the markets and customers we know best, or we can act like entrepreneurs and leaders and go after new markets and customers who don't exist yet.

How do we do that? The formula was constantly repeated to me in China, in the form of a question: "Can you be fast, flexible, and decisive?"

Many potential partners indicated to me that DuPont was their first choice, but if we could not move fast they would pursue other options. While this is an old bargaining ploy, I believe it *is* their honest position. They are very impatient to take advantage of new economic freedom and to establish their organizations as role models in an emerging economy. They are committed to speed, know they can find technology somewhere, and have remarkable self-confidence — all the hallmarks of entrepreneurship.

---

> Established companies should not encourage employee entrepreneurs to make hasty decisions or invest in unprofitable projects.

---

What about flexibility? In China many of our businesses are evaluating different ways of doing business and distribution systems that are quite different from standard practices. These opportunities often involve small investments with local customers and distributors who wish to align with us. There are risks in such an approach compared to our role in North America and Europe, where we are primarily a materials supplier. Once again, we face a choice: Will we do things differently, or will we do business in a way that satisfies us instead of the customer?

As for decisiveness, the clear concern in all of my discussions was, is DuPont really prepared to act? Established companies should not encourage employee entrepreneurs to make hasty decisions or invest in unprofitable projects. But today's business environment is such that when opportunities present themselves, we must assign adequate resources and good people, gather the necessary data, and make a prompt decision to proceed — or assume a competitor will.

---

> If employees are to think like entrepreneurs, they have to understand that no job is secure if the business isn't growing.

---

Speed, flexibility, and decisiveness are central to entrepreneurship. How do we get our employees to act in that spirit? There are two characteristics of the entrepreneur we must make part of the everyday reality of our employees.

The first is that the personal well-being, security, and reward of the entrepreneur are tied directly to the success of the business. In many old-line manufacturing companies, the industrial culture of the second half of the 20th century has been one in which most employees were insulated from the success or failure of the businesses in which they worked. But if employees are to think like entrepreneurs, they have to understand that no job is secure if the business isn't growing. Their livelihoods are tied to business success.

---

Not all characteristics of the classic entrepreneur have a place in a large corporate setting.

---

The second characteristic of the entrepreneur that we have to make a reality in our companies is direct contact with the customer. We have to take away the big mechanisms in traditional corporate organizations that prevent people from knowing, understanding, and responding directly to customer needs.

At the same time, not all characteristics of the classic entrepreneur have a place in a large corporate setting. For example, no one can have absolute free rein in a large, complex organization. For us the entrepreneurial spirit has to flourish within a strong corporate team with the power and capability to make world-class contributions to society.

That power and capability is still very real. A few months ago I was asked by *The Washington Post* how an "elephant" like DuPont can compete with the small, rapid-response companies—the "gazelles" of the business world? I responded: Did you ever see an elephant charge? Large corporate organizations have resources, knowledge, and business power that independent entrepreneurs—gazelles—can only dream about.

We all know of cases where companies are succeeding internationally because they balance the clout of a big organization with the speed and aggressiveness of a smaller business unit. Neither is a substitute for the other in today's environment. Managing the creative tension between the two will be the model of the successful global enterprise in the decades ahead. But it will only work if our employees begin to think like entrepreneurs and are given the opportunity to act that way.

Chairman of British Airways and an influential voice in directing Great Britain's economic policy, Lord Colin Marshall of Knightsbridge is one of the most prominent business leaders in Europe. After college and a stint with the Orient Steam Navigation Company, he joined Hertz in 1958 as a management trainee. Eventually he was promoted to general manager of the Mexico operations and then assistant to the president in New York. In 1964 Lord Marshall jumped cars to Avis, where he became regional manager/vice president Europe and then president of the company in 1975 and CEO in 1976. Avis was taken over by another firm three years later and he was made cochairman, but in 1983 Lord Marshall elected to join British Airways as CEO.

At British Airways, Lord Marshall has had to contend with fierce competition due to the deregulation of the airline industry and Richard Branson's upstart company Virgin Atlantic, in addition to successfully privatizing (in 1987) and streamlining the once-bloated, government-owned airline. While an "unashamed free-trader," he campaigns for stricter regulation of the industry when it comes to environmental and noise pollution. To deal with heightened competition and the need to be socially conscious, Lord Marshall, who is now chairman of the company, espouses self-management: "British Airways has moved towards this management evolution because we know that to succeed in the deregulated marketplace, our unit costs must be among the lowest; and our levels of efficiency and quality, must be among the very best, if not the highest."

Self-management simply pushes more responsibility to the front lines and therefore eliminates layers of management, creating a flat organization. The key is for employees to keep an eye on each other. "The underlying self-management process in the workplace essentially involves cross-functional checks and controls among internal suppliers and customers," Lord Marshall writes in *Self-Management* and is one of several points he touches on in describing how to manage in this new era of heightened competitiveness.

# Self-Management
## *Lord Colin Marshall*
## *of Knightsbridge*

At British Airways . . . we have long recognised that the day of multiple levels of management—the deep management hierarchy—was coming to an end. It was expensive, held up response time and, most importantly, distanced the business from its customers.

Technology has taken over a very large amount of the processing traditionally carried out by managers and layers of hierarchy became redundant. We moved to what used to be known as the "flat" company, where management is driven out of the centre towards the marketplace. The old structure in which the market was at the bottom of the chain was literally turned on its head so that everything started with the customer.

Self-management is now the essential driving force because—apart from anything else—the control and supervision of others adds immense, unnecessary cost. Having said that, there is still the need for integration, controls and what we might call exception management, which the traditional structure provides.

British Airways has moved towards this management evolution because we know that to succeed in the deregulated marketplace, our unit costs must be among the lowest; and our levels of efficiency and quality, must be among the very best, if not the highest.

It is by no means exclusive to us, but in my book the role of management consists of three key functions; Leadership—the responsibility for charting direction; Stewardship—the process of keeping the business's resources on course; and Administration—making the planned procedures work.

---

Self-management is now the essential driving force because—apart from anything else—the control and supervision of others adds immense, unnecessary cost.

---

None of them, it goes without saying, can stand alone, but they must work hand in glove with one another, under the superstructure of strategic development, structural planning and financial control provided by the representatives of shareholders, the board of directors.

As the use of technology increases and the process of self-management steps up, the role of managers is changing and their numbers are being reduced, in some cases quite drastically.

---

Management consists of three key functions; Leadership—the responsibility for charting direction; Stewardship—the process of keeping the business's resources on course; and Administration—making the planned procedures work.

---

Along with many other companies, British Airways has found that the layered hierarchy defined by traditional management functions needs to be replaced by fewer numbers of all-round managers covering each responsibility.

The underlying self-management process in the workplace essentially involves cross-functional checks and controls among internal suppliers and customers.

The result of this kind of change is that the distance between the top level of management and the company at large is significantly reduced. Communication is faster and more effective, with direct implications for flexibility, market response, efficiency and—where necessary—change of strategic direction.

These people are the global managers we need to develop, encourage and retain. In the airline we have been doing this for some years now through a rigorous programme of education and training, including our own MBA course run in conjunction with Lancaster University; through critical path career planning; and through performance-related incentives.

It is worth mentioning that, under the new regime of corporate governance which has emerged in this country, executive loyalty schemes, whether stock options or the new long-term incentive plans, are now all tied to very specific performance criteria.

---

At the end of the day, lasting loyalty, commitment and enthusiasm come from good leadership. The best people are attracted to exciting companies, not necessarily to exciting pay packets, alone.

---

The more measured tone of new corporate governance now at play in Britain does not diminish belief in the value of management and employee shareholding through schemes which encourage and assist share acquisition. Ownership over the long-term is a very strong incentive.

Retaining key people is one of the themes at this conference* and it is right that such expensive assets should be protected. Nevertheless, the movement of people cannot be restricted and there is an upside to executive loss. If the underlying company culture is right, the departing executive will carry much goodwill, influence and persisting loyalty out into the marketplace. I have seen interesting networks develop among former British Airways people who have left to go to important positions in other companies, with benefits of many kinds accruing to the airline. Wherever people may go, whatever change of course their career paths take, it is important that—like good schools or universities—companies must cultivate an environment of practice and philosophy which nobody ever truly leaves.

At the end of the day, lasting loyalty, commitment and enthusiasm come from good leadership. The best people are attracted to exciting companies, not necessarily to exciting pay packets, alone.

Finally, anybody wanting to see the new era of competitive intent at work in British business need only call in at Shakespeare's Globe Theatre in London this Summer. There, you might have heard, the Cranfield School of Management will be running an unusual series of courses.

Apparently, the idea is for business people to study and act out themes from Shakespeare plays. One of the courses, for example, is entitled "Stepping into Leadership with Henry V." Just imagine what executives inspired by the bloody battle of Agincourt might do for British competitiveness in the Single Market. No doubt there is another course on something like "Trust and delegation for subordinates with Julius Caesar." Or "Reputation Management with Othello." Although in these days of keeping a tight rein on overheads, a course on "Controlling the headcount with Henry VIII" might be the most popular.

---

*This selection is from a speech delivered at a conference celebrating The Conference Board's twentieth anniversary of operating in Europe.

The idea has certainly caught on and suggestions for the syllabus are rattling around the Board rooms of London. For instance, study of Hamlet is recommended if your desired quality is knowing what you are supposed to be doing in a business environment that never seems to stand still, with its goalposts forever on the move. But the one I support is the desired quality available from studying Macbeth: "Avoiding becoming obsessed with power, to the extent that your wife encourages you to murder the Chairman."

# EMMANUEL A. KAMPOURIS

Emmanuel Kampouris, recently retired CEO of American Standard, is truly "a man of the world." He was born in Egypt and studied in Great Britain, where he earned a masters in law from Oxford University in 1957. Five years later found him in Athens, Greece, working for a manufacturing company. He joined American Standard's plumbing products subsidiary in Greece in 1966 and later became the group's managing director. Finally, he came to the United States in 1979 to serve as vice president of American Standard's Building Products group. The board appointed him president and CEO in 1989 and chairman in 1993.

Unfortunately, in 1988 Black & Decker had made a hostile takeover bid for American Standard, which makes plumbing equipment and supplies, and air conditioning units, among other products. As Kampouris recalls, "We had tremendous cash penetration but no debt, and there was nothing very exciting going on. Easy prey, really." The company's management team elected to opt for a leveraged buyout. The recession in the early 1990s complicated matters. The key to turning around the company was maximizing return on working capital, and to do so Kampouris introduced demand-flow technology. The process has been described as "just-in-time plus," which not only involves tight inventory management, but reorganization of the entire manufacturing process to minimize costs.

By 1995 the company's earnings were solid and Kampouris, who studies the Bible for both moral lessons and management advice, was ready to once again take the company public and to look overseas for growth. "China in the year 2000 is going to be the largest plumbing market in the world," he said. "It's humid and hot. They need sanitation. There's one loo on every floor, not every apartment." The turnaround of American Standard was so impressive that Jack Welch, the king of reengineering, dispatched a series of teams to investigate. Kampouris describes his reengineering experience in *A Case Study in Reengineering,* including his discovery that "the basic, underlying principle is the elimination of non-value-added activities."

# A Case Study in Reengineering

*Emmanuel A. Kampouris*

In 1988, Black & Decker made a surprise bid to take over American Standard. At that time, Black & Decker was about half our size. To counter the bid, we privatized our company through a leveraged buyout. We borrowed approximately $3 billion, eliminated our pension plan, and formed an employee stock ownership plan (ESOP). Employees owned about 25 percent of the company, and with the eventual appreciation of the stock, the ESOP turned out to be an excellent investment for everyone.

Although the takeover threat had been thwarted, we still faced another disturbing fact: We had no contingency plan for a potential recession. We tried to liquidate the only asset we had—$650 million in working capital—to ensure our survival should a recession occur, which would cause all three of our businesses—air conditioning, automotive, and plumbing—to suffer. Attacking working capital was indeed the only solution, but we did not have a way of doing it. So we initiated a global search to find techniques that would help us.

## INVENTORY TURNS ESCALATE

American Standard found a disciplined method called "demand flow," which pulls material through a process that essentially focuses on the customer. The basic, underlying principle is the elimination of non-value-added activities. At American Standard, we discovered that in our manufacturing processes we were spending 80–90 percent of our time on non-value-added activities. To eliminate these activities meant rearranging every one of our manufacturing facilities worldwide. Integral in the demand-flow discipline is the allowance for flexibility so that customers could receive what they wanted, when they wanted it, and as frequently as they wanted it. This discipline dramatically improved both our quality and productivity, resulting in market-share gains while reducing our working capital, which was, of course, our primary target through the dramatic reduction of inventories in all of our manufacturing facilities worldwide. At the time, inventory turns stood at about 3.0 turns. We set a global target of doubling that number, virtually halving the amount of inventory, within three years. To achieve that goal, we trained 30,000 people; conducted courses in seven different languages; changed our management structure, as well as our measurement and compensation systems; redesigned all of our facilities; eliminated supervision on the factory floor; and dramatically stepped up our communications. By the end of 1992, we had reached 6.0 inventory turns overall; by 1995, we hit 11 turns. All of this resulted in an inventory savings of $400 million and saved about 5 million square feet of space.

Within specific divisions, we achieved impressive gains:

- In the United States, the residential air conditioning business' inventory turns increased from 2.5 to more than 8.
- Also in the United States, another one of our Kentucky air conditioning businesses grew its business by 50 percent without adding any floor space; inventory turns soared from 6 to 20.

- In England, inventory turns at American Standard's Westinghouse Air Brake Company climbed from 5 to 40.
- In Germany, the air brake and electronics business for the truck and bus industry improved its inventory turns from 6 to 23, and subsequently improved its on-time delivery from 37 percent to 95 percent.

The fact that we were able to implement demand-flow techniques is not as important as what resulted: namely, our survival through a recession, our ability to continue our growth on a global basis, continued investment in new products and technology, and improved customer service. Today, we are aiming for 15 inventory turns by 1998. If we achieve that goal with our current balance sheet ratios, we will eliminate working capital from our balance sheet, meaning we can grow our business without investing in working capital, and do all of this while dramatically improving customer service, which has always been one of our primary objectives.

---

We discovered that in our manufacturing processes we were spending 80–90 percent of our time on non-value-added activities.

---

## CHANGE FROM TOP TO BOTTOM

We then tried to apply these same concepts of reducing cycle time and performing only value-added work to the office, but here we encountered a large stumbling block: the hierarchical organization. This type of organization prevented a holistic approach, so we decided to transform American Standard into a process-managed organization that revolves around three processes: the operational process, the enabling process, and the coaching process. We changed titles

269

and organizations and applied incentives and metrics to the specific process organization.

---

When senior managers personally exemplify integrity and demonstrate their willingness to sacrifice, they can create the trust needed and hence the environment necessary to undergo extensive reengineering. Without that trust, the effort will fail.

---

To ensure success, we implemented a major training program, which simultaneously helped us to communicate the extensive changes taking place. We began internal benchmarking to evaluate our effectiveness and train employees in the new processes. In order to formalize this activity, we formed the American Standard College. Employees from around the world can attend weekly classes (via satellite in the future), thus continuously receiving training in the demand-flow techniques. Similar courses and training are available for manufacturing associates at every facility.

The results of American Standard's reengineering have been overwhelmingly positive. For example, in Germany it used to take four weeks to enter an order because the process was complicated and had to flow through various countries; today, it takes one hour. Shipments from inventory decreased from five days to one, and the overall manufacturing cycle for certain products fell from two months to two days.

The only way a company can execute a program of this magnitude is to have the unequivocal commitment of senior managers. This must be done by providing clear direction and continuous communication; explaining how and why changes are being made; providing all the necessary tools, funds, and training; and rewarding collective—not individual—achievement. When senior managers personally exemplify integrity and demonstrate their willingness to sacrifice, they can create the trust needed and hence the environment necessary to undergo extensive reengineering. Without that trust, the effort will fail.

Tom Peters and Robert H. Waterman coauthored *In Search of Excellence,* which was an instant best-seller in 1982 and went on to become the most successful management book of all time, spending three years on *The New York Times* best-seller list and selling millions worldwide.

The Maryland native attended Cornell University, where he played lacrosse and earned a bachelor's degree in 1965 and a master's degree in industrial engineering in 1966. Business had to wait as he joined the war in Vietnam as a member of the navy's construction battalion. Peters then continued his education, earning an M.B.A. and a Ph.D. from Stanford University. In between, Peters joined the venerable consulting firm McKinsey & Company in 1974. There he met Waterman.

*In Search of Excellence* struck a chord with American business managers in part because at the time Japanese firms were receiving all the accolades; however, Peters and Waterman were highlighting 60 successful *U.S.* businesses and identifying eight shared qualities that made them so. The two authors discovered that the companies they studied "worked hard to keep things simple in a complex world. They persisted. They insisted on top quality. They fawned on their customers. They listened to their employees and treated them like adults. . . . They allowed some chaos in return for quick action and regular experimentation."

Peters left McKinsey the year before the book was published, and on the heels of its success he founded his own consulting firm, the Tom Peters Group. By 1985 the Tom Peters group was generating $5 million in revenue merely from Peters's speaking engagements, publishing books by others, and selling audio and video tapes (mostly by Peters). One of his more recent messages: You have to put the employee first, not the customer. "Success depends a lot on more intelligence at the front line. And intelligence and commitment at the front line come only if you literally make each employee a partner in the process." This message is at the forefront in *Letting Go of Controls.* He concludes, "We need to give up 'control,' and lots of it, to stand even a chance of gaining control in these tumultuous times."

# Letting Go of Controls
## *Tom Peters*

Although we might debate one flavor or another of monetary policy, or varying degrees of strictness in antitrust enforcement, few executives would challenge the ideas underlying Adam Smith's "invisible hand." After all, the United States' matchless standard of living is the result of millions of invisible hands, stretching back centuries.

The power of the invisible hand, we all know, is its invisibility. Masses of people, largely unknown to one another, make self-interested choices, which turn out to coincide with the greatest good.

"The market economy," according to Smith's modern-day interpreter and 1974 Nobel prize winner in economics, F.A. Hayek, succeeds precisely because it "is not the product of deliberate design. It far surpasses the reach of our understanding." In the marketplace, "unintended consequences are paramount." That is, what we don't know and the fact that we don't "know" it—those millions of self-interested choices by strangers—are the very engines of economic progress. Indeed, the presence and intrusion of controllers bent upon comprehension destroy the invisibility and quickly sap the vitality of Smith's market Eden. To try to know destroys the machine, perversely enough.

But although we understand the concept of the invisible hand at a gut level, we continue to have intellectual problems with accepting that incomprehensibility and unintended consequences *per se* power the economy. There is another problem as well: While we may be able to accept the concept for the economy, we have a devil of a time transferring the notion across the moat and into the company.

---

Our hesitation in truly decentralizing our companies is analogous to the Soviets' reluctance to fully switch to a market economy; we both have trouble believing that complex systems work better without central controllers.

---

Consider decentralization. The idea of pursuing decentralization is considered hardly worth the bother of further explanation. We're for it. We know what it means. But I'm not so sure. When decentralization really works, as at 3M Company, it minimizes hierarchical impedance and allows the market winds to blow a gale inside the firm; it allows "incomprehensibility" and "unintended consequences" to hold sway and move the firm forward vigorously, if via a zigzag path. To tell the truth, most of us find the idea of placing our company's fate in invisible hands to be plain scary.

Our hesitation in truly decentralizing our companies is analogous to the Soviets' reluctance to fully switch to a market economy; we both have trouble believing that complex systems work better without central controllers. Despite the invisibility that is decentralization's ultimate power, the benefits of decentralizing companies are clear.

## MORE INFORMATION PROCESSED

Market economies, in their maddeningly imprecise fashion, process much more information than do "command" economies. Instead of central plans and numerous controllers, there's the hurly-burly of middlemen, opportunists, and entrepreneurs—all jostling to take advantage of scarcities, short-term price distortions, emergent technologies, and subtle consumer preferences. (What controller would have foreseen the "need" for hundreds of styles of running shoes?)

So, too, in the truly decentralized firm: For example, people at the front line, with little fuss, seek out others both inside and outside the corporation to obtain useful, timely information to solve problems or take advantage of fleeting opportunities. This additional volume of useful information is "invisible" and hence unseen by senior managers, which gives most of them the heebie-jeebies. In the centralized firm, by contrast, rigid and segregated information-processing rituals restrict the volume, timeliness, breadth, and usefulness of information flowing to those who need it most.

## Less Distorted Information

Hierarchies distort, abstract, and delay information processing—by definition. Consider Hewlett-Packard Company. After a several year bout of centralization, the firm recently returned to its more decentralized roots. The reason: Centralized rituals were causing unacceptable delays in decision-making in computer markets where product life cycles' length had collapsed to months. Decentralized operations allow the largest possible number of people to use unfiltered, "real-time" information directly from the source, whether he be a customer, distributor, vendor, or fellow front-line employee in another function.

## More Parallel Processing

Computer mavens are agog over massively parallel processing of information, which appears to be many times more effective than traditional sequential processing. In markets, parallel processing is the norm. Suppliers, producers, middlemen, and consumers deal regularly with one another and the same information all at the same time. In truly decentralized corporate operations, in which formal barriers between functions, divisions, and outsiders have been demolished, engineers, accountants, marketers, sales people, and manufacturers from various entities (supplier, corporation, distributor, customer) work "all at once" to try things, fix things, and exploit opportunities. There is no better example than telecommunications upstart MCI Communications Corporation. Traditional middle management is virtually nonexistent at MCI, and a host of devices, including a vigorous E-mail system, induce wide-open, no-holds-barred communication across, inside, up, down, and beyond official borders. Alternatively, centralized operations by and large process information sequentially: One functional fiefdom deals with an issue; then it's passed on to the next in due—read delayed—course.

## MORE FRONT-LINE-TO-FRONT-LINE CONTACT

In decentralized organizations, workers nearest the action make up their own minds about whom they need to deal with in order to behave most effectively and efficiently. Usually that means dealing with others at the front (other functions, divisions, outsiders) because they have fresher, less-distorted information. I recall a visit to an old General Motors Corporation plant a year or so ago. Undergoing a revolutionary management transition, it had encouraged work teams to be in direct contact with the customer, in this case, GM assembly plants; the team I chatted with has installed a hot line from their operations to a GM work team in an assembly plant hundreds of miles away. It simply amounts to more front-to-front communication than in centralized operations.

The result, it's important to note, is more than additive. Such rich contacts over time lead to cumulative individual, group, and multigroup learning and to increased readiness to respond to unforeseen difficulties or opportunities without the intervention of intermediate-level "processors"—that is, staff experts and middle managers.

---

In decentralized organizations, workers nearest the action make up their own minds about whom they need to deal with in order to behave most effectively and efficiently.

---

## SHORTER FEEDBACK LOOPS

When you're close to the scene and getting in your licks, you hear more quickly about whether a new product or new technique works. You can adjust faster, toss out useless schemes faster, and improve faster. Market economies perform well because feedback loops are short and signals are rapidly provided (sales or a lack thereof, for instance) that inform the largest number of people that they are on the money, off the money, or halfway in between, giving impetus for an immediate next act. At Pepsico Inc., for example, unit managers don't have to wait for orders from headquarters. They move instantly in response to the slightest market tremor: Failure to act is a far more unforgivable sin than failure to check with the higher-ups.

## INCREASED AT BATS

Success at anything is a function of the number of times we try something. Like baseball, market economies succeed by maximizing the number of tries by individuals, entrepreneurs, and firms. The same holds within a firm. Assuming equally energetic and talented people in a centralized and decentralized corporation (a lousy assumption—the best people tend to gravitate to more empowered, decentralized environments), the decentralized one wins hands down: Less time and effort are expended processing information through the hierarchy, and more time and effort are directed to marketplace "at bats" and real-time problem-solving. 3M, Apple Computer Inc., MCI, and Pepsico are among the best of the big firms at understanding this. Are they smarter than the rest? Not as I see it. They simply get more going—that is, get in more swings—and as a result more balls drop between the outfielders for hits.

---

When you're close to the scene and getting in your licks, you hear more quickly about whether a new product or new technique works.

---

## HIGHER ACCOUNTABILITY

Since information is less distorted, feedback loops are shorter, and there are more tries in a market economy, accountability is automatically maximized. So, too, in the corporation: In the rigid, hierarchical, pre-just-in-time world at Harley-Davidson Motor Company, for instance, six months of parts inventory hung from an advanced, centralized material-handling system on the plant's roof. The producer of handlebars, say, was unaccountable—precisely because the handlebars she made today wouldn't be used by a final assembler for 180 days. Now, with only a few minutes of in-plant inventory, the assembler screams bloody murder if there's a handlebar defect—and knows whom to scream at. And the person screamed at can respond, because her out-of-adjustment machine only started causing problems an hour ago, rather than six months ago.

## LESS CONTROL

The Soviet economy is and has been "under control." Yet it recently reported shortages among 996 of 1,000 basic consumer goods. No one, starting with Secretary of the Treasury Nicholas Brady, understands the U.S. economy, yet virtually nothing is out of stock. Our economy is "out of control" in common-sense terms—it's thoroughly incomprehensible to anyone, complex macroeconomic models notwithstanding. And that's precisely why it's, in fact, in control. The Soviet economy, on the other hand, is in control in a common-sense fashion (you can point to a detailed plan for everything) and out of control in fact. And it's out of control precisely because it *is* comprehensible.

---

I do acknowledge that decentralization can be overdone. Usually, however, it is because we only half do it.

---

The story is the same for the corporation: 3M is out of control by most standards—thousands of unseen, internal entrepreneurs are beavering away on odds and ends of projects, following the company's "make a little, sell a little, make a little more" beacon. But 3M is in control compared with corporations in general, most of which, like the Russian economy, are guided by comprehensible master plans that shrivel the human spirit, delay useful signals, and reduce at bats.

## MORE UNFAIRNESS

F.A. Hayek is clear that marketplace victory does not always, or perhaps even often, go to those who "deserve it." Instead, victory goes to those who happen to be in the right place at the right time. Controlled economies (and corporations) tend to work on the "deserve it" principle; their orderly, hyperrational approaches fall far short of maximizing the possibility of the largely lucky accidents we call progress—the Apple II, Post-it Notes, FedEx delivery service, CNN. Truly decentralized enterprises maximize the odds of the firm getting lucky by putting more people in the market's way.

Is there no downside to decentralization? Can't it be overdone? Campbell Soup Company under CEO Gordon McGovern took on an "at bats" strategy with a vengeance for several years. Many say he went too far, and costs and basics got out of control amid an entrepreneurial frenzy at the once stodgy firm.

---

We need to give up "control," and lots of it, to stand even a chance of gaining control in these tumultuous times.

---

I don't know the ins and outs of Campbell's story. But I do acknowledge that decentralization can be overdone. Usually, however, it is because we only half do it. We may introduce a flurry of new product entrepreneurship, but then don't allow the full blast of market wind to scour the firm. Most often, eye-catching financial incentives that rivet attention on profit as well as novelty are overlooked.

In any event, my experience is clear: Many executives lose their nerve and quit far short of tapping decentralization's full power. Asea Brown Boveri Ltd.'s chairman, Percy Barnevik, reports that he has broken his 240,000-person giant into roughly 4,500 profit centers (in 1,200 business units) with only 50 people on average in each. The whole affair is overseen by an unencumbered 100-person corporate staff. How do you rank by that standard?

Most important, this discussion takes on special significance these days. With product life cycles dramatically com-
pressed, information sources burgeoning, the speed of
information transmission accelerating, new technologies
sprouting, and entrepreneurs from around the world pop-
ping up by the bushel each week, the need to get in more
licks, faster—that is, try more, fail more, do more—is growing by the day. For most companies that should mean revis-
iting the basic, usually unexamined ideas that lie beneath
well-oiled market economies, and then turning corporate
decentralization on paper (our normal state) into radical
decentralization in practice (still the exception). We need to
give up "control," and lots of it, to stand even a chance of
gaining control in these tumultuous times.

# Acknowledgments

While searching for essays and speeches for the Business Wisdom series of anthologies, I noticed more than a few superlative pieces that had appeared in publications by The Conference Board. I set most of them aside, hoping to work with The Conference Board on a separate collection someday—and fortunately, that day came. Foremost, I want to thank Randy Poe for his initial enthusiasm for the project and for his help once it was under way. Melissa Berman and Carol Estoppey also provided immeasurable help in the research and the shaping of the book. Of course, I can't forget Ruth Mills and Ed Knappman, who both helped so much in launching the project. Thanks also to Airié Dekidjiev, my editor at Wiley, for adding punch to the collection. As the years and words accumulate, Diana, Pierson, Alex, and Julia provide the energy to keep on trucking—here's to another word or two in the new millennium.

# Appendix A
## *About The Conference Board*

The Conference Board was created in the early 1900s — an era of economic and social turmoil. At the beginning of this century, expanding technology, newly formed labor unions, and a wave of government regulations were drastically changing the business environment.

Many business leaders worried that the excesses and abuses of some employers, media attacks on business, militant trade unionists, and public ignorance about economic issues were triggering a severe backlash against business. In 1915, Magnus Alexander, a prominent General Electric executive, convened a meeting of 23 business leaders in upstate New York. They discussed strategies to improve relationships with employees, the general public, and the media.

The group proposed the creation of an organization fully devoted to objective research about real-life business conditions. "We do not need a propaganda machine, but a credible fact-finding organization," Alexander said.

In 1916, these executives created The National Industrial Conference Board (later to be called The Conference Board). This totally new-wave organization was formed to conduct unbiased research on major management practices and economic issues, encourage the sharing of business knowledge across every industry, and bring together executives to discuss timely issues. Research findings would be made available not only to business executives but also to the public, via the media. Alexander became the first president of the new organization.

Later, Dr. Leonard Silk, an authority on the U.S. economy and a member of the editorial board of *The New York Times*, wrote: "The Conference Board represented a new direction for American industry: A body dedicated to discovering and spreading accurate and objective information about business and the economy, in the belief that the truth would better serve the interests of its members than propaganda. Its guiding principle was 'Let there be light.' "

From its beginnings, The Conference Board conducted pioneering research into an astonishing range of economic issues. The Conference Board was the first organization to establish national and regional cost of living indexes (1918), which were later gifted to the U.S. Government. These barometers led to the creation of the Consumer Price Index. In 1996, The Conference Board became the first private-sector organization given responsibility for a major U.S. Government economic series — the Leading Economic Indicators.

To broaden its reach, The Conference Board expanded its operations to Canada in 1954. The Conference Board of Canada was formed to serve the needs of Canadian-based organizations. It is now an affiliated, self-supporting organization. In 1977, The Conference Board opened a European office in Brussels. Since then, The Conference Board Europe has become a major, fully integrated part of the Board's global business network, with representation in the major business capitals.

Steadily, The Conference Board has become a major source of economic and management intelligence. Its Leading Economic Indicators, Consumer Confidence Index, Help-Wanted Advertising Index and Business Confidence Index are heavily used by business, government, and media to gauge business trends and design strategy. The organization is now launching a series of leading indicators for more than 20 major nations. As the *Bloomberg News* reported: "When The Conference Board talks, even the Federal Reserve Board listens."

The Conference Board also is a worldwide authority on global economic trends, corporate governance, institutional investment, executive compensation, business ethics, performance excellence, organization structure, management capabilities, corporate citizenship, and productivity.

Because of its global credibility, The Conference Board is a major speaking platform for leaders, from presidents of the United States to the CEOs of major worldwide companies. Seven of the last eight presidents of the United States have addressed Conference Board events. More than 3,000 chief executives have spoken to Conference Board audiences over the last three decades.

Since 1995, The Conference Board has rapidly globalized its activities. The Conference Board now has corporate members in 67 nations and operates programs throughout North America, Europe, Asia-Pacific, and the Middle East. Nearly 1,000 of its corporate members and one-third of its trustees, who are the leaders of major corporations, are based outside the United States.

The Conference Board's conferences, featuring leaders from business, government, and the not-for-profit sector, are now held in virtually all areas of the world. They attract more than 12,000 executives annually. One of the most popular programs at The Conference Board are its Management Centers and Councils, which link more than 3,000 senior executives from around the world. These executives head major business functions in their companies and meet regularly to share ideas and find solutions to common problems.

The Conference Board's non-partisan, not-for-profit structure has helped make it the world's most widely quoted private source of business intelligence. Today, virtually every issue of importance to twenty-first century business executives is examined in Conference Board reports, forecasts, conferences, and councils. While The Conference Board's mission has remained the same for eight decades, its scale and scope have multiplied as the 23 original corporate members have grown a hundredfold.

For more information, visit The Conference Board's web site — www.conference-board.org.

Randall Poe
Executive Director of Communications
The Conference Board

# Appendix B
## Research by The Conference Board

The purpose of this section is to present *some* of the key findings of The Conference Board's research that is only briefly referred to in the introductions to the eight parts of this collection. For more information concerning these reports and The Conference Board's other research initiatives, please contact The Conference Board at 212-759-0900 or www.conference-board.org.

### THE CEO CHALLENGE:
### TOP MARKETPLACE AND MANAGEMENT ISSUES
### (REPORT #1244-99-RR)

This 1999 study was sponsored by Heidrick & Struggles and conducted by The Conference Board. A one-page survey was mailed or faxed to CEOs around the world and 656 responded. They were asked to select their top three marketplace and top three management challenges for their companies in the next year from a list of about 15 issues in each category.

*Survey Results*

| The CEO Challenge: Top Marketplace and Management Issues | | | 656 CEO responses |
|---|---|---|---|
| MARKETPLACE | % | MANAGEMENT | % |
| Downward pressure on your prices | 48 | Customer loyalty/retention | 40 |
| Changes in type/level of competition | 43 | Managing mergers/acquisitions/ alliances | 30 |

| MARKETPLACE | % | MANAGEMENT | % |
|---|---|---|---|
| Industry consolidation | 41 | Reducing costs | 30 |
| Changing technology | 25 | Engaging employees in the | |
| Shortages of key skills | 23 | company's vision/values | 29 |
| Changes in supply/ distribution systems | 22 | Increasing flexibility and speed | 26 |
| Access to/cost of capital | 17 | Developing and retaining potential leaders | 24 |
| Regulatory issues (labor, market access, etc.) | 15 | Increasing innovation | 24 |
| Impact of the Internet | 15 | Competing for talent | 23 |
| Instability in emerging markets | 15 | Improving the stock price multiple | 19 |
| Pressure from institutional investors | 8 | Making investment/capital allocation decisions | 17 |
| Environment, health & safety issues | 7 | Top management and/or board succession | 9 |
| Currency issues | 5 | Transferring knowledge, ideas and practices | 9 |
| Inadequate education systems | 3 | Communicating across cultures | 6 |
| Effects of corruption | 1 | Leveraging diversity (inc. cultural diversity) | 2 |
| | | Community relations across multiple regions | 1 |
| | | Helping employees achieve work/life balance | 1 |

# ALIGNING STRATEGIC PERFORMANCE MEASURES AND RESULTS (REPORT #1261-99-RR)

This 1999 research report, sponsored by A.T. Kearney, is based on insights from chief financial officers, corporate strategists, a survey of 113 companies, as well as a review of current business literature. Part of its purpose was to evaluate the importance of strategic performance measures. Companies were asked to rank their top financial and nonfinancial measures.

*Survey Results*

## Is Strategic Performance Measurement An Important Issue in Your Company?

Yes    92%
No    8

## Who Receives Communication About SPM Targets?

*Percent receiving communication and feedback about SPMs*

Board members   56% / 41
Senior managers   63 / 58
Division managers   61 / 57
Business unit managers   56 / 49
All employees   33 / 26

■ Communication
▨ Feedback

## Top Financial Strategic Performance Measures

*Stock price relative to competitors*

| | Over past three years: | | | Over next three years: |
|---|---|---|---|---|

Cash flow — past: 24%, 4 — next: 27%, 6
Return on capital employment — past: 29, 10 — next: 26, 11
Economic profit — past: 19, 9 — next: 26, 9
Total shareholder return — past: 17, 10 — next: 23, 14
Operating margin — past: 35, 13 — next: 21, 5
Revenue — past: 12, 4 — next: 19, 3
EPS — past: 23, 11 — next: 16, 7
Other — past: 12, 1 — next: 10, 3
Share price — past: 8, 4 — next: 9, 4
Dividend yield — past: 2, 1 — next: 1, 1

■ Ranked among top three strategic performance measures

▨ Ranked as top strategic performance measure

## Top Non-Financial Strategic Performance Measures

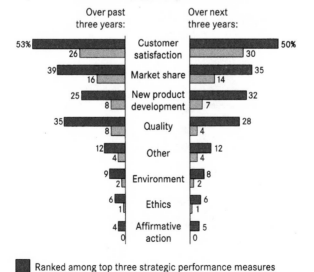

| | Over past three years: | | | Over next three years: |
|---|---|---|---|---|

Customer satisfaction — past: 53%, 26 — next: 50%, 30
Market share — past: 39, 16 — next: 35, 14
New product development — past: 25, 8 — next: 32, 7
Quality — past: 35, 8 — next: 28, 4
Other — past: 12, 4 — next: 12, 4
Environment — past: 9, 2 — next: 8, 2
Ethics — past: 6, 1 — next: 6, 1
Affirmative action — past: 4, 0 — next: 5, 0

■ Ranked among top three strategic performance measures

▨ Ranked as top strategic performance measure

# CONSUMER EXPECTATIONS ON THE SOCIAL ACCOUNTABILITY OF BUSINESS (REPORT #1255-99-RR)

This July 1999 research project involved a 12-page telephone interview of U.S. consumers. One thousand interviews (584 women; 416 men) were completed from a representative sample of 2,600 households and reflected the demographics of the larger sample. They were asked how they form favorable or unfavorable impressions of large companies. Environics, Inc. developed the survey with The Prince of Wales Business Leaders Forum; it was also fielded in more than 20 other countries.

*Survey Results*

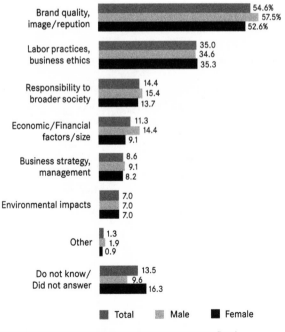

Consumers Care More About Brand Quality and
Company Image and Reputation Than They Do
About Company Management or Business Strategy

| | Total | Male | Female |
|---|---|---|---|
| Brand quality, image/reputation | 54.6% | 57.5% | 52.6% |
| Labor practices, business ethics | 35.0 | 34.6 | 35.3 |
| Responsibility to broader society | 14.4 | 15.4 | 13.7 |
| Economic/Financial factors/size | 11.3 | 14.4 | 9.1 |
| Business strategy, management | 8.6 | 9.1 | 8.2 |
| Environmental impacts | 7.0 | 7.0 | 7.0 |
| Other | 1.3 | 1.9 | 0.9 |
| Do not know/Did not answer | 13.5 | 9.6 | 16.3 |

Note: Totals do not equal 100 percent because up to two answers were allowed.

## Consumers Reward Companies They Consider Socially Responsible in the Marketplace

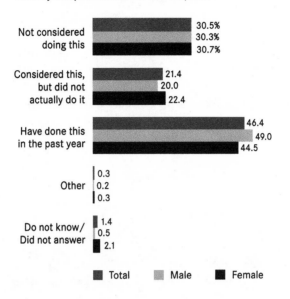

| | |
|---|---|
| Not considered doing this | 30.5% / 30.3% / 30.7% |
| Considered this, but did not actually do it | 21.4 / 20.0 / 22.4 |
| Have done this in the past year | 46.4 / 49.0 / 44.5 |
| Other | 0.3 / 0.2 / 0.3 |
| Do not know/ Did not answer | 1.4 / 0.5 / 2.1 |

■ Total   ■ Male   ■ Female

## Consumers Punish Companies They Do Not Consider Socially Responsible in the Marketplace

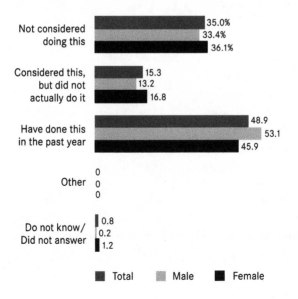

| | |
|---|---|
| Not considered doing this | 35.0% / 33.4% / 36.1% |
| Considered this, but did not actually do it | 15.3 / 13.2 / 16.8 |
| Have done this in the past year | 48.9 / 53.1 / 45.9 |
| Other | 0 / 0 / 0 |
| Do not know/ Did not answer | 0.8 / 0.2 / 1.2 |

■ Total   ■ Male   ■ Female

## MANAGING THE CORPORATE BRAND
## (REPORT #1214-98-RR)

This 1998 research report is, in part, the result of a study questionnaire that was mailed in the spring of 1997 to approximately 800 large companies in the United States and Europe. Survey responses were received from 106 firms. The purpose of the study was to determine the importance of a corporate brand and its role in a company's performance. More than a dozen leading companies helped develop and support the research.

*Survey Results*

### FACTORS INFLUENCING THE SUCCESS OF BRAND STRATEGY

**Strong leadership and support from CEO and senior management is seen as key to brand strategy.**

| | |
|---|---|
| Leadership/support from CEO | 85%* |
| Championship of the brand by others in senior management | 74 |
| Consistency in communicating brand/ identity message | 73 |
| Strength of the brand logo/identity message | 73 |
| Distinctive corporate culture serving as a foundation for brand promise | 63 |
| Effective integration of delivery of brand messages across media/markets | 63 |
| Effective use of visuals/imagery to support the brand | 62 |
| Ability to create buy-in among frontline managers | 61 |
| Availability of adequate resources to support the brand | 59 |
| Ability to create buy-in among broad spectrum of employees | 57 |
| Ability to create a distinctive brand personality | 57 |
| Unique attributes of the company's products/ services | 57 |

Effective alignment across functions to deliver
brand message to customers        54
Ability to capture the brand in a slogan        40
Ability to create buy-in among business partners    37

*Percent rating these factors "highly" important to success
N = 106

## BEHIND THE NUMBERS: SEVEN CRITICAL FACTORS FOR BRAND STRATEGY SUCCESS

Further analysis of responses highlights which factors contribute to a winning brand strategy. When compared with other respondents, those companies reporting success were significantly more likely to rate 7 of the 15 factors as highly important to their success. Three concern the creation and presentation of the brand, areas that can be influenced by the brand manager and advertising agency or other creative partners. More surprising is that four are tied to the organization, its culture, and its support for the brand:

### Brand Presentation

1. The strength of the brand logo/identity system
2. The effective use of visuals and imagery
3. The ability to capture the brand in a slogan

### Organizational Support

4. CEO leadership and support
5. A distinctive corporate culture that serves as a platform for the brand promise
6. The ability to obtain support from a broad spectrum of employees
7. The alignment of brand messages across functions

## GLOBAL CORPORATE ETHICS PRACTICES
## (REPORT #1243-99-RR)

This 1999 corporate ethics study is based on the responses of 120 companies from around the world. One purpose of the study was to better understand the existing standards for global business practices and to determine who sets the standards within a company and why. In addition to corporate sponsors, a working group of more than 20 organizations worldwide participated in supporting the research.

*Survey Results*

KEY FINDINGS

(Percent of companies)

**Business Justification for Ethics Codes**

| | |
|---|---|
| Establish core principles for global operations | 66% |
| Promote employee professionalism | 58 |
| Limit legal risks | 58 |

**Strategic Justification for Ethics Codes**

| | |
|---|---|
| Legal incentives | 56 |
| Changing legal requirements | 55 |
| Growing company involvement in regions with different cultural or political traditions | 42 |

**Subjects Addressed by Ethics Codes**

*For employees*

| | |
|---|---|
| Bribery/improper payments | 92 |
| Conflict of interest | 92 |
| Security of proprietary information | 92 |

*For suppliers/vendors*

| | |
|---|---|
| Giving gifts | 48 |
| Receiving gifts | 46 |
| Bribery/improper payments | 45 |

*For joint venture partners*

| | |
|---|---|
| Bribery/improper payments | 27 |
| Conflict of interest | 26 |
| Giving gifts | 26 |

## Dominant Code Rationales

| | |
|---|---|
| United States — Instrumental | 64 |
| Europe — Values/mission | 60 |
| Latin America — Instrumental | 50 |
| Canada — Values/mission | 40 |
| Japan — Legal compliance; values/mission | 33 |

## Participants in Code Drafting

| | |
|---|---|
| CEO | 95 |
| General counsel | 92 |
| Human resources | 86 |

## Code Distribution Practices
*(Copy of code given to all employees)*

| | |
|---|---|
| 1998 | 90 |
| 1991 | 77 |
| 1987 | 67 |

ORGANIZING FOR GLOBAL COMPETITIVENESS:
THE CORPORATE HEADQUARTERS DESIGN
(REPORT #1233-99-RR)

This 1999 research report sought to answer the following questions posed by the 15 sponsoring companies: How should corporate headquarters add value? How might it be organized? How can the performance of corporate headquarters be measured and assessed? The answers to these questions, among others, are based on the responses of 89 companies.

*Survey Results*
Eighty-five percent of corporate headquarters have undergone one or more significant reorganizations in the 1990s.

### HQ ROLES COMPANIES ARE STRENGTHENING:

| | |
|---|---|
| Executive selection and development | 92% |
| Best practices exchange | 86 |
| Strategic planning | 84 |
| Government/public relations | 83 |
| Finance | 80 |
| Information technology | 76 |
| Brand management | 74 |

## MANAGEMENT IS MOST LIKELY STRENGTHENING THESE ROLES BECAUSE OF CONCERNS ABOUT:

- increased competition
- globalization
- impact of IT technologies
- customer influence
- changing regulatory laws
- M&A and alliance activity

## DRIVERS OF CHANGE

The three most important drivers of organizational and/or role changes are:

| | |
|---|---|
| Greater speed | 54% |
| Bring about greater organizational clarity and enhance accountability | 48 |
| Improve integration | 21 |

## MAJOR WAYS THAT CORPORATE HEADQUARTERS ADDS VALUE

*Note:* Multiple responses given

# Notes

Paul A. Allaire:

Allaire, Paul. "The Xerox Method of Duplicating Success." *The Journal for Quality and Participation,* January/February 1998.

Inglesby, Tom. "An Interview with Paul Allaire." *Manufacturing Systems,* January 1992.

Moreau, Dan. "Xerox Tries to Duplicate Its Glory Days." *Kiplinger's Personal Finance Magazine,* April 1994.

"Paul Allaire." *Chief Executive,* 1997.

*Who's Who in America.* Wilmette, IL: Marquis Who's Who, 1996.

Warren G. Bennis:

"In Conversation with Warren Bennis." *Director,* September 1997.

Johnson, James A. "Warren Bennis, Chairman, The Leadership Institute." *Journal of Healthcare Management,* July/August 1998.

Loeb, Marshall. "Where Leaders Come From." *Fortune,* September 19, 1994.

Romano, Catherine. "Interview: Warren Bennis." *Management Review,* January 1997.

*Who's Who in America.* Wilmette, IL: Marquis Who's Who, 1996.

Michael R. Bonsignore:

Bonsignore, Michael. "Wanted: Company Owners." *Across the Board,* July/August 1997.

Clow, Robert. "Michael Bonsignore of Honeywell: Turning Up the Heat." *Institutional Investor,* April 1998.

Ettorre, Barbara. "The Insider." *Chief Executive,* January/February 1997.

Sellers, Patricia. "The Boss's Other Life." *Fortune,* November 24, 1997.

I. MacAllister Booth:

Booth, I. MacAllister. "Toward the New Image of Employee Decision Making." *The Conference Board's President's Series,* no. 7.

Byrnes, Nanette, and Adrienne Hardman. "Cold Shower." *Financial World,* September 28, 1993.

Chakravarty, Subrata N. "The Vindication of Edwin Land." *Forbes*, May 4, 1987.

Lawrence A. Bossidy:
Doherty, Jacqueline. "Still Going." *Barron's*, April 26, 1999.
"Larry Bossidy Won't Stop Pushing." *Fortune*, January 13, 1997.
Seigle, Greg. "AlliedSignal, Honeywell Merger to Create Defence Electronics Giant." *Jane's Defence Weekly*, June 16, 1999.
Tulley, Shawn. "So, Mr. Bossidy, We Know You Can Cut, Now Show Us How to Grow." *Fortune*, August 21, 1995.

Richard Branson:
"Behind Branson." *The Economist*, February 21, 1998.
Branson, Richard. *Losing My Virginity*. New York: Times Business, 1998.
Branson, Richard. "Risk Taking." *Journal of General Management*, Winter 1985.
Flynn, Julia, with Wendy Zellner, Larry Light, and Joseph Weber. "Then Came Branson." *Business Week*, October 26, 1998.

Warren E. Buffett:
Buffett, Warren. "Mr. Buffett on the Stock Market." *Fortune*, November 22, 1999.
Hagstron, Robert G. *The Warren Buffett Way: Investment Strategies of the World's Greatest Investor*. New York: John Wiley & Sons, Inc., 1995.
Lowe, Janet. *Warren Buffett Speaks*. New York: John Wiley & Sons, Inc., 1997.

Peter F. Drucker:
Crainer, Stuart. "Prophet of the Information Age." *Management Today*, January 1999.
*Current Biography Yearbook, 1964*. New York: The H.W. Wilson Company, 1964.
*Who's Who in America*. Wilmette, IL: Marquis Who's Who, 1996.

William T. Esrey:
Chakravarty, Subrata N. "Nimble Upstart." *Forbes*, May 8, 1995.
Chakravarty, Subrata N. "The Quiet Corner." *Forbes*, February 23, 1998.
Rosenberg, Martin. "Sprinting to the Future." *Utility Business*, December 1998.

Raymond V. Gilmartin:
Barrett, Amy, with Larry Armstrong. "Merck Takes Some Growth Pills." *Business Week*, October 12, 1998.
*Who's Who in America*. Wilmette, IL: Marquis Who's Who, 1996.

Melvin R. Goodes:

Goodes, Melvin R. "What Would You Do if Your Name Were on the Building?" *Chief Executive Speeches* 1, no. 1, 1992.

Herrera, Stephan. "The Forbes Platinum List." *Forbes*, January 11, 1999.

*Who's Who in America*. Wilmette, IL: Marquis Who's Who, 1996.

Katherine Graham:

*Current Biography Yearbook, 1971*. New York: The H.W. Wilson Company, 1971.

Graham, Katherine. *Personal History*. New York: Alfred A. Knopf, 1997.

Crawford H. Greenewalt:

Colby, Gerald. *Du Pont Dynasty: Behind the Nylon Curtain*. Secaucus, NJ: Lyle Stuart Inc., 1984.

"The Wizards of Wilmington." *Time*, April 16, 1951.

Andrew S. Grove:

"Man of the Year." *Time*, December 29, 1997–January 5, 1998.

Palmer, Jay. "Zero Hour." *Barron's*, October 4, 1999.

Schlender, Brent. "The Incredible, Profitable Career of Andy Grove." *Fortune*, April 27, 1998.

Robert D. Haas:

Dugan, Sean M. "Levi Strauss & Co. Site Doesn't Pan Out, But the Rush Isn't Over Yet." *Infoworld*, November 22, 1999.

Mitchell, Russell. "Managing by Values." *Business Week*, August 1, 1994.

Mitchell, Russell. "A Mild-Mannered Maverick Puts His Brand on Levi's." *Business Week*, August 1, 1994.

"The Quiet American." *The Economist*, November 8, 1997.

Wilson, Marianne. "Levi's Fashions a New Attitude." *Chain Store Age*, October 1999.

Joseph M. Juran:

Butman, John. *Juran: A Lifetime of Influence*. New York: John Wiley & Sons, Inc., 1997.

Kirker, Tracy Benson. "The Teacher's Still a Student." *Industry Week*, May 2, 1994.

Stewart, Thomas A. "A Conversation with Joseph Juran." *Fortune*, January 11, 1999.

*Who's Who in America*. Wilmette, IL: Marquis Who's Who, 1996.

Emmanuel A. Kampouris:

Reingold, Jennifer, and John Kimelman. "Nerves of Steel." *Financial World*, May 23, 1995.

Tully, Shawn. "American Standard: Prophet of Zero Working Capital." *Fortune*, June 13, 1994.

*Who's Who in America*. Wilmette, IL: Marquis Who's Who, 1996.

James P. Kelly:

Barron, Kelly. "Logistics in Brown." *Forbes*, January 10, 1999.

Bernstein, Aaron, with Nicole Harris. "This Package Is a Heavy One for the Teamsters." *Business Week*, August 25, 1997.

Greenhouse, Steve. "United Parcel Asks Clinton to Intervene in Walkout." *The New York Times*, August 11, 1997.

King, Julia. "UPS Delivers the Goods with IPO." *Computerworld*, November 22, 1999.

McTague. "D.C. Current." *Barron's*, March 8, 1999.


Jim Koch:

Lieber, Ronald B. "Beating the Odds." *Fortune*, March 31, 1997.

"New Brewery Has Family History." *Beverage Industry*, January 1998.

Prince, Greg W. "A Second Look at Koch." *Beverage World*, December 31, 1994.

Theodore, Sarah. "Still Crazy About Craft Beer." *Beverage Industry*, January 1998.

Warner, Judy. "Soul Searching for Samuel Adams." *Adweek*, November 2, 1998.


Jennifer Laing:

Elliott, Stuart. "Delta Airlines Dismisses Saatchi & Saatchi." *The New York Times*, September 9, 1997.

Elliott, Stuart. "Fresh from London: Saatchi & Saatchi's New Chief Executive in the U.S. Is Off to a Fast Start." *The New York Times*, March 19, 1997.

McCarthy, Michael. "Saatchi Plans Creative Dept. Reunion." *Adweek*, March 24, 1997.


Richard G. LeFauve:

Bradsher, Keith. "G.M. Announces Two Steps to Streamline Its Operations." *The New York Times*, March 11, 1997.

Gardner, Greg. "At Saturn Everyone's a Brand Manager." *Ward's Auto World*, October 1996.

"Logistics as a Competitive Weapon." *Chief Executive*, November/December 1994.

O'Toole, Jack. *Forming the Future: Lessons from the Saturn Corporation.* Cambridge, MA: Blackwell Publishers, Inc., 1996.


Jon C. Madonna:

"Been There, Seen It, Done That." *Accountancy*, February 1997.

"Leadership and Empowerment for Total Quality." *The CPA Journal*, December 1991.

James P. Manzi:
Bierch, Richard. "Found on the Internet: Life After Lotus." *U.S. News & World Report*, May 20, 1996.
Darrow, Barbara. "IBM-Lotus Honeymoon Got Off to Rocky Start." *Computer Reseller News*, June 3, 1996.
Rifkin, Glenn. "Profile: Jim Manzi." *Computerworld*, July 13, 1992.
Shore, Joel. "Jim Manzi." *Computer Reseller News*, November 14, 1994.
*Who's Who in America*. Wilmette, IL: Marquis Who's Who, 1996.

Rebecca P. Mark:
Corwin, Judy. "Global Perspectives from Enron's Rebecca Mark." *Baylor Business Review*, Spring 1999.
*Current Biography*, May 1999.

Lord Colin Marshall of Knightsbridge:
British Airways Plc company records.
Moore, Alison. "Review of IABC UK's First Annual Conference." *Communication World*, April/May 1998.

Arjay Miller:
"From the Executive Suite to Halls of Ivy." *Business Week*, July 19, 1969.
Lamm, Michael. "The '49 Car that Saved Ford Motor." *The New York Times*, September 10, 1999.
"Miller of Ford and Stanford." *Fortune*, August 1968.

Charles D. Miller:
Barrett, Amy. "The Loved One." *Financial World*, February 18, 1992.
Darlin, Damon. "Thank You, 3M." *Forbes*, September 25, 1995.
Miller, Charles D. "Seeking the Service Grail." *Financial Executive*, July/August 1993.
*Who's Who in America*. Wilmette, IL: Marquis Who's Who, 2000.

J. Irwin Miller:
Harris, T. George. "Egghead in the Diesel Industry." *Fortune*, October 1957.
Miller, J. Irwin. "The Service Ethic." *Executive Excellence*, October 1992.

Akio Morita:
Morita, Akio. *Made in America: Akio Morita and Sony*. New York: E.P. Dutton, 1986.
Ohmae, Kenichi. "Guru of Gadgets: Akio Morita." *Time*, December 7, 1998.

Tom Peters:
*Current Biography Yearbook, 1994*. New York: The H.W. Wilson Company, 1994.
Stevens, Tim. "Service with Soul." *Industry Week*, February 5, 1996.

Howard J. Morgens:
"How Morgens Makes P&G No. 1." *Business Week*, July 21, 1973.
"Is the Soap Leader Getting Soft?" *Business Week*, July 19, 1969.
"Proud to Be an Organization Man." *Forbes*, May 15, 1972.

Simon Ramo:
Louis, Arthur M. "The U.S. Business Hall of Fame." *Fortune*, April 2, 1984.
Ramo, Simon. *The Business of Science*. New York: Hill and Wang, 1988.

Anita Roddick:
Dignam, Conor. "Roddick Attacks Shell's Ethical Ads." *Marketing*, September 30, 1999.
O'Byrne, Robert. "Jolly Green Giant." *The Irish Times*, November 4, 1997.
Roddick, Anita. *Body and Soul: Profits with Principles*. New York: Crown Publishers, Inc., 1991.
Roddick, Anita. "Four Letter Words." *Executive Excellence*, February 1998.

Robert Townsend:
Buchalter, Gail. "Up to What?" *Forbes*, March 24, 1986.
*Current Biography Yearbook 1970*. New York: The H.W. Wilson Company, 1970.
Quinn, Judy. "Lessons from a Geezer." *Incentive*, December 1994.
Townsend, Robert. *Up the Organization*. New York: Alfred A. Knopf, 1970.

Charles B. Wang:
Weld, Royal. "Interview: The Global Marketer: Charles Wang." *Sales and Marketing Management*, May 1999.
Weld, Royal. "Software Giant's Hardware Kings." *Industry Week*, February 15, 1999.

Edgar S. Woolard:
Norman, James R. "Switching Strategies." *Forbes*, July 4, 1994.
Reisch, Marc S. "SCI Medal Goes to Edgar Woolard." *Chemical and Engineering News*, October 12, 1998.
Shapiro, Lynn. "Du Pont's Woolard Earns Analyst's Nod." *Chemical Marketing Reporter*, June 1, 1992.
*Who's Who in America*. Wilmette, IL: Marquis Who's Who, 1994.

# Credits and Sources

"Leadership through Quality at Xerox" by Paul A. Allaire, from the 1991 75th Symposium Series: Leadership and Empowerment for Total Quality.

"Leaders and Visions: Orchestrating the Corporate Culture" by Warren G. Bennis, from the 1986 Corporate Culture and Change Conference.

"The Quality Experience at Honeywell" by Michael R. Bonsignore, from the 1996 Quality Conference.

"Much Ado About Worker Participation" by I. MacAllister Booth, from the 1994 Human Resources Conference.

"Why Do We Waste Time Doing This?" by Lawrence A. Bossidy, from *Across the Board*, May 1991.

"The Virgin Iconoclast," an interview with Richard Branson, by Manfred F. R. Kets de Vries, from *Across the Board*, February 1996.

"Track Record Is Everything" by Warren E. Buffett, from *Across the Board*, October 1991.

"The Rise of the Knowledge Worker" by Peter F. Drucker, from the 1996 Growth Conference.

"Leadership in the Next Century" by William T. Esrey, from the 1998 New Leadership Conference. Reprinted in *Chief Executive Digest* 2, no. 4, 1998.

"An Ethics Prescription for Success" by Raymond V. Gilmartin, from the 1998 Business Ethics Conference. Reprinted in *Chief Executive Digest* 2, no. 4, 1998.

"How to Create an Internal Corporate Brand" by Melvin R. Goodes, from the 1999 Corporate Image Conference. Reprinted in *Chief Executive Digest* 3, no. 1, 1999.

"If 'Business Credibility' Means Anything" by Katherine Graham, from *Business Credibility: The Critical Factors*, a report on conference proceedings, January 15, 1976.

"A Philosophy of Business Leadership" by Crawford H. Greenewalt, from the 1965 International Industrial Conference.

"Elephants Can So Dance" by Andrew S. Grove, from *Across the Board*, February 1987.

"Ethics: A Global Business Challenge" by Robert D. Haas, from *Chief Executive Speeches* 3, no. 1, 1994.

"Strategies for World-Class Quality" by Joseph M. Juran, from *Sustaining Total Quality*, 1993.

"A Case Study in Engineering" by Emmanuel A. Kampouris, from the 1996 Business Reengineering Conference. Reprinted in *Chief Executive Digest* 1, no. 1, 1997.

"Growing a Global Delivery System" by James P. Kelly, from the 1997 Growth Conference. Reprinted in *Chief Executive Digest* 1, no. 4.

"Brewing Up Growth: An Innovator's Tale" by Jim Koch, from the 1996 Growth Conference.

"Keeping an Endangered Relationship Alive" by Jennifer Laing, from the 1999 Advertising Conference. Reprinted in *Chief Executive Digest* 3, no. 4, 1999.

"Leaving the Comfort Zone" by Richard G. LeFauve, from the 1995 Managing Change Conference.

"Measure, Monitor and Improve Quality" by Jon C. Madonna, from the 1996 Quality Conference.

"Beyond Strategy: A View from the Top" by James P. Manzi, from the 1994 Strategic Management Conference.

"Risky Business" by Rebecca P. Mark, from the 1997 Strategic Management Conference. Reprinted in *Chief Executive Digest* 1, no. 2, 1997.

"Self-Management" by Lord Colin Marshall of Knightsbridge, from a speech delivered to The Conference Board Europe Dinner, April 20, 1999.

"Human Values in the Computer Age" by Arjay Miller, from the 1976 Systems Society Conference. Reprinted in *The Conference Board Record*, January 1968.

"Using Strategic Planning to Lead the Corporation" by Charles D. Miller, from 1991 Strategic Management Conference.

"Company Social Responsibility—Too Much or Not Enough?" by J. Irwin Miller, from *The Conference Board Record*, April 1964.

"Advertising from a Management Viewpoint" by Howard J. Morgens, from the Eighth Annual Marketing Conference, September 15, 1960.

"Moving Up in Marketing by Getting Down to Basics" by Akio Morita, from *The Conference Board Record*, December 1974.

"Letting Go of Controls" by Tom Peters, from *Across the Board*, June 1991.

"The Computer in Management" by Simon Ramo, from *The Conference Board Record*, February 1974.

"Not Free Trade but fair Trade" by Anita Roddick, from *Across the Board*, June 1994.

"Townsend's Third Degree in Leadership" by Robert Townsend, from the 1985 Strategic Planning Conference. Reprinted in *Across the Board*, June 1985.

"What CEOs Don't Know . . ." by Charles B. Wang, from *Across the Board*, June 1995.

"Did You Ever See an Elephant Charge?" by Edgar S. Woolard Jr., from the *Business Week* Symposium of Chief Executive Officers. Reprinted in *Across the Board*, June 1995.

# Index